Git Version Control Cookbook

90 hands-on recipes that will increase your productivity when using Git as a version control system

Aske Olsson

Rasmus Voss

[PACKT] open source
PUBLISHING
community experience distilled

BIRMINGHAM - MUMBAI

Git Version Control Cookbook

First published: July 2014

Production reference: 1170714

Published by Packt Publishing Ltd.
Livery Place
35 Livery Street
Birmingham B3 2PB, UK.

ISBN 978-1-78216-845-4

www.packtpub.com

Cover image by Benoit Benedetti (benoit.benedetti@gmail.com)

Credits

Authors

Aske Olsson

Rasmus Voss

Reviewers

Kenneth Geisshirt

Shashikant Vaishnav

Commissioning Editor

Martin Bell

Acquisition Editor

Rebecca Youé

Content Development Editor

Govindan K

Technical Editors

Manal Pednekar

Anand Singh

Copy Editors

Mradula Hegde

Gladson Monteiro

Adithi Shetty

Project Coordinator

Shipra Chawhan

Proofreaders

Simran Bhogal

Maria Gould

Ameesha Green

Paul Hindle

Indexers

Hemangini Bari

Mariammal Chettiyar

Mehreen Deshmukh

Tejal Soni

Priya Subramani

Production Coordinator

Nitesh Thakur

Cover Work

Nitesh Thakur

About the Authors

Aske Olsson has more than 10 years of experience in the software industry. With a background as an electrical engineer, he has used every tool available for development, from a soldering iron over Assembly, C, and Java programming to different SCM, build- and issue-tracking systems.

Aske has worked for Nokia for 6 years, where he was one of the leading forces behind complex tool transformation and renewal projects. Among them was a broad adoption of Git SCM, Gerrit Code Review, and Jenkins CI.

Currently, Aske works at Schantz, a company developing advanced IT solutions for the financial sector. He develops and maintains their continuous delivery pipeline.

Aske is also one of the four founding partners in the software development tools and processes company Switch-Gears ApS, where he helps customers, large and small, increase the maturity and productivity of their software delivery efforts by moving the customers from legacy tools and working modes to modern open source based tools and processes.

Aske has more than 4 years of experience working with Git, and since 2011, he has been teaching Git in regular training sessions, from basic Git to its advanced usage.

First, I would like to thank my wife and two kids (soon to be three) for supporting me and putting up with me while writing this book.

I would also like to thank Rasmus Voss for co-authoring the book with me. Last but not least, I would like to thank Knud Poulsen, Emanuele Zattin, Lars Pedersen, and the rest of the tool renewal team at Nokia for all the good discussions around Git.

Rasmus Voss is specialized in continuous integration, software releasing, and process automation. His vast knowledge on these areas has been built by a 10-year career in Nokia mobile phones in Copenhagen, Denmark and Beijing, China, where he started optimizing autotesting for the Series 30 platform. He later moved to software releasing and became part of the team that upgraded the software delivery chain from an old version control system CM Synergy to Git, incorporating Gerrit for code review and Jenkins for single commit verification, software releasing, and much more. Rasmus spent 2 years in China working for Nokia where he sparred with developers, release managers, test engineers, and leaders to optimize the process so that developers could spend time coding and testers knew what they were testing.

Today, Rasmus has his own company VossCon, where he consults with companies on how to make the most of developers and testers by optimizing software releasing, providing visibility in the delivery chain, upgrading the tool chain, automating tedious processes, and training developers. He also holds courses on Git, Gerrit, and Jenkins.

First and foremost, I would like to thank my wife and four kids for putting up with me and the stress it has been moving back to Denmark while starting a company, writing a book, and also trying to be the best family father I could be.

I would also like to thank Nokia for the career opportunities they gave me. Thanks to Aske Olsson for co-authoring the book with me. Thanks to Jonas Christensen from Schneider Electric who signed the first contract for my company. Thanks to Knud Poulsen for introducing me to Git, Gerrit, and Jenkins.

About the Reviewers

Kenneth Geisshirt is a chemist by education and a geek by nature. He has been programming for the last three decades. For more than 20 years, he has been using Unix and Linux as his primary operating system.

He is currently working at Realm, a small database company. He is working on language bindings (Python, Objective C, Node.js, and so on), and Git is an integrated tool in his daily work flow.

Kenneth has reviewed books on Vim, Linux system programming, and Octave. He has also written books on PAM and Linux, and numerous featured articles on open source software.

Shashikant Vaishnav was born and brought up in a desert town of Jodhpur, Rajasthan, India. He is currently a contract developer at Click Here Media, United Kingdom.

His research interests primarily focus on the areas of technology in education and developing software that takes into consideration the needs of elementary learners.

He has also been involved with Moodle LMS for quite a long time as a student. While being an undergraduate, he participated in Google's Summer of Code program and integrated Apache Solr with Moodle. He also participated as a mentor in the Google Code-in 2013 program for Sugar Labs.

He completed his undergraduate degree at Government Engineering College, Bikaner, with a Bachelor of Engineering and Technology in Computer Science in 2013. In college, he formed a group named LUGB (Linux User Group Bikaner).

Besides his academics focus, he harbors a deep interest for music and sports. He loves to blog about his experiences with open source technology, travel, and life. To allure himself at times, he reads spiritual books, does photography, and hacks around with open source stuff.

> I want to thank Packt Publishing for giving me the opportunity to contribute towards this great effort.

www.PacktPub.com

Support files, eBooks, discount offers, and more

You might want to visit www.PacktPub.com for support files and downloads related to your book.

Did you know that Packt offers eBook versions of every book published, with PDF and ePub files available? You can upgrade to the eBook version at www.PacktPub.com and as a print book customer, you are entitled to a discount on the eBook copy. Get in touch with us at service@packtpub.com for more details.

At www.PacktPub.com, you can also read a collection of free technical articles, sign up for a range of free newsletters and receive exclusive discounts and offers on Packt books and eBooks.

http://PacktLib.PacktPub.com

Do you need instant solutions to your IT questions? PacktLib is Packt's online digital book library. Here, you can access, read and search across Packt's entire library of books.

Why Subscribe?

- ► Fully searchable across every book published by Packt
- ► Copy and paste, print and bookmark content
- ► On demand and accessible via web browser

Free Access for Packt account holders

If you have an account with Packt at www.PacktPub.com, you can use this to access PacktLib today and view nine entirely free books. Simply use your login credentials for immediate access.

Table of Contents

Preface

Git is the clear leader in the new paradigm of distributed version control systems. Originally developed by Linus Torvalds as a source control management (SCM) system for the Linux kernel to replace the proprietary SCM BitKeeper, Git has since conquered most of the open source world and is also used by lots of organizations for their private/proprietary projects.

This book is designed to give you practical recipes for everyday Git usage. The recipes can be used directly or as an inspiration for you. The book will cover the Git data model through practical recipes and in-depth explanations so you get a deeper understanding of the internal workings of Git. This book will show you the following topics:

- ▶ Working with the history. With Git, you have all the history stored locally. Use it to search through the history, view the history, find the last commit touching a particular line, and so on.
- ▶ Using branches effectively with options and strategies to push, pull, and merge.
- ▶ Storing and extracting additional metadata in the Git repository.
- ▶ Disaster recovery: local and global.

Git Version Control Cookbook gives you precise step-by-step instructions to various common and uncommon Git operations. The book can help ease your daily work with Git by providing recipes for common issues, useful tips and tricks, and in-depth clarifications of why and how they work.

What this book covers

Chapter 1, *Navigating Git*, shows how Git stores files and commits. Examples will visually show you the data model and how to navigate the history and database with simple commands.

Chapter 2, *Configuration*, shows how a lot can be configured in Git and how configuration targets are set, the different configuration levels, and some useful targets.

Chapter 3, Branching, Merging, and Options, will give you a deeper understanding of branching and the options for easy push/pull targets. It also shows you the different merge strategies and some tips on how to record merge resolutions.

Chapter 4, Rebase Regularly and Interactively, and Other Use Cases, shows you how rebasing can be used instead of merging along with a lot of other use cases of rebase: cleaning up the history before publishing, testing single commits, and so on.

Chapter 5, Storing Additional Information in Your Repository, takes you on a tour of Git notes. It will show you how to tie additional information to a commit, and how to use and see this information again.

Chapter 6, Extracting Data from the Repository, will show you how to extract statistics and other metadata from the repository.

Chapter 7, Enhancing Your Daily Work with Git Hooks, Aliases, and Scripts, contains a collection of recipes to help you automate much of the tedious daily work.

Chapter 8, Recovering from Mistakes, walks you through several recovery scenarios, from local undo, to where-is-my-old-commit, to global recovery scenarios.

Chapter 9, Repository Maintenance, is a collection of recipes that concern the maintenance and management of repositories, from forcing garbage collection, over-splitting, and joining repositories to complete history rewriting.

Chapter 10, Patching and Offline Sharing, shows you how to work offline with Git and share the work by means other than pushing and pulling.

Chapter 11, Git Plumbing and Attributes, has a collection of recipes that show you how to utilize the filter feature of Git and a small collection of recipes that cover some of the useful but not widely known plumbing commands.

Chapter 12, Tips and Tricks, is a collection of recipes that covers various topics, from simple tips to displaying the current branch in your prompt to advanced Git tools, such as bisect and stash.

What you need for this book

To follow and recreate the recipes from this book, you will need a computer preferably running a *NIX operating system. You will need Git installed, preferably Git Version 1.8 or later.

If you are a Windows user, we recommend the Git Extensions package, which ships both a graphical and textual (bash) Git interface. The latter is required for the recipes in this book.

Who this book is for

This book targets both developers, as well as professional build/release managers who want a practical guide for the next level of Git. There is something for everyone. Starting with the Git data model and advancing through branching to metadata and hooks, all through an easy-to-read recipe structure, the transition from simple everyday use cases to advanced repository handling is smooth. The book can be easily read and understood by readers from all categories. The book requires basic knowledge of common GNU/Linux tools and shell/bash scripting.

Conventions

In this book, you will find a number of text styles that distinguish between different kinds of information. Here are some examples of these styles and an explanation of their meaning.

Code words in text, database table names, folder names, filenames, file extensions, pathnames, dummy URLs, user input are shown as follows: "Again, we will use the JGit repository with the master branch pointing to b14a939."

Any command-line input or output is written as follows:

```
$ git log -G"isOutdated" --oneline
```

New terms and **important words** are shown in bold. Words that you see on the screen, in menus or dialog boxes for example, appear in the text like this: "We can just write the commit message in the field in the bottom of the screen and hit **Commit**."

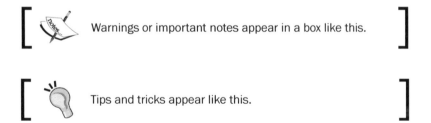

Warnings or important notes appear in a box like this.

Tips and tricks appear like this.

Reader feedback

Feedback from our readers is always welcome. Let us know what you think about this book—what you liked or may have disliked. Reader feedback is important for us to develop titles that you really get the most out of.

To send us general feedback, simply send an e-mail to feedback@packtpub.com, and mention the book title through the subject of your message.

If there is a topic that you have expertise in and you are interested in either writing or contributing to a book, see our author guide on www.packtpub.com/authors.

Customer support

Now that you are the proud owner of a Packt book, we have a number of things to help you to get the most from your purchase.

Downloading the example code

You can download the example code files for all Packt books you have purchased from your account at `http://www.packtpub.com`. If you purchased this book elsewhere, you can visit `http://www.packtpub.com/support` and register to have the files e-mailed directly to you.

Errata

Although we have taken every care to ensure the accuracy of our content, mistakes do happen. If you find a mistake in one of our books—maybe a mistake in the text or the code—we would be grateful if you would report this to us. By doing so, you can save other readers from frustration and help us improve subsequent versions of this book. If you find any errata, please report them by visiting `http://www.packtpub.com/support`, selecting your book, clicking on the **errata submission form** link, and entering the details of your errata. Once your errata are verified, your submission will be accepted and the errata will be uploaded to our website, or added to any list of existing errata, under the Errata section of that title.

Piracy

Piracy of copyright material on the Internet is an ongoing problem across all media. At Packt, we take the protection of our copyright and licenses very seriously. If you come across any illegal copies of our works, in any form, on the Internet, please provide us with the location address or website name immediately so that we can pursue a remedy.

Please contact us at `copyright@packtpub.com` with a link to the suspected pirated material.

We appreciate your help in protecting our authors, and our ability to bring you valuable content.

Questions

You can contact us at `questions@packtpub.com` if you are having a problem with any aspect of the book, and we will do our best to address it.

1
Navigating Git

In this chapter, we will cover the following topics:

- ▸ Git's objects
- ▸ The three stages
- ▸ Viewing the DAG
- ▸ Extracting fixed issues
- ▸ Getting a list of the changed files
- ▸ Viewing the history with Gitk
- ▸ Finding commits in the history
- ▸ Searching through the history code

Introduction

In this chapter, we will take a look at Git's data model. We will learn how Git references its objects and how the history is recorded. We will learn how to navigate the history, from finding certain text snippets in commit messages to the introduction of a certain string in the code.

The data model of Git is different from other common **version control systems** (**VCSs**) in the way Git handles its data. Traditionally, a VCS will store its data as an initial file followed by a list of patches for each new version of the file.

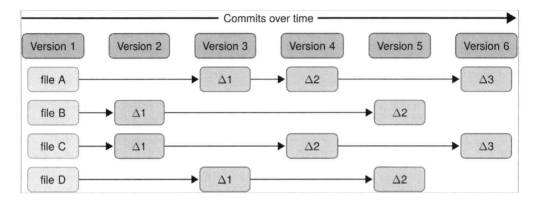

Git is different; instead of the regular file and patches list, Git records a snapshot of all the files tracked by Git and their paths relative to the repository root, that is, the files tracked by Git in the file system tree. Each commit in Git records the full tree state. If a file does *not* change between commits, Git will not store the file once more; instead, Git stores a link to the file.

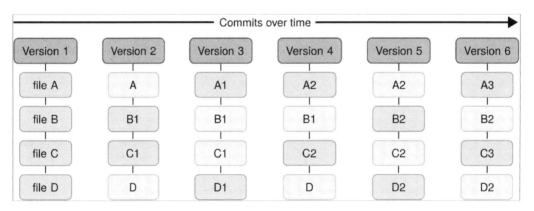

This is what makes Git different from most other VCSs, and in the following chapters, we will explore some of the benefits of this powerful model.

The way Git references the files and directories it tracks is directly built into the data model. In short, the Git data model can be summarized as shown in the following diagram:

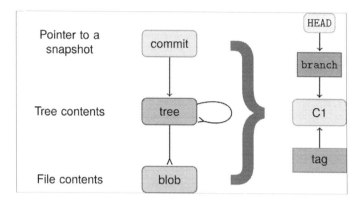

The commit object points to the root tree. The root tree points to subtrees and files. Branches and tags point to a commit object and the HEAD object points to the branch that is currently checked out. So for every commit, the full tree state and snapshot are identified by the root tree.

Git's objects

Now that you know Git stores every commit as a full tree state or snapshot, let's look closer at the object's Git store in the repository.

Git's object storage is a key-value storage, the key being the ID of the object and the value being the object itself. The key is an SHA-1 hash of the object, with some additional information such as size. There are four types of objects in Git, branches (which are not objects, but are important), and the special HEAD pointer that refers to the branch/commit currently checked out. The four object types are as follows:

- Files, or blobs as they are also called in the Git context
- Directories, or trees in the Git context
- Commits
- Tags

We will start by looking at the most recent commit object in the repository we just cloned, keeping in mind that the special HEAD pointer points to the branch currently checked out.

Getting ready

To view the objects in the Git database, we first need a repository to be examined.
For this recipe, we will clone an example repository located here:

```
$ git clone https://github.com/dvaske/data-model.git
$ cd data-model
```

Now you are ready to look at the objects in the database, we will start by looking first at the commit object, then the trees, the files, and finally the branches and tags.

How to do it...

Let's take a closer look at the object's Git stores in the repository.

The commit object

The special Git object HEAD always points to the current snapshot/commit, so we can use that as a target for our request of the commit we want to have a look at:

```
$ git cat-file -p HEAD
tree 34fa038544bcd9aed660c08320214bafff94150b
parent a90d1906337a6d75f1dc32da647931f932500d83
author Aske Olsson <aske.olsson@switch-gears.dk> 1386933960 +0100
committer Aske Olsson <aske.olsson@switch-gears.dk> 1386941455 +0100


This is the subject line of the commit message


It should be followed by a blank line then the body, which is this text.
Here you can have multiple paragraphs etc. and explain your commit. It's
like an email with subject and body, so get people's attention in the
subject
```

The cat-file command with the -p option pretty prints the object given on the command line; in this case, HEAD, which points to master, which in turn points to the most-recent commit on the branch.

We can now see the commit object, consisting of the root tree (tree), the parent commit object's ID (parent), author and timestamp information (author), committer and timestamp information (committer), and the commit message.

The tree object

To see the tree object, we can run the same command on the tree, but with the tree ID (`34fa038544bcd9aed660c08320214bafff94150b`) as the target:

```
$ git cat-file -p 34fa038544bcd9aed660c08320214bafff94150b
100644 blob f21dc2804e888fee6014d7e5b1ceee533b222c15    README.md
040000 tree abc267d04fb803760b75be7e665d3d69eeed32f8    a_sub_directory
100644 blob b50f80ac4d0a36780f9c0636f43472962154a11a    another-file.txt
100644 blob 92f046f17079aa82c924a9acf28d623fcb6ca727    cat-me.txt
100644 blob bb2fe940924c65b4a1cefcbdbe88c74d39eb23cd    hello_world.c
```

We can also specify that we want the tree object from the commit pointed to by HEAD, by specifying `git cat-file -p HEAD^{tree}`, which would give the same results as the previous one. The special notation `HEAD^{tree}` means that from the reference given, (HEAD) recursively dereferences the object at the reference until a tree object is found. The first tree object is the root tree object found from the commit pointed to by the `master` branch, which is pointed to by HEAD. A generic form of the notation is `<rev>^<type>` and will return the first object of `<type>` searching recursively from `<rev>`.

From the tree object, we can see what it contains: file type/permissions, type (`tree`/`blob`), ID, and pathname:

Type/ Permissions	Type	ID/SHA-1	Pathname
100644	blob	f21dc2804e888fee6014 d7e5b1ceee533b222c15	README.md
040000	tree	abc267d04fb803760b75 be7e665d3d69eeed32f8	a_sub_ directory
100644	blob	b50f80ac4d0a36780f9c 0636f43472962154a11a	another-file. txt
100644	blob	92f046f17079aa82c924 a9acf28d623fcb6ca727	cat-me.txt
100644	blob	bb2fe940924c65b4a1ce fcbdbe88c74d39eb23cd	hello-world.c

The blob object

Now, we can investigate the blob (file) object. We can do it using the same command, giving the blob ID as target for the `cat-me.txt` file:

```
$ git cat-file -p 92f046f17079aa82c924a9acf28d623fcb6ca727


This is the content of the file: "cat-me.txt."


Not really that exciting, huh?
```

This is simply the content of the file, which we will also get by running a normal `cat cat-me.txt` command. So, the objects are tied together, blobs to trees, trees to other trees, and the root tree to the commit object, all by the SHA-1 identifier of the object.

The branch

The branch object is not really like any other Git objects; you can't print it using the `cat-file` command as we can with the others (if you specify the `-p` pretty print, you'll just get the commit object it points to):

```
$ git cat-file master
usage: git cat-file (-t|-s|-e|-p|<type>|--textconv) <object>
   or: git cat-file (--batch|--batch-check) < <list_of_objects>


<type> can be one of: blob, tree, commit, tag.
...
$ git cat-file -p master
tree 34fa038544bcd9aed660c08320214bafff94150b
parent a90d1906337a6d75f1dc32da647931f932500d83
...
```

Instead, we can take a look at the branch inside the `.git` folder where the whole Git repository is stored. If we open the text file `.git/refs/heads/master`, we can actually see the commit ID the `master` branch points to. We can do this using `cat` as follows:

```
$ cat .git/refs/heads/master
34acc370b4d6ae53f051255680feaefaf7f7850d
```

We can verify that this is the latest commit by running `git log -1`:

```
$ git log -1
commit 34acc370b4d6ae53f051255680feaefaf7f7850d
```

```
Author: Aske Olsson <aske.olsson@switch-gears.dk>
Date:    Fri Dec 13 12:26:00 2013 +0100

    This is the subject line of the commit message
...
```

We can also see that HEAD is pointing to the active branch by using cat with the .git/HEAD file:

```
$ cat .git/HEAD
ref: refs/heads/master
```

The branch object is simply a pointer to a commit, identified by its SHA-1 hash.

The tag object

The last object to be analyzed is the tag object. There are three different kinds of tags: a lightweight (just a label) tag, an annotated tag, and a signed tag. In the example repository, there are two annotated tags:

```
$ git tag
v0.1
v1.0
```

Let's take a closer look at the v1.0 tag:

```
$ git cat-file -p v1.0
object 34acc370b4d6ae53f051255680feaefaf7f7850d
type commit
tag v1.0
tagger Aske Olsson <aske.olsson@switch-gears.dk> 1386941492 +0100

We got the hello world C program merged, let's call that a release 1.0
```

As you can see, the tag consists of an object, which in this case is the latest commit on the master branch, the object's type (both, commits, and blobs and trees can be tagged), the tag name, the tagger and timestamp, and finally a tag message.

How it works...

The Git command `git cat-file -p` will pretty print the object given as an input. Normally, it is not used in everyday Git commands, but it is quite useful to investigate how it ties together the objects. We can also verify the output of `git cat-file`, by rehashing it with the Git command `git hash-object`; for example, if we want to verify the commit object at HEAD (`34acc370b4d6ae53f051255680feaefaf7f7850d`), we can run the following command:

```
$ git cat-file -p HEAD | git hash-object -t commit --stdin
34acc370b4d6ae53f051255680feaefaf7f7850d
```

If you see the same commit hash as HEAD pointing towards you, you can verify whether it is correct with `git log -1`.

There's more...

There are many ways to see the objects in the Git database. The `git ls-tree` command can easily show the contents of trees and subtrees and `git show` can show the Git objects, but in a different way.

See also

> ▶ For further information about Git plumbing, see *Chapter 11, Git Plumbing and Attributes*, almost at the end of this book.

The three stages

We have seen the different objects in Git but how do we create them? In this example, we'll see how to create a blob, tree, and commit object in the repository. We'll learn about the three stages of creating a commit.

Getting ready

We'll use the same `data-model` repository as seen in the last recipe:

```
$ git clone https://github.com/dvaske/data-model.git
$ cd data-model
```

How to do it...

First, we'll make a small change to the file and check `git status`:

```
$ echo "Another line" >> another-file.txt
$ git status
On branch master
Your branch is up-to-date with 'origin/master'.

Changes not staged for commit:
  (use "git add <file>..." to update what will be committed)
  (use "git checkout -- <file>..." to discard changes in working
directory)

    modified:   another-file.txt

no changes added to commit (use "git add" and/or "git commit -a")
```

This, of course, just tells us that we have modified `another-file.txt` and we need to use `git add` to stage it. Let's add the `another-file.txt` file and run `git status` again:

```
$ git add another-file.txt
$ git status
On branch master
Your branch is up-to-date with 'origin/master'.

Changes to be committed:
  (use "git reset HEAD <file>..." to unstage)

    modified:   another-file.txt
```

The file is now ready to be committed, just as you have probably seen before. But what happened during the `add` command? The `add` command, generally speaking, moves files from the working directory to the staging area, but more than this actually happens, though you don't see it. When a file is moved to the staging area, the SHA-1 hash of the file is created and the blob object is written to Git's database. This happens for all the files added and every time a file is added, but if nothing changes for a file, this means it is already stored in the database. At first, this might seem that the database is growing quickly, but this is not the case. Garbage collection kicks in at times, compressing and cleaning up the database and keeping only the objects that are required.

We can edit the file again and run `git status`:

```
$ echo 'Whoops almost forgot this' >> another-file.txt
$ git status
On branch master
Your branch is up-to-date with 'origin/master'.

Changes to be committed:
  (use "git reset HEAD <file>..." to unstage)

  modified:    another-file.txt

Changes not staged for commit:
  (use "git add <file>..." to update what will be committed)
  (use "git checkout -- <file>..." to discard changes in working
directory)

  modified:    another-file.txt
```

Now, the file shows up both in the **Changes to be committed** and **Changes not staged for commit** sections. This looks a bit weird at first, but there is of course an explanation. When we added the file the first time, the content of it was hashed and stored in Git's database. The changes from the second change of the file have not yet been hashed and written to the database; it only exists in the working directory. Therefore, the file shows up in both the **Changes to be committed** and **Changes not staged for commit** sections; the first change is ready to be committed, the second is not. Let's also add the second change:

```
$ git add another-file.txt
$ git status
On branch master
Your branch is up-to-date with 'origin/master'.

Changes to be committed:
  (use "git reset HEAD <file>..." to unstage)

  modified:    another-file.txt
```

Now, all the changes we have made to the file are ready to be committed and we can record a commit:

```
$ git commit -m 'Another change to another file'
[master 55e29e4] Another change to another file
 1 file changed, 2 insertions(+)
```

How it works...

As we learned previously, the `add` command creates the blob object, the tree, and commit objects; however, they are created when we run the `commit` command. We can view these objects with the `cat-file` command, as we saw in the previous recipe:

```
$ git cat-file -p HEAD
tree 162201200b5223d48ea8267940c8090b23cbfb60
parent 34acc370b4d6ae53f051255680feaefaf7f7850d
author Aske Olsson <aske@schantz.com> 1401744547 +0200
committer Aske Olsson <aske@schantz.com> 1401744547 +0200

Another change to another file
```

The root-tree object from the commit is:

```
$ git cat-file -p HEAD^{tree}
100644 blob f21dc2804e888fee6014d7e5b1ceee533b222c15    README.md
040000 tree abc267d04fb803760b75be7e665d3d69eeed32f8    a_sub_directory
100644 blob 35d31106c5d6fdb38c6b1a6fb43a90b183011a4b    another-file.txt
100644 blob 92f046f17079aa82c924a9acf28d623fcb6ca727    cat-me.txt
100644 blob bb2fe940924c65b4a1cefcbdbe88c74d39eb23cd    hello_world.c
```

From the previous recipe, we know the SHA-1 of the root tree was `34fa038544bcd9aed660c08320214bafff94150b` and of the `another-file.txt` file was `b50f80ac4d0a36780f9c0636f43472962154a11a`, and as expected, they changed in our latest commit when we updated the `another-file.txt` file. We added the same file, `another-file.txt`, twice before we created the commit, recording the changes to the history of the repository. We also learned that the `add` command creates a blob object when called. So in the Git database, there must be an object similar to the content of `another-file.txt` the first time we added the file to the staging area. We can use the `git fsck` command to check for dangling objects, that is, objects that are not referred by other objects or references:

```
$ git fsck --dangling
Checking object directories: 100% (256/256), done.
dangling blob ad46f2da274ed6c79a16577571a604d3281cd6d9
```

Let's check the contents of the blob using the following command:

```
$ git cat-file -p ad46f2da274ed6c79a16577571a604d3281cd6d9
This is just another file
Another line
```

The blob is, as expected, similar to the content of `another-file.txt` when we added it to the staging area the first time.

The following diagram describes the tree stages and the commands used to move between the stages:

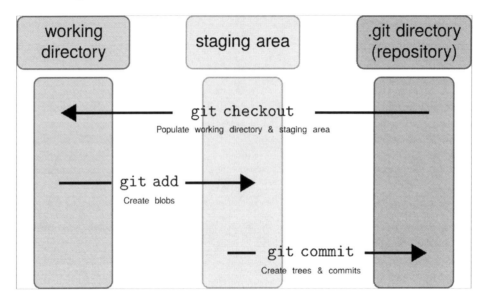

See also

► For more examples and information on the `cat-file`, `fsck`, and other plumbing commands, see *Chapter 11, Git Plumbing and Attributes*.

Viewing the DAG

The history in Git is formed from the commit objects; as development advances, branches are created and merged, and the history will create a directed acyclic graph, the DAG, due to the way Git ties a commit to its parent commit. The DAG makes it easy to see the development of a project based on the commits. Please note that the arrows in the following diagram are dependency arrows, meaning that each commit points to its parent commit(s), hence the arrows point in the opposite direction of time:

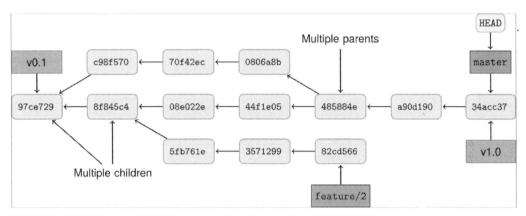

A graph of the example repository with abbreviated commit IDs

Viewing the history (the DAG) is built into Git by its `git log` command. There are also a number of visual Git tools that can graphically display the history. This section will show some features of `git log`.

Getting ready

We will use the example repository from the last section and ensure that the master branch is pointing to `34acc37`:

```
$ git checkout master && git reset --hard 34acc37
```

In the previous command, we only use the first seven characters (`34acc37`) of the commit ID; this is fine as long as the abbreviated ID used is unique in the repository.

How to do it...

The simplest way to see the history is to use the `git log` command; this will display the history in reverse chronological order. The output is paged through `less` and can be further limited, for example, by providing only the number of commits in history to be displayed:

```
$ git log -3
```

This will display the following result:

```
commit 34acc370b4d6ae53f051255680feaefaf7f7850d
Author: Aske Olsson <aske.olsson@switch-gears.dk>
Date:    Fri Dec 13 12:26:00 2013 +0100

    This is the subject line of the commit message.


    It should be followed by a blank line then the body, which is this
text. Here
    you can have multiple paragraphs etc. and explain your commit. It's
like an
    email with subject and body, so get people's attention in the subject

commit a90d1906337a6d75f1dc32da647931f932500d83
Author: Aske Olsson <aske.olsson@switch-gears.dk>
Date:    Fri Dec 13 12:17:42 2013 +0100

    Instructions for compiling hello_world.c

commit 485884efd6ac68cc7b58c643036acd3cd208d5c8
Merge: 44f1e05 0806a8b
Author: Aske Olsson <aske.olsson@switch-gears.dk>
Date:    Fri Dec 13 12:14:49 2013 +0100

    Merge branch 'feature/1'

    Adds a hello world C program.
```

 Turn on colors in the Git output by running `git config --global color.ui auto`.

By default, `git log` prints the commit, author's name and e-mail ID, timestamp, and the commit message. However, the information isn't very graphical, especially if you want to see branches and merges.

To display this information and limit some of the other data, you can use the following options with `git log`:

```
$ git log --decorate --graph --oneline --all
```

The previous command will show one commit per line (`--oneline`) identified by its abbreviated commit ID and the commit message subject. A graph will be drawn between the commits depicting their dependency (`--graph`). The `--decorate` option shows the branch names after the abbreviated commit ID, and the `--all` option shows all the branches, instead of just the current one(s).

```
$ git log --decorate --graph --oneline --all
* 34acc37 (HEAD, tag: v1.0, origin/master, origin/HEAD, master) This is
the sub...
* a90d190 Instructions for compiling hello_world.c
*   485884e Merge branch 'feature/1'
...
```

This output, however, gives neither the timestamp nor author information, due to the way the `--oneline` option formats the output.

Fortunately, the `log` command gives us the possibility to create our own output format. So, we can make a history view similar to the previous. The colors are made with the `%C<color-name>text-be-colored%Creset` syntax: including the author and timestamp information, and some colors to display it nicely:

```
$ git log --all --graph --pretty=format:\
'%Cred%h%Creset -%C(yellow)%d%Creset %s %Cgreen(%ci) %C(bold
blue)<%an>%Creset'
```

This is a bit cumbersome to write, but luckily it can be made as an alias so you only have to write it once:

```
git config ----global alias.graph "log --all --graph
--pretty=format:'%Cred%h%Creset -%C(yellow)%d%Creset %s %Cgreen(%ci)
%C(bold blue)<%an>%Creset'"
```

 Now, all you need to do is call `git graph` to show the history as you saw previously.

How it works...

Git traverses the DAG by following the parent IDs (hashes) from the given commit(s). The options passed to `git log` can format the output in different ways; this can serve several purposes, for example, to give a nice graphical view of the history, branches, and tags, as seen previously, or to extract specific information from the history of a repository to use, for example, in a script.

See also

▸ For more information about configuration and aliases, see *Chapter 2, Configuration*.

Extracting fixed issues

A common use case when creating a release is to create a release note, containing among other things, the bugs fixed in the release. A good practice is to write in the commit message if a bug is fixed by the commit. A better practice is to have a standard way of doing it, for example, a line with the string `"Fixes-bug: "` followed by the bug identifier in the last part of the commit message. This makes it easy to compile a list of bugs fixed for a release note. The JGit project is a good example of this; their bug identifier in the commit messages is a simple `"Bug: "` string followed by the bug ID.

This recipe will show you how to limit the output of `git log` to list just the commits since the last release (tag), which contains a bug fix.

Getting ready

Clone the JGit repository using the following command lines:

```
$ git clone https://git.eclipse.org/r/jgit/jgit
$ cd jgit
```

If you want the exact same output as in this example, reset your `master` branch to the following commit, `b14a93971837610156e815ae2eee3baaa5b7a44b`:

```
$ git checkout master && git reset --hard b14a939
```

How to do it...

You are now ready to look through the commit log for commit messages that describe the bugs fixed. First, let's limit the log to only look through the history since the last tag (release). To find the last tag, we can use `git describe`:

```
$ git describe
v3.1.0.201310021548-r-96-gb14a939
```

The preceding output tells us three things:

- ▸ The last tag was `v3.1.0.201310021548-r`
- ▸ The number of commits since the tag were `96`
- ▸ The current commit in abbreviated form is `b14a939`

Now, the log can be parsed from HEAD to `v3.1.0.201310021548-r`. But just running `git log 3.1.0.201310021548-r..HEAD` will give us all the 96 commits, and we just want the commits with commit messages that contain `"Bug: xxxxxx"` for our release note. The xxxxxx is an identifier for the bug, for example, a number. We can use the `--grep` option with `git log` for this purpose: `git log --grep "Bug: "`. This will give us all the commits with `"Bug: "` in the commit message; all we need now is just to format it to something we can use for our release note.

Let's say we want the release note format to look like the following template:

```
Commit-id: Commit subject
Fixes-bug: xxx
```

Our command line so far is as follows:

```
$ git log --grep "Bug: " v3.1.0.201310021548-r..HEAD
```

This gives us all the bug fix commits, but we can format this to a format that is easily parsed with the `--pretty` option. First, we will print the abbreviated commit ID `%h`, followed by a separator of our choice `|`, then the commit subject `%s`, (first line of the commit message), followed by a new line `%n`, and the body, `%b`:

```
--pretty="%h|%s%n%b"
```

The output of course needs to be parsed, but that's easy with regular Linux tools such as `grep` and `sed`:

First, we just want the lines that contain "|" or "Bug: ":

```
grep -E "\||Bug: "
```

Then, we replace these with `sed`:

```
sed -e 's/|/: /' -e 's/Bug:/Fixes-bug:/'
```

The entire command put together gives:

```
\$ git log --grep "Bug: " v3.1.0.201310021548-r..HEAD --pretty="%h|%s%n%b"
| grep -E "\||Bug: " | sed -e 's/|/: /' -e 's/Bug:/Fixes-bug:/'
```

The previous set of commands gives the following output:

```
f86a488: Implement rebase.autostash
Fixes-bug: 422951
7026658: CLI status should support --porcelain
Fixes-bug: 419968
e0502eb: More helpful InvalidPathException messages (include reason)
Fixes-bug: 413915
f4dae20: Fix IgnoreRule#isMatch returning wrong result due to missing
reset
Fixes-bug: 423039
7dc8a4f: Fix exception on conflicts with recursive merge
Fixes-bug: 419641
99608f0: Fix broken symbolic links on Cygwin.
Fixes-bug: 419494
...
```

Now, we can extract the bug information from the bug tracker and put the preceding code in the release note as well, if necessary.

How it works...

First, we limit the `git log` command to only show the range of commits we are interested in, then we further limit the output by filtering the `"Bug: "` string in the commit message. We pretty print the string so we can easily format it to a style we need for the release note and finally find and replace with `grep` and `sed` to completely match the style of the release note.

There's more...

If we just wanted to extract the bug IDs from the commit messages and didn't care about the commit IDs, we could have just used `grep` after the `git log` command, still limiting the log to the last tag:

```
$ git log  v3.1.0.201310021548-r..HEAD | grep "Bug: "
```

If we just want the commit IDs and their subjects but not the actual bug IDs, we can use the `--oneline` feature of `git log` combined with the `--grep` option:

```
$ git log --grep "Bug: " --oneline  v3.1.0.201310021548-r..HEAD
```

Getting a list of the changed files

As seen in the previous recipe where a list of fixed issues was extracted from the history, a list of all the files that have been changed since the last release can also easily be extracted. The files can be further filtered to find those that have been added, deleted, modified, and so on.

Getting ready

The same repository and HEAD position (HEAD pointing to `b14a939`) as seen in the previous recipe will be used. The release is also the same, which is `v3.1.0.201310021548-r`.

How to do it...

The following command lists all the files changed since the last release (`v3.1.0.201310021548-r`):

```
$ git diff --name-only v3.1.0.201310021548-r..HEAD
org.eclipse.jgit.packaging/org.eclipse.jgit.target/jgit-4.3.target
org.eclipse.jgit.packaging/org.eclipse.jgit.target/jgit-4.4.target
org.eclipse.jgit.pgm.test/tst/org/eclipse/jgit/pgm/DescribeTest.java
org.eclipse.jgit.pgm.test/tst/org/eclipse/jgit/pgm/FetchTest.java
org.eclipse.jgit.pgm/src/org/eclipse/jgit/pgm/Describe.java
...
```

How it works...

The `git diff` command operates on the same revision range as `git log` did in the previous recipe. By specifying `--name-only`, Git will only give the paths of the files as output changed by the commits in the range specified.

There's more...

The output of the command can be further filtered; if we only want to show which files have been deleted in the repository since the last commit, we can use the `--diff-filter` switch with `git diff`:

```
$ git diff --name-only --diff-filter=D  v3.1.0.201310021548-r..HEAD
org.eclipse.jgit.junit/src/org/eclipse/jgit/junit/
SampleDataRepositoryTestCase.java
org.eclipse.jgit.packaging/org.eclipse.jgit.target/org.eclipse.jgit.
target.target
org.eclipse.jgit.test/tst/org/eclipse/jgit/internal/storage/file/GCTest.
java
```

There are also switches for the files that have been added (A), copied (C), deleted (D), modified (M), renamed (R), and so on.

See also

▶   For more information, visit the help page by running `git help diff`

Viewing history with Gitk

We saw earlier how we can view the history (the DAG) and visualize it with the use of `git log`. However, as the history grows, the terminal representation of the history can be a bit cumbersome to navigate. Fortunately, there are a lot of graphical tools around Git, one of them being Gitk, which works on multiple platforms (Linux, Mac, and Windows).

This recipe will show you how to get started with Gitk.

Getting ready

Make sure you have Gitk installed:

```
$ which gitk
/usr/local/bin/gitk
```

If nothing shows up, Gitk in not installed on your system, or at least is not available on your $PATH.

Change the directory to the `data-model` repository from the objects and DAG examples. Make sure the master branch is checked out and pointing to 34acc37:

```
$ git checkout master && git reset --hard 34acc37
```

How to do it...

In the repository, run `gitk --all` `&` to bring up the Gitk interface. You can also specify the commit range or branches you want similar to `git log` or provide `--all` to see everything:

```
$ gitk --all &
```

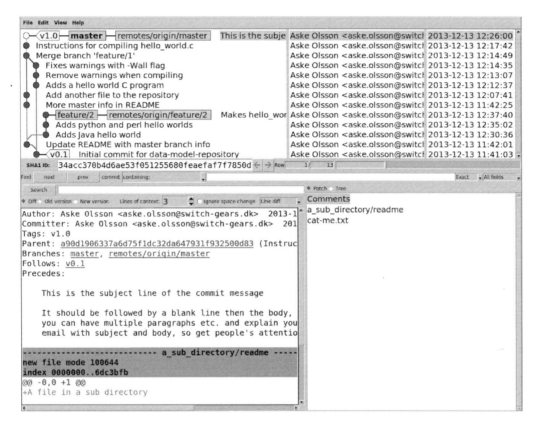

How it works...

Gitk parses the information for every commit and the objects attached to it to provide an easy graphical information screen that shows a graph of the history, author, and timestamp for each commit. In the bottom half, the commit message and the patches for each file changed and the list of files changed by the selected commit are displayed.

Though very lightweight and fast, Gitk is a very powerful tool. There are many different context menus regarding clicking on a commit, a branch, or a tag in the history view. You can create and delete branches, revert and cherry-pick commits, diff selected commits, and much more.

There's more...

From the interface, you can perform a find and search. Find looks through the history and search looks through the information displayed in the lower half of Gitk for the currently highlighted commit.

Finding commits in history

You already saw in the previous recipe how we can filter the output of `git log` to only list commits with the string `"Bug: "` in the commit message. In this example, we will use the same technique to find specific commits in the entire history.

Getting ready

Again, we will use the JGit repository, trying to find commits related to the keyword `"Performance"`. In this recipe, we will look through the entire history, so we don't need the master branch to point to a specific commit.

How to do it...

As we tried earlier, we can use the `--grep` option to find specific strings in commit messages. In this recipe, we look at the entire history and search every commit that has `"Performance"` in its commit message:

```
$ git log --grep "Performance" --oneline --all
9613b04 Merge "Performance fixes in DateRevQueue"
84afea9 Performance fixes in DateRevQueue
7cad0ad DHT: Remove per-process ChunkCache
d9b224a Delete DiffPerformanceTest
e7a3e59 Reuse DiffPerformanceTest support code to validate algorithms
fb1c7b1 Wait for JIT optimization before measuring diff performance
```

How it works...

In this example, we specifically ask Git to consider all of the commits in the history, by supplying the `--all` switch. Git runs through the DAG and checks whether the `"Performance"` string is included in the commit message. For an easy overview of the results, the `--oneline` switch is also used to limit the output to just the subject of the commit message. Hopefully then the commit(s) we needed to find can be identified from this much shorter list of commits.

Note that the search is case sensitive; had we searched for `"performance"` (all in lower case), the list of commits would have been very different:

```
$ git log --grep "performance" --oneline --all
5ef6d69 Use the new FS.exists method in commonly occuring places
2be6927 Always allocate the PackOutputStream copyBuffer
437be8d Simplify UploadPack by parsing wants separately from haves
e6883df Enable writing bitmaps during GC by default.
374406a Merge "Fix RefUpdate performance for existing Refs"
f1dea3e Fix RefUpdate performance for existing Refs
84afea9 Performance fixes in DateRevQueue
8a9074f Implement core.checkstat = minimal
130ad4e Delete storage.dht package
d4fed9c Refactored method to find branches from which a commit is
reachable
...
```

There's more...

We also could have used the find feature in Gitk to find the same commits. Open Gitk with the `--all` switch, type `Performance` in the **Find** field and hit *Enter*. This will highlight the commits in the history view and you can navigate to the previous/next result by pressing *Shift + up arrow*, *Shift + down arrow*, or the buttons next to the **Find** field. You will still, however, be able to see the entire history in the view with the matching commits highlighted:

Searching through history code

Sometimes it is not enough; by just looking through the commit messages in the history, you may want to know which commits touched a specific method or variable. This is also possible using `git log`. You can perform a search for a string, for example, a variable or method, and `git log` will give you the commits, adding or deleting the string from the history. In this way, you can easily get the full commit context for the piece of code.

Getting ready

Again, we will use the JGit repository with the master branch pointing to `b14a939`:

```
$ git checkout master && git reset --hard b14a939
```

How to do it...

We would like to find all the commits that have changes made to lines that contain the method `"isOutdated"`. Again, we will just display the commits on one line each then we can check them individually later:

```
$ git log -G"isOutdated" --oneline
f32b861 JGit 3.0: move internal classes into an internal subpackage
c9e4a78 Add isOutdated method to DirCache
797ebba Add support for getting the system wide configuration
ad5238d Move FileRepository to storage.file.FileRepository
4c14b76 Make lib.Repository abstract and lib.FileRepository its
implementation
c9c57d3 Rename Repository 'config' as 'repoConfig'
5c780b3 Fix unit tests using MockSystemReader with user configuration
cc905e7 Make Repository.getConfig aware of changed config
```

Eight commits have patches that involve the string `"isOutdated"`.

How it works...

Git traverses the history, the DAG, looking at each commit for the string `"isOutdated"` in the patch between the parent commit and the current commit. This method is quite convenient to find out when a given string was introduced or deleted and to get the full context and commit at that point in time.

There's more...

The `-G` option used with `git log` will look for differences in the patches that contain added or deleted lines that match the given string. However, these lines could also have been added or removed due to some other refactoring/renaming of a variable or method. There is another option that can be used with `git log`, `-S`, which will look through the difference in the patch text similar to the `-G` option, but only match commits where there is a change in the number of occurrences of the specified string, that is, a line added or removed, but not added and removed.

Let's see the output of the `-S` option:

```
$ git log -S"isOutdated" --oneline
f32b861 JGit 3.0: move internal classes into an internal subpackage
c9e4a78 Add isOutdated method to DirCache
797ebba Add support for getting the system wide configuration
ad5238d Move FileRepository to storage.file.FileRepository
4c14b76 Make lib.Repository abstract and lib.FileRepository its
implementation
5c780b3 Fix unit tests using MockSystemReader with user configuation
cc905e7 Make Repository.getConfig aware of changed config
```

The search matches seven commits, whereas the search with the –G option matches eight commits. The difference is the commit with the ID `c9c57d3` is only found with the –G option in the first list. A closer look at this commit shows that the `isOutdated` string is only touched due to renaming of another object, and this is why it is filtered away from the list of matching commits in the last list when using the –S option. We can see the content of the commit with the `git show` command, and use `grep -C4` to limit the output to just the four lines before and after the search string:

```
$ git show c9c57d3 | grep -C4 "isOutdated"
@@ -417,14 +417,14 @@ public FileBasedConfig getConfig() {
            throw new RuntimeException(e);
        }
      }
-    if (config.isOutdated()) {
+    if (repoConfig.isOutdated()) {
        try {
-            loadConfig();
+            loadRepoConfig();
        } catch (IOException e) {
```

2
Configuration

In this chapter, we will cover the following topics:

- ▶ Configuration targets
- ▶ Querying the existing configuration
- ▶ Templates
- ▶ A .git directory template
- ▶ A few configuration examples
- ▶ Git aliases
- ▶ The refspec exemplified

Configuration targets

In this section, we will look at the different layers that can be configured. The layers are:

- ▶ `SYSTEM`: This layer is system-wide and found in `/etc/gitconfig`
- ▶ `GLOBAL`: This layer is global for the user and found in `~/.gitconfig`
- ▶ `LOCAL`: This layer is local to the current repository and found in `.git/config`

Getting ready

We will use the `jgit` repository for this example; clone it or use the clone you already have from *Chapter 1, Navigating Git*, as shown in the following command:

```
$ git clone https://git.eclipse.org/r/jgit/jgit
$ cd jgit
```

How to do it...

In the previous example, we saw how we could use the command `git config --list` to list configuration entries. This list is actually made from three different levels of configuration that Git offers: system-wide configuration, `SYSTEM`; global configuration for the user, `GLOBAL`; and local repository configuration, `LOCAL`.

For each of these configuration layers, we can query the existing configuration. On a Windows box with a default installation of the Git extensions, the different configuration layers will look approximately like the following:

```
$ git config --list --system
core.symlinks=false
core.autocrlf=true
color.diff=auto
color.status=auto
color.branch=auto
color.interactive=true
pack.packsizelimit=2g
help.format=html
http.sslcainfo=/bin/curl-ca-bundle.crt
sendemail.smtpserver=/bin/msmtp.exe
diff.astextplain.textconv=astextplain
rebase.autosquash=true


$ git config --list --global
merge.tool=kdiff3
mergetool.kdiff3.path=C:/Program Files (x86)/KDiff3/kdiff3.exe
diff.guitool=kdiff3
difftool.kdiff3.path=C:/Program Files (x86)/KDiff3/kdiff3.exe
core.editor="C:/Program Files (x86)/GitExtensions/GitExtensions.exe"
fileeditor
core.autocrlf=true
credential.helper=!\"C:/Program Files (x86)/GitExtensions/
GitCredentialWinStore/git-credential-winst
ore.exe\"
user.name=Aske Olsson
user.email=aske.olsson@switch-gears.dk
```

```
$ git config --list --local
core.repositoryformatversion=0
core.filemode=false
core.bare=false
core.logallrefupdates=true
core.symlinks=false
core.ignorecase=true
core.hidedotfiles=dotGitOnly
remote.origin.url=https://git.eclipse.org/r/jgit/jgit
remote.origin.fetch=+refs/heads/*:refs/remotes/origin/*
branch.master.remote=origin
branch.master.merge=refs/heads/master
```

We can also query a single key and limit the scope to one of the three layers, by using the following command:

```
$ git config --global user.email
aske.olsson@switch-gears.dk
```

We can set the e-mail address of the user to a different one for the current repository:

```
$ git config --local user.email aske@switch-gears.dk
```

Now, listing the GLOBAL layer user.email will return aske.olsson@switch-gears.dk, listing LOCAL gives aske@switch-gears.dk, and listing user.email without specifying the layer gives the effective value that is used in the operations on this repository, in this case, the LOCAL value aske@switch-gears.dk. The effective value is the value, which takes precedence when needed. When two or more values are specified for the same key, but on different layers, the lowest layer takes precedence. When a configuration value is needed, Git will first look in the LOCAL configuration. If not found here, the GLOBAL configuration is queried. If it is not found in the GLOBAL configuration, the SYSTEM configuration is used. If none of this works, the default value in Git is used.

In the previous example, user.email is specified in both the GLOBAL and LOCAL layers. Hence, the LOCAL layer will be used.

How it works...

Querying the three layers of configuration simply returns the content of the configuration files: /etc/gitconfig for system-wide configuration, ~/.gitconfig for user-specific configuration, and .git/config for repository-specific configuration. When not specifying the configuration layer, the returned value will be the effective value.

There's more...

Instead of setting all the configuration values on the command line by the key value, it is possible to set them by just editing the configuration file directly. Open the configuration file in your favorite editor and set the configuration you need, or use the built-in `git config -e` repository to edit the configuration directly in the Git-configured editor. You can set the editor to the editor of your choice either by changing the $EDITOR environment variable or with the `core.editor` configuration target, for example:

```
$ git config --global core.editor vim
```

Querying the existing configuration

In this example, we will look at how we can query the existing configuration and set the configuration values.

Getting ready

We'll use `jgit` again by using the following command:

```
$ cd jgit
```

How to do it...

To view all the effective configurations for the current Git repository, run the following command:

```
$ git config --list
user.name=Aske Olsson
user.email=askeolsson@switch-gears.dk
core.repositoryformatversion=0
core.filemode=false
core.bare=false
core.logallrefupdates=true
remote.origin.url=https://git.eclipse.org/r/jgit/jgit
remote.origin.fetch=+refs/heads/*:refs/remotes/origin/*
branch.master.remote=origin
branch.master.merge=refs/heads/master
```

The previous output will of course reflect the user running the command. Instead of Aske Olsson as the name and the e-mail, the output should reflect your settings.

If we are just interested in a single configuration item, we can just query it by its `section.key` or `section.subsection.key`:

```
$ git config user.name
Aske Olsson
$ git config remote.origin.url
https://git.eclipse.org/r/jgit/jgit
```

How it works...

Git's configuration is stored in plaintext files, and works like a key-value storage. You can set/query by key and get the value back. An example of the text-based configuration file is shown as follows (from the `jgit` repository):

```
$ cat .git/config
[core]
        repositoryformatversion = 0
        filemode = false
        bare = false
        logallrefupdates = true
[remote "origin"]
        url = https://git.eclipse.org/r/jgit/jgit
        fetch = +refs/heads/*:refs/remotes/origin/*
[branch "master"]
        remote = origin
        merge = refs/heads/master
```

There's more...

It is also easy to set configuration values. Just use the same syntax as you did when querying the configuration, except you need to add an argument to the value. To set a new e-mail address on the LOCAL layer, we can execute the following command line:

```
git config user.email askeolsson@example.com
```

The LOCAL layer is the default if nothing else is specified. If you require whitespaces in the value, you can enclose the string in quotation marks, as you would do when configuring your name:

```
git config user.name "Aske Olsson"
```

You can even set your own configuration, which does not have any effect on the core Git, but can be useful for scripting/builds and so on:

```
$ git config my.own.config "Whatever I need"
```

List the value

```
$ git config my.own.config
Whatever I need
```

It is also very easy to delete/unset configuration entries:

```
$ git config --unset my.own.config
```

List the value

```
$ git config my.own.config
```

Templates

In this example, we will see how to create a template commit message that will be displayed in the editor when creating a commit. The template is only for the local user and not distributed with the repository in general.

Getting ready

In this example, we will use the example repository from *Chapter 1, Navigating Git*:

```
$ git clone https://github.com/dvaske/data-model.git
$ cd data-model
```

We'll use the following code as a commit message template for commit messages:

```
Short description of commit

Longer explanation of the motivation for the change

Fixes-Bug: Enter bug-id or delete line
Implements-Requirement: Enter requirement-id or delete line
```

Save the commit message template in $HOME/.gitcommitmsg.txt. The filename isn't fixed and you can choose a filename of your liking.

How to do it...

To let Git know about our new commit message template, we can set the configuration variable `commit.template` to point at the file we just created with that template; we'll do it globally so it is applicable to all our repositories:

```
$ git config --global commit.template $HOME/.gitcommitmsg.txt
```

Now, we can try to change a file, add it, and create a commit. This will bring up our preferred editor with the commit message template preloaded:

```
$ git commit


Short description of commit


Longer explanation of the motivation for the change


Fixes-Bug: Enter bug-id or delete line
Implements-Requirement: Enter requirement-id or delete line


# Please enter the commit message for your changes. Lines starting
# with '#' will be ignored, and an empty message aborts the commit.
# On branch master
# Changes to be committed:
#   (use "git reset HEAD <file>..." to unstage)
#
#   modified:   another-file.txt
#
~
~
"\.git/COMMIT_EDITMSG" 13 lines, 396 characters
```

We can now edit the message according to our commit and save to complete the commit.

How it works...

When `commit.template` is set, Git simply uses the content of the template file as a starting point for all commit messages. This is quite convenient if you have a commit-message policy as it greatly increases the chances of the policy being followed. You can even have different templates tied to different repositories, since you can just set the configuration at the local level.

A .git directory template

Sometimes, having a global configuration isn't enough. You will also need to trigger the execution of scripts (also known as Git hooks), exclude files, and so on. It is possible to achieve this with the template option set to `git init`. It can be given as a command-line option to `git clone` and `git init`, or as the `$GIT_TEMPLATE_DIR` environment variable, or as the configuration option `init.templatedir`. It defaults to `/usr/share/git-core/templates`. The template option works by copying files in the template directory to the `.git` (`$GIT_DIR`) folder after it has been created. The default directory contains sample hooks and some suggested exclude patterns. In the following example, we'll see how we can set up a new template directory, and add a commit message hook and exclude file.

Getting ready

First, we will create the template directory. We can use any name we want, and we'll use `~/.git_template`, as shown in the following command:

```
$ mkdir ~/.git_template
```

Now, we need to populate the directory with some template files. This could be a hook or an exclude file. We will create one hook file and an exclude file. The hook file is located in `.git/hooks/name-of-hook` and the exclude file in `.git/info/exclude`. Create the two directories needed, `hooks` and `info`, as shown in the following command:

```
$ mkdir ~/.git_template/{hooks,info}
```

To keep the sample hooks provided by the default template directory (the Git installation), we copy the files in the default template directory to the new one. When we use our newly created template directory, we'll override the default one. So, copying the default files to our template directory will make sure that except for our specific changes, the template directory is similar to the default one, as shown in the following command:

```
$ cd ~/.git_template/hooks
$ cp /usr/share/git-core/templates/hooks/* .
```

We'll use the `commit-msg` hook as the example hook:

```
#!/bin/sh
MSG_FILE="$1"
echo "\nHi from the template commit-msg hook" >> $MSG_FILE
```

The hook is very simple and will just add `Hi from the template commit-msg hook` to the end of the commit message. Save it as `commit-msg` in the `~/.git_template/hooks` directory and make it executable by using the following command:

```
chmod +x ~/.git_template/hooks/commit-msg
```

Now that the commit message hook is done, let's also add an exclude file to the example. The exclude file works like the `.gitignore` file, but is not tracked in the repository. We'll create an exclude file that excludes all the `*.txt` files, as follows:

```
$ echo *.txt > ~/.git_template/info/exclude
```

Now, our template directory is ready for use.

How to do it...

Our template directory is ready and we can use it, as described earlier, as a command-line option, an environment variable or, as in this example, to be set as a configuration:

```
$ git config --global init.templatedir ~/.git_template
```

Now, all Git repositories we create using `init` or `clone` will have the default files of the template directory. We can test if it works by creating a new repository as follows:

```
$ git init template-example
$ cd template-example
```

Let's try to create a `.txt` file and see what `git status` tells us. It should be ignored by the exclude file from the template directory:

```
$ echo "this is the readme file" > README.txt
$ git status
```

The exclude file worked! You can put in the file endings yourself or just leave it blank and keep to the `.gitignore` files.

To test if the `commit-msg` hook also works, let's try to create a commit. First, we need a file to commit. So, let's create that and commit it as follows:

```
$ echo "something to commit" > somefile
$ git add somefile
$ git commit -m "Committed something"
```

We can now check the history with `git log`:

```
$ git log -1
commit 1f7d63d7e08e96dda3da63eadc17f35132d24064
Author: Aske Olsson <aske.olsson@switch-gears.dk>
Date:    Mon Jan 6 20:14:21 2014 +0100

    Committed something


    Hi from the template commit-msg hook
```

How it works...

When Git creates a new repository, either via `init` or `clone`, it will copy the files from the template directory to the new repository when creating the directory structure. The template directory can be defined either by a command-line argument, environment variable, or configuration option. If nothing is specified, the default template directory will be used (distributed with the Git installation). By setting the configuration as a `--global` option, the template directory defined will apply to all of the user's (new) repositories. This is a very nice way to distribute the same hooks across repositories, but it also has some drawbacks. As the files in the template directory are only copied to the Git repositories, updates to the template directory do not affect the existing repositories. This can be solved by running `git init` in each existing repository to reinitialize the repository, but this can be quite cumbersome. Also, the template directory can enforce hooks on some repositories where you don't want them. This is quite easily solved by simply deleting the hook files in `.git/hooks` of that repository.

See also

> ► For more information on hooks in Git, please refer to *Chapter 7, Enhancing Your Daily Work with Git Hooks, Aliases, and Scripts*

A few configuration examples

There are configuration targets in the core Git system. In this section, we'll take a closer look at a few of them that might be useful in your daily work.

We'll look at the following three different configuration areas:

► Rebase and merge setup

► Expiry of objects

► Autocorrect

Getting ready

In this exercise, we'll just set a few configurations. We'll use the data model repository from *Chapter 1, Navigating Git*:

```
$ cd data-model
```

How to do it...

Let's take a closer look at the previously mentioned configuration areas.

Rebase and merge setup

By default, when performing `git pull`, a merge commit will be created if the history of the local branch has diverged from the remote one. However, to avoid all these merge commits, a repository can be configured so it will default to rebase instead of merging when doing `git pull`. Several configuration targets related to the option exist as follows:

▶ `pull.rebase`: This configuration, when set to `true`, will pull to rebase the current branch on top of the fetched one when performing a `git pull`. It can also be set to `preserve` so that the local merge commit will not be flattened in the rebase, by passing `--preserve-merges` to `git rebase`. The default value is `false` as the configuration is not set. To set this option in your local repository, run the following command:

```
$ git config pull.rebase true
```

▶ `branch.autosetuprebase`: When this configuration is set to `always`, any new branch created with `<git branch` or `git checkout` that tracks another branch will be set up to pull to rebase (instead of merge). The valid options are as follows:

  ❑ `never`: This is set to pull to rebase (default)
  ❑ `local`: This is set to pull to rebase for local tracked branches
  ❑ `remote`: This is set to pull to rebase for remote tracked branches
  ❑ `always`: This is set to pull to rebase for all tracked branches

To set this option for all the new branches regardless of tracking remote or local branches, run the following command:

```
$ git config branch.autosetuprebase always
```

- ▶ `branch.<name>.rebase`: This configuration, when set to `true`, applies only to the `<name>` branch and tells Git to pull to rebase when performing `git pull` on the given branch. It can also be set to `preserve` so that the local merge commit will not be flattened when running `git pull`. By default, the configuration is not set for any branch. To set the `feature/2` branch in the repository to default to rebase instead of merge, we can run the following command:

```
$ git config branch.feature/2.rebase true
```

Expiry of objects

By default, Git will perform garbage collection on unreferenced objects and clean `reflog` for entries, both of which are older than 90 days. For an object to be referenced, something must point to it; a tree, a commit, a tag, a branch, or some of the internal Git bookkeeping like `stash` or `reflog`. There are three settings that can be used to change this time as follows:

- ▶ `gc.reflogexpire`: This is the general setting to know for how long a branch's history is kept in `reflog`. The default time is 90 days. The setting is a length of time, for example, `10 days, 6 months` and it can be turned completely off with the value `never`. The setting can be set to match a `refs` pattern by supplying the pattern in the configuration setting. `gc.<pattern>.reflogexpire`: This pattern can, for example, be `/refs/remotes/*` and the expire setting would then only apply for those refs.

- ▶ `gc.reflogexpireunreachable`: This setting controls how long the `reflog` entries that are not a part of the current branch history should be available in the repository. The default value is `30 days`, and similar to the previous option, it is expressed as a length of time or set to `never` in order to turn it off. This setting can, as the previous one, be set to match a `refs` pattern.

- ▶ `gc.pruneexpire`: This option tells `git gc` to prune objects older than the value. The default is `2.weeks.ago`, and the value can be expressed as a relative date like `3.months.ago`. To disable the grace period, the value `now` can be used. To set a non-default expiry date only on remote branches, use the following command:

```
$ git config gc./refs/remote/*.reflogexpire never
$ git config gc./refs/remote/*.reflogexpireunreachable "2 months"
```

We can also set a date so `git gc` will prune objects sooner:

```
$ git config gc.pruneexpire 3.days.ago
```

Autocorrect

This configuration is useful when you get tired of messages like the following one just because you made a typo on the keyboard:

```
$ git statis
git: 'statis' is not a git command. See 'git --help'.


Did you mean this?
        status
```

By setting the configuration to `help.autocorrect`, you can control how Git will behave when you accidentally send a typo to it. By default, the value is `0` and it means to list the possible options similar to the input (if `statis` is given `status` will be shown). A negative value means to immediately execute the corresponding command. A positive value means to wait the given number of deciseconds (0.1 sec) before running the command, (so there is some amount of time to cancel it). If several commands can be deduced from the text entered, nothing will happen. Setting the value to half a second gives you some time to cancel a wrong command, as follows:

```
$ git config help.autocorrect 5
$ git statis
WARNING: You called a Git command named 'statis', which does not exist.
Continuing under the assumption that you meant 'status'
in 0.5 seconds automatically...
# On branch master
# Changes to be committed:
#   (use "git reset HEAD <file>..." to unstage)
#
#       modified:   another-file.txt
#
```

How it works...

Setting the configuration targets will change the way Git behaves. The previous examples describe a few useful methods to get Git to act differently than its default behavior. You should be sure when you are changing a configuration that you completely understand what that configuration does. So, check the Git configuration help page by using `git help config`.

There's more...

There are a lot of configuration targets available in Git. You can run `git help config` and a few pages down all of them are displayed and explained.

Git aliases

An alias is a nice way to configure long and/or complicated Git commands to represent short useful ones. An alias is simply a configuration entry under the alias section. It is usually configured to `--global` to apply it everywhere.

Getting ready

In this example, we will use the `jgit` repository, which was also used in *Chapter 1, Navigating Git*, with the `master` branch pointing at `b14a93971837610156e815ae2eee3baaa5b7a44b`. Either use the clone from *Chapter 1, Navigating Git*, or clone the repository again, as follows:

```
$ git clone https://git.eclipse.org/r/jgit/jgit
$ cd jgit
$ git checkout master && git reset --hard b14a939
```

How to do it...

First, we'll create a few simple aliases, then a couple of more special ones, and finally a couple of aliases using external commands. Instead of writing `git checkout` every time we need to switch branches, we can create an alias of that command and call it `git co`. We can do the same for `git branch`, `git commit`, and `git status` as follows:

```
$ git config --global alias.co checkout
$ git config --global alias.br branch
$ git config --global alias.ci commit
$ git config --global alias.st status
```

Now, try to run `git st` in the `jgit` repository as follows:

```
$ git st
# On branch master
nothing to commit, working directory clean
```

The alias method is also good to create the Git commands you think are missing in Git. One of the common Git aliases is `unstage`, which is used to move a file out of the staging area, as shown in the following command:

```
$ git config --global alias.unstage 'reset HEAD --'
```

Try to edit the `README.md` file in the root of the `jgit` repository and add it in the root. Now, `git status/git st` should display something like the following:

```
$ git st
# On branch master
# Changes to be committed:
#   (use "git reset HEAD <file>..." to unstage)
#
#       modified:   README.md
#
```

Let's try to unstage `README.md` and then look at `git st` as follows:

```
$ git unstage README.md
Unstaged changes after reset:
M       README.md
```

```
$ git st
# On branch master
# Changes not staged for commit:
#   (use "git add <file>..." to update what will be committed)
#   (use "git checkout -- <file>..." to discard changes in working directory)
#
#       modified:   README.md
#
no changes added to commit (use "git add" and/or "git commit -a")
```

A common use case for aliases is to format the history of Git in specific ways. Let's say you want the number of lines added and deleted for each file in the commit displayed along with some common commit data. For this, we can create the following alias so we don't have to type everything each time:

```
$ git config --global alias.ll "log --pretty=format:\"%C(yellow)%h%Cred%d %Creset%s %Cgreen(%cr) %C(bold blue)<%an>%Creset\" --numstat"
```

Now, we can execute `git ll` in the terminal and get a nice stat output, as shown in the following command:

```
$ git ll
b14a939 (HEAD, master) Prepare 3.3.0-SNAPSHOT builds (8 days ago)
<Matthias Sohn>
6          6          org.eclipse.jgit.ant.test/META-INF/MANIFEST.MF
1          1          org.eclipse.jgit.ant.test/pom.xml
3          3          org.eclipse.jgit.ant/META-INF/MANIFEST.MF
1          1          org.eclipse.jgit.ant/pom.xml
4          4          org.eclipse.jgit.archive/META-INF/MANIFEST.MF
2          2          org.eclipse.jgit.archive/META-INF/SOURCE-MANIFEST.MF
1          1          org.eclipse.jgit.archive/pom.xml
6          6          org.eclipse.jgit.console/META-INF/MANIFEST.MF
1          1          org.eclipse.jgit.console/pom.xml
12         12         org.eclipse.jgit.http.server/META-INF/MANIFEST.MF
...
```

It is also possible to use an external command instead of a Git command. So, small shell scripts and so on can be embedded. To create an alias with an external command, the alias must start with an exclamation mark `!`. The examples can be used when resolving conflicts from a rebase or merge. In your `~/.gitconfig` file under [alias], add the following:

```
editconflicted = "!f() {git ls-files --unmerged | cut -f2 | sort -u ; };
$EDITOR 'f'"
```

This will bring up your configured `$EDITOR` with all the files that are in the conflict state due to the merge/rebase. This quickly allows you to fix the conflicts and get on with the merge/rebase.

In the `jgit` repository, we can create two branches at an earlier point in time and merge these two branches:

```
$ git branch A 03f78fc
$ git branch B 9891497
$ git checkout A
Switched to branch 'A'

$ git merge B
```

Now, you'll see that this fails to perform the merge, and you can run `git st` to check the status ses of a lot of files that are in a conflicted state, `both modified`. To open and edit all the conflicted files, we can now run `git editconflicted`. This brings up $EDITOR with the files. If your environment variable isn't set, use `EDITOR=<you-favorite-editor>` export to set it.

For this example, we don't actually resolve the conflicts. Just check that the alias works and you're ready for the next alias.

Now that we have solved all the merge conflicts, it is time to add all of those files before we conclude the merge. Luckily, we can create an alias that can help us with that, as follows:

```
addconflicted = "!f() { git ls-files --unmerged | cut -f2 | sort -u ; };
git add 'f'"
```

Now, we can run `git addconflicted`. Later, `git status` will tell us that all the conflicted files are added:

```
$ git st
On branch A
All conflicts fixed but you are still merging.
  (use "git commit" to conclude merge)


Changes to be committed:

    modified:   org.eclipse.jgit.console/META-INF/MANIFEST.MF
    modified:   org.eclipse.jgit.console/pom.xml
    modified:   org.eclipse.jgit.http.server/META-INF/MANIFEST.MF
    modified:   org.eclipse.jgit.http.server/pom.xml
    modified:   org.eclipse.jgit.http.test/META-INF/MANIFEST.MF
    modified:   org.eclipse.jgit.http.test/pom.xml
...
```

Now we can conclude the merge with git commit:

```
$ git commit
[A 94344ae] Merge branch 'B' into A
```

How it works...

Git simply runs the command the alias is short for. It is very convenient for long Git commands, or Git commands that are hard to remember exactly how to write. Now, all you have to remember is the alias and you can always look in the configuration file for it.

There's more...

Another way to create a kind of Git alias is to make a shell script and save the file with the name `git-<your-alias-name>`. Make the file executable and place it somewhere in your `$PATH`. You can now run that file simply by running `git <your-alias-name>` from the command line.

The refspec exemplified

Though the refspec isn't the first thing that comes to mind when thinking about the Git configuration, it is actually quite close. In a lot of the Git commands the refspec is used, but often implicitly, that is, the refspec is taken from the configuration file. If you don't remember setting a refspec configuration, you are probably right, but if you cloned the repository or added a remote, you'll have a section in `.git/config`, which looks something like the following (this is for the Jgit repository):

```
[remote "origin"]
        url = https://git.eclipse.org/r/jgit/jgit
        fetch = +refs/heads/*:refs/remotes/origin/*
```

The fetch line contains the configured refspec to fetch for this repository.

Getting ready

In this example, we'll be using the `jgit` repository as our server repository, but we have to make a clone of it to a bare repository so we can push it. You can't push to the checked out branch on a non-bare repository as this can overwrite the work area and index.

Create a bare repository from the `jgit` repository and create a new Git repository where we can play with the refspec as follows:

```
$ git clone --bare https://git.eclipse.org/r/jgit/jgit jgit-bare.git
$ git init refspec-tests
$ cd refspec-tests
$ git remote add origin ../jgit-bare.git
```

We also need to change the branch names on some of the branches to match the example for name spacing; the following will rename the `stable-xxx` branches to `stable/xxx`:

```
$ for br in $(git branch  -a | grep "stable-"); do new=$(echo $br| sed
's/-/\//'); git branch $new $br; done
```

In the previous shell scripting, the $new and $br variables aren't placed in double quotes (") as good practice for shell scripting would otherwise suggest. This is okay as the variables reflect the names of the branches in the repository and branch names cannot contain spaces.

How to do it...

Let us set up our new repository to only fetch the master branch. We do this by changing the fetch line under [remote "origin"] in the configuration file (.git/config), as follows:

```
[remote "origin"]
        url = ../jgit-bare.git
        fetch = +refs/heads/master:refs/remotes/origin/master
```

Now, we will only fetch the master branch and not all the other branches when executing a git fetch, git pull, or a git remote update origin, as follows:

```
$ git pull
remote: Counting objects: 44033, done.
remote: Compressing objects: 100% (6927/6927), done.
remote: Total 44033 (delta 24063), reused 44033 (delta 24063)
Receiving objects: 100% (44033/44033), 9.45 MiB | 5.70 MiB/s, done.
Resolving deltas: 100% (24063/24063), done.
From ../jgit-bare
 * [new branch]      master       -> origin/master
From ../jgit-bare
 * [new tag]         v0.10.1      -> v0.10.1
 * [new tag]         v0.11.1      -> v0.11.1
 * [new tag]         v0.11.3      -> v0.11.3
...
$ git branch -a
* master
  remotes/origin/master
```

Let's also set up a separate refspec to fetch all the stable/* branches to the local repository as follows:

```
[remote "origin"]
        url = ../jgit-bare.git
        fetch = +refs/heads/master:refs/remotes/origin/master
        fetch = +refs/heads/stable/*:refs/remotes/origin/stable/*
```

Now, fetch the branches locally, as shown in the following command:

```
$ git fetch
From ../jgit-bare
 * [new branch]      stable/0.10 -> origin/stable/0.10
 * [new branch]      stable/0.11 -> origin/stable/0.11
 * [new branch]      stable/0.12 -> origin/stable/0.12
 * [new branch]      stable/0.7 -> origin/stable/0.7
 * [new branch]      stable/0.8 -> origin/stable/0.8
 * [new branch]      stable/0.9 -> origin/stable/0.9
 * [new branch]      stable/1.0 -> origin/stable/1.0
 * [new branch]      stable/1.1 -> origin/stable/1.1
 * [new branch]      stable/1.2 -> origin/stable/1.2
 * [new branch]      stable/1.3 -> origin/stable/1.3
 * [new branch]      stable/2.0 -> origin/stable/2.0
 * [new branch]      stable/2.1 -> origin/stable/2.1
 * [new branch]      stable/2.2 -> origin/stable/2.2
 * [new branch]      stable/2.3 -> origin/stable/2.3
 * [new branch]      stable/3.0 -> origin/stable/3.0
 * [new branch]      stable/3.1 -> origin/stable/3.1
 * [new branch]      stable/3.2 -> origin/stable/3.2
```

We can also set up push refspecs that specify where branches are pushed to by default. Let's create a branch called develop and create one commit, as shown in the following commands:

```
$ git checkout -b develop
Switched to a new branch 'develop'
$ echo "This is the developer setup, read carefully" > readme-dev.txt
$ git add readme-dev.txt
$ git commit -m "adds readme file for developers"
[develop ccb2f08] adds readme file for developers
1 file changed, 1 insertion(+)
 create mode 100644 readme-dev.txt
```

Now, let's create a push refspec that will send the contents of the `develop` branch to `integration/master` on origin:

```
[remote "origin"]
    url = ../jgit-bare.git
    fetch = +refs/heads/master:refs/remotes/origin/master
    fetch = +refs/heads/stable/*:refs/remotes/origin/stable/*
    push = refs/heads/develop:refs/remotes/origin/integration/master
```

Let us push our commit on develop as follows:

```
$ git push
Counting objects: 4, done.
Compressing objects: 100% (2/2), done.
Writing objects: 100% (3/3), 345 bytes | 0 bytes/s, done.
Total 3 (delta 1), reused 0 (delta 0)
To ../jgit-bare.git
 * [new branch]      develop -> origin/integration/master
```

As the `integration/master` branch didn't exist on the remote side, it was created for us.

How it works...

The format of the refspec is in the form of `<source>:<destination>`. For a fetch refspec, this means that `<source>` is the source on the remote side and `<destination>` is `local`. For a push refspec, `<source>` is `local` and `<destination>` is `remote`. The refspec can be prefixed by a + to indicate that the ref pattern can be updated even though it isn't a fast-forward update. It is not possible to use partial globs in the refspec pattern, as shown in the following line:

```
fetch = +refs/heads/stable*:refs/remotes/origin/stable*
```

But it is possible to use namespacing. That's why we had to rewrite the `stable-xxx` branches to `stable/xxx` to fit as a namespace pattern:

```
fetch = +refs/heads/stable/*:refs/remotes/origin/stable/*
```

3
Branching, Merging, and Options

In this chapter, we will cover the following recipes:

- ▶ Managing your local branches
- ▶ Branches with remotes
- ▶ Forcing a merge commit
- ▶ Using git rerere to merge Git conflicts
- ▶ The difference between branches

Introduction

If you are developing a small application in a big corporation as a developer, or you are trying to wrap your head around an open source project from GitHub, you have already been using branches with Git.

Most of the time, you may just be working on a local `develop` or `master` branch and didn't care so much about other branches.

In this chapter, we will show you different branch types and how to work with them.

Managing your local branches

Suppose you are just having your local Git repository, and you have no intentions at the moment to share the code with others; however, you can easily share this knowledge while working with a repository with one or more remotes. Local branches with no remotes work exactly in this fashion. As you can see in the examples, we are cloning a repository, thus we have a remote.

Let's start by creating a few local branches.

Getting ready

Use the following command to clone the `jgit` repository to match:

```
$ git clone https://git.eclipse.org/r/jgit/jgit
$ cd jgit
```

How to do it...

Perform the following steps to manage your local branches:

1. Whenever you start working on a bug fix or a new feature in your project, you should create a branch. You can do so using the following code:

    ```
    $ git branch newBugFix
    $ git branch
    * master
      newBugFix
    ```

2. The `newBugFix` branch points to the current HEAD I was on at the time of the creation. You can see the HEAD with `git log -1`:

    ```
    $ git log -1 newBugFix --format=format:%H
    25fe20b2dbb20cac8aa43c5ad64494ef8ea64ffc
    ```

3. If you want to add a description to the branch, you can do it with the `--edit-description` option for the `git branch` command:

    ```
    $ git branch --edit-description newBugFix
    ```

4. The previous command will open an editor where you can type in a description:

    ```
    Refactoring the Hydro controller
    The hydro controller code is currently horrible needs to be refactored.
    ```

5. Close the editor and the message will be saved.

How it works...

Git stores the information in the local `git config` file; this also means that you cannot push this information to a remote repository.

To retrieve the description for the branch, you can use the `--get` flag for the `git config` command:

```
$ git config --get branch.newBugFix.description
Refactoring the Hydro controller
The hydro controller code is currently horrible needs to be refactored.
```

This will be beneficial when we automate some tasks in *Chapter 7, Enhancing Your Daily Work with Git Hooks, Aliases, and Scripts*.

> Remember to perform a checkout of `newBugFix` before you start working on it. This must be done with the Git checkout of `newBugFix`.

The branch information is stored as a file in `.git/refs/heads/newBugFix`:

```
$ cat .git/refs/heads/newBugFix
25fe20b2dbb20cac8aa43c5ad64494ef8ea64ffc
```

Note that it is the same commit hash we retrieved with the `git log` command

There's more...

Maybe you want to create specific branches from specific commit hashes. The first thought might be to check out the commit, and then create a branch; however, it is much easier to use the `git branch` command to create the branches without checking out the commits:

1. If you need a branch from a specific commit hash, you can create it with the `git branch` command as follows:

```
$ git branch anotherBugFix 979e346
$ git log -1 anotherBugFix --format=format:%h
979e346
$ git log -1 anotherBugFix --format=format:%H
979e3467112618cc787e161097986212eaaa4533
```

2. As you can see, the abbreviated commit hash is shown when you use h, and the full commit hash is shown when you use H. You can see the abbreviated commit hash is the same as the one used to create the branch. Most of the time, you want to create and start working on the branch immediately:

```
$ git checkout -b lastBugFix 979e346
Switched to a new branch 'lastBugFix'
```

3. Git switches to the new branch immediately after it creates the branch. Verify with Gitk to see whether the lastBugFix branch is checked out and another BugFix branch is at the same commit hash:

```
$ gitk
```

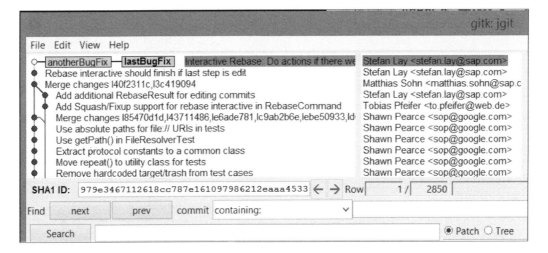

4. Instead of using Gitk, you can also add -v to the git branch command or even another v.

```
$ git branch -v
  anotherBugFix 979e346 Interactive Rebase: Do actions if
* lastBugFix    979e346 Interactive Rebase: Do actions if
  master        25fe20b Add missing package import for jg
  newBugFix     25fe20b Add missing package import for jg
```

5. With `-v`, you can see the abbreviated commit hash for each branch and with `-vv`, you can also see that the `master` branch tracks the `origin/master` branch:

```
$ git branch -vv
  anotherBugFix 979e346 Interactive Rebase: Do actions if e
* lastBugFix    979e346 Interactive Rebase: Do actions if e
  master        25fe20b [origin/master] Add missing package
  newBugFix     25fe20b Add missing package import for g
```

Branches with remotes

At some point, it is very likely that you have cloned somebody's repository. This means you have an associated remote. The remote is usually called origin because it is where the source originated from.

While working with Git and remotes, you will get some benefits from Git.

We can start with `git status` and see what we get while working with the remote.

Getting ready

1. We will start by checking out a local branch that tracks a remote branch:

   ```
   $ git checkout -b remoteBugFix --track origin/stable-3.2
   Branch remoteBugFix set up to track remote branch stable-3.2 from
   origin.
   Switched to a new branch 'remoteBugFix'
   ```

2. The previous command creates and checks out the `remoteBugFix` branch that will track the `origin/stable-3.2` branch. So, for instance, executing `git status` will automatically show how different your branch is from `origin/stable-3.2`, and it will also show whether your branch's HEAD can be fast forwarded to the HEAD of the remote branch or not.

3. To provide an example of how the previous step works, we need to do some manual work that will simulate this situation. First, we find a commit:

   ```
   $ git log -10 origin/stable-3.2 --oneline
   f839d38 Prepare post 3.2.0 builds
   699900c JGit v3.2.0.201312181205-r
   0ff691c Revert "Fix for core.autocrlf=input resulting in modified
   fil
   ```

> 1def0a1 Fix for core.autocrlf=input resulting in modified file and
> un
>
> 0ce61ca Canonicalize worktree path in BaseRepositoryBuilder if set
> vi
>
> be7942f Add missing @since tags for new public methods in Config
>
> ea04d23 Don't use API exception in RebaseTodoLine
>
> 3a063a0 Merge "Fix aborting rebase with detached head" into
> stable-3.
>
> e90438c Fix aborting rebase with detached head
>
> 2e0d178 Add recursive variant of Config.getNames() methods

4. The command will list the last 10 commits on the `stable-3.2` branch from the remote origin. The `--oneline` option will show the abbreviated commit hash and the commit subject. For this recipe, we will be using the following commit:

   ```
   $ git reset --hard 2e0d178
   HEAD is now at 2e0d178 Add recursive variant of Config.getNames()
   m
   ```

5. This will reset the `remoteBugFix` branch to the `2e0d178` commit hash. We are now ready to continue using the free benefits of Git when we have a remote tracking branch.

We are resetting to a commit that is accessible from the `origin/stable-3.2` remote tracking branch; this is done to simulate that we have performed a Git fetch and new commits were downloaded for the `origin/stable-3.2` branch.

How to do it...

Here, we will try a few commands that assist you when you have a remote tracking branch:

1. Start by executing `git status`:

   ```
   $ git status
   On branch remoteBugFix
   Your branch is behind 'origin/stable-3.2' by 9 commits, and can be
   fast-forwarded.
     (use "git pull" to update your local branch)
     nothing to commit, working directory clean
   ```

Git is very descriptive when you have a tracking branch and you use `git status`. As you can see from the message, you can use `git pull` to update your local branch, which we will try in the next example. Now, we will just perform the merge:

 The `git pull` command is just a `git fetch` command and then a `git merge` command with the remote tracking branch.

```
$ git merge origin/stable-3.2

Updating 2e0d178..f839d38

Fast-forward

 .../org/eclipse/jgit/api/RebaseCommandTest.java      | 213
++++++++++

 .../src/org/eclipse/jgit/api/RebaseCommand.java      |  31 +--

 .../jgit/errors/IllegalTodoFileModification.java     |  59 ++++++

 .../eclipse/jgit/lib/BaseRepositoryBuilder.java      |   2 +-

 .../src/org/eclipse/jgit/lib/Config.java             |   2 +

 .../src/org/eclipse/jgit/lib/RebaseTodoLine.java     |  16 +-

 6 files changed, 266 insertions(+), 57 deletions(-)

 create mode 100644 org.eclipse.jgit/src/org/eclipse/jgit/errors/
Ille
```

2. From the output, you can see it is a fast-forward merge, as Git predicted in the output of `git status`.

There's more...

You can also add a remote to an existing branch, which is very handy when you realize that you actually wanted a remote tracking branch but forgot to add the tracking information while creating the branch:

1. Start by creating a local branch at the `2e0d17` commit:

```
$ git checkout -b remoteBugFix2 2e0d17


Switched to a new branch 'remoteBugFix2'
```

2. The `remoteBugFix2` branch is just a local branch at the moment with no tracking information; to set the tracking branch, we need to use `--set-upstream-to` or `-u` as a flag to the `git branch` command:

```
$ git branch --set-upstream-to origin/stable-3.2
Branch remoteBugFix2 set up to track remote branch stable-3.2 from origin.
```

3. As you can see from the Git output, we are now tracking the `stable-3.2` branch from the origin:

```
$ git status
On branch remoteBugFix2
Your branch is behind 'origin/stable-3.2' by 9 commits, and can be fast-forwarded.
  (use "git pull" to update your local branch)


nothing to commit, working directory clean
```

4. You can see from the Git output that you are nine commits ahead, and you can use `git pull` to update the branch. Remember that a `git pull` command is just a `git fetch` command, and then a `git merge` command with the upstream branch, which we also call the remote tracking branch:

```
$ git pull
remote: Counting objects: 1657, done
remote: Finding sources: 100% (102/102)
remote: Total 102 (delta 32), reused 98 (delta 32)
Receiving objects: 100% (102/102), 65.44 KiB | 0 bytes/s, done.
Resolving deltas: 100% (32/32), completed with 19 local objects.
From https://git.eclipse.org/r/jgit/jgit
   25fe20b..50a830f  master      -> origin/master
First, rewinding head to replay your work on top of it...
Fast-forwarded remoteBugFix2 to
f839d383e6fbbda26729db7fd57fc917fa47db44.
```

5. From the output, you can see the branch has been fast forwarded to the `f839d383e6fbbda26729db7fd57fc917fa47db44` commit hash, which is equivalent to `origin/stable-3.2`. You can verify this with `git log`:

```
$ git log -1 origin/stable-3.2  --format=format:%H
f839d383e6fbbda26729db7fd57fc917fa47db44
```

Forcing a merge commit

If you are reading this book, you might have seen a lot of basic examples of software delivery chains and branching models. It is very likely that you have been trying to use different strategies and found that none of them completely supports your scenario, which is perfectly fine as long as the tool can support your specific workflow.

Git supports almost any workflow. I have often encountered a situation that requires a merge commit while merging a feature, even though it can be done with a fast-forward merge. Those who requested it often use it to indicate that you have actually merged in a feature and want to store the information in the repository.

 Git has fast and easy access to all the commit messages, so the repository should be used as a journal, not just a *backup* of the source code.

Getting ready

Start by checking out a local branch remoteOldbugFix that tracks origin/stable-3.1:

```
$ git checkout -b remoteOldBugFix --track origin/stable-3.1

Branch remoteOldBugFix set up to track remote branch stable-3.1
from Switched to a new branch 'remoteOldBugFix'
```

How to do it...

The following steps will show you how to force a merge commit:

1. To force a merge commit, you need to use the `--no-ff` flag, `no-ff` is no fast forward. We will also use `--quiet` for minimizing the output and `--edit` to allow us to edit the commit message. Unless you have a merge conflict, Git will create the merge commit for you automatically:

```
$ git merge origin/stable-3.2 --no-ff --edit --quiet

Auto-merging

org.eclipse.jgit.test/tst/org/eclipse/jgit/test/resources/
SampleDat

Removing org.eclipse.jgit.test/tst/org/eclipse/jgit/internal/
storage/file/GCTe

Auto-merging org.eclipse.jgit.packaging/org.eclipse.jgit.target/
jgit-4.3.target
```

2. The commit message editor will open, and you can write a commit message. Closing the editor creates the merge commit and we are done.

3. To verify this, you can reset back to `origin/stable-3.1` and perform the merge without the `--no-ff` flag:

   ```
   $ git reset --hard  remotes/origin/stable-3.1
   HEAD is now at da6e87b Prepare post 3.1.0 builds
   ```

4. Now, perform the merge with the following command:

   ```
   $ git merge origin/stable-3.2 --quiet
   ```

5. You can see the difference using Gitk. The following screenshot shows the fast forward merge, as you can see our `remoteOldBugFix` branch points to `origin/stable-3.2`:

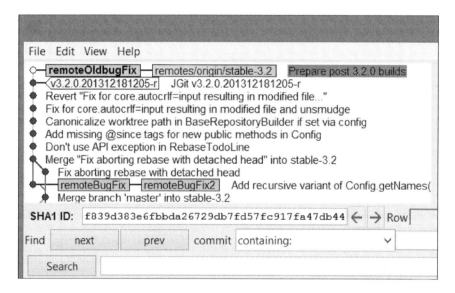

6. The following screenshot shows the merge commit we forced Git to create. My branch `remoteOldBugFix` is ahead of `remotes/origin/stable-3.2`, and the I performed the commit:

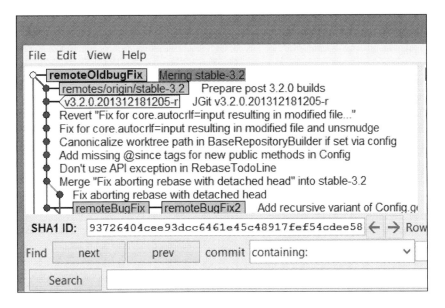

There's more...

Although most branching scenarios expect you to completely merge branches, there are situations when while working in a real environment, you only need to merge specific pieces of one branch into another branch. Using the `--no-commit` option, Git will make the merge and stop before committing, allowing you to modify and add files to the merge commit before committing.

As in example, I have been working with projects where versions of strings have been updated in the `feature` branch but not in the `master` branch. So, an automatic merge into `master` would replace the current version string used on the `master` branch, which in my case was not the intention:

1. Start by checking out a local `remotePartlyMerge` branch that tracks `origin/stable-2.3`:

   ```
   $ git checkout -b remotePartlyMerge --track origin/stable-2.3
   Branch remotePartlyMerge set up to track remote branch stable-2.3
   from origin.
   Switched to a new branch 'remotePartlyMerge'
   ```

2. Then, to create the merge and allow you to decide what will be part of the commit, you can use `--no-commit`:

   ```
   $ git merge origin/stable-3.1  --no-ff --no-commit
    a lot of output….
     Automatic merge went well; stopped before committing as
   requested
   ```

3. Again, Git is very informative; you can see from the output that everything went well and Git stopped before committing as requested. To continue, let's pretend we didn't want the `org.eclipse.jgit.test` directory to be part of the merge commit. To achieve this, we reset the directory using the `git reset <path>` command:

   ```
   $ git reset ./org.eclipse.jgit.test
   Unstaged changes after reset:
   M        org.eclipse.jgit.test/.gitignore
    A lot of output
   M        org.eclipse.jgit.test/tst/org/eclipse/jgit/util/io/
   AutoCRLFOutputStreamTest.java
   ```

4. You can see from the output that you have unstaged changes after the reset; this is exactly what we want. You can check which unstaged changes you have by running `git status`. Now, we will just finish the merge:

   ```
   $ git commit -m "Merging stable-3.1 without org.eclipse.jgit.test"
   [remotePartlyMerge 396f32a] Merging stable-3.1 without
   ```

5. The merge commit is complete. If you run a `git status` command now, you will still have the unstaged changes in you work area. To verify whether the result is as expected, we can use `diff` for this with `git diff` to show that the file is as it is on the `origin/stable-2.3` branch:

   ```
   $ git diff  origin/stable-2.3 ./org.eclipse.jgit.test
   ```

6. There is no output from `diff`; this is the expected result. We are telling the `diff` command to diff our current `HEAD` commit and branch `origin/stable-2.3`, and we only care about the diffs in `./org.eclipse.jgit.test`:

 If you don't specify `HEAD`, you will diff with your current WA, and the `diff` command will have a lot of output as you have unstaged changes.

Using git rerere to merge known conflicts

While working on a feature branch, you probably like to merge daily or maybe more often, but often when you work on long-living feature branches, you end up in a situation where you have the same conflict occurring repeatedly.

Here, you can use `git rerere` which stands for *reuse recorded resolution*. Git `rerere` is not enabled by default but can be enabled with the following command:

```
$ git config rerere.enabled true
```

 You can configure it globally by adding `--global` to the `git config` command.

How to do it...

Perform the following steps to merge the known conflicts:

1. In the `jgit` repository folder, start by checking out a branch that tracks `origin/stable-2.2`:

   ```
   git checkout -b rerereExample --track origin/stable-2.2
   ```

2. Now, change the maven-compiler-plugin version to something personalized such as `2.5.2` like this is in line 211. If you run `git diff`, you should get a result very similar to the following:

   ```
   $ git diff
   diff --git a/pom.xml b/pom.xml
   index 085e00f..d5aec17 100644
   --- a/pom.xml
   +++ b/pom.xml
   ```

```
@@ -208,7 +208,7 @@


        <plugin>
          <artifactId>maven-compiler-plugin</artifactId>
-          <version>2.5.1</version>
+          <version>2.5.2</version>
        </plugin>


        <plugin>
```

3. Now add the file and create a commit:

```
$ git add pom.xml
$ git commit -m "Update maven-compiler-plugin to 2.5.2"
[rerereExample d474848] Update maven-compiler-plugin to 2.5.2
 1 file changed, 1 insertion(+), 1 deletion(-)
```

4. Store you current commit in a backup branch named `rerereExample2`:

```
$ git branch rerereExample2
```

   Here, `git branch rerereExample2` is just storing the current commit as a branch, as we need to use that for rerere example number 2.

5. Now, we need to perform the first merge that will fail on auto merge. Then, we can solve that. After solving it, we can reuse the merge resolution to solve the same problem in the future:

```
$ git merge --no-ff v3.0.2.201309041250-rc2
A lot of output …
Automatic merge failed; fix conflicts and then commit the result.
```

6. As we have `git rerere` enabled, we can use `git rerere status` to see which files or paths will be recorded:

```
$ git rerere status
pom.xml
```

7. Edit the `pom.xml` file and solve the merge conflict so that you can get the diff output shown as follows. You have to remove the line with `2.5.1` and the merge markers:

 Merge markers are lines that begin with `<<<<<<`, `>>>>>>`, or `======`; these lines indicate the points where Git could not perform an auto merge.

```
$ git diff v3.0.2.201309041250-rc2 pom.xml
diff --git a/pom.xml b/pom.xml
index 60cb0c8..faa7618 100644
--- a/pom.xml
+++ b/pom.xml
@@ -226,7 +226,7 @@

          <plugin>
            <artifactId>maven-compiler-plugin</artifactId>
-           <version>3.1</version>
+           <version>2.5.2</version>
          </plugin>

          <plugin>
```

8. Mark the merge as complete by adding `pom.xml` to the staging area and run `git commit` to finish the merge:

```
$ git commit
Recorded resolution for 'pom.xml'.
[rerereExample 9b8725f] Merge tag 'v3.0.2.201309041250-rc2' into rerereExample
```

9. Note the recorded resolution for the `pom.xml` output from Git; this will not be here without enabling `git rerere`. Git has recorded this resolution to this particular merge conflict and will also record how to solve this. Now, we can try and rebase the change to another branch.

10. Start by checking out the `rerereExample2` branch from our repository:

    ```
    $ git checkout rerereExample2
    Switched to branch 'rerereExample2'
    ```

11. Try to rebase your change on top of the `origin/stable-3.2` branch:

    ```
    $ git rebase origin/stable-3.2
    First, rewinding head to replay your work on top of it...
    Applying: Update maven-compiler-plugin to 2.5.2
    Using index info to reconstruct a base tree...
    M       pom.xml
    Falling back to patching base and 3-way merge...
    Auto-merging pom.xml
    CONFLICT (content): Merge conflict in pom.xml
    Resolved 'pom.xml' using previous resolution.
    Failed to merge in the changes.
    Patch failed at 0001 Update maven-compiler-plugin to 2.5.2
    The copy of the patch that failed is found in:
        c:/Users/Rasmus/repos/jgit/.git/rebase-apply/patch


    When you have resolved this problem, run "git rebase --continue".
    If you prefer to skip this patch, run "git rebase --skip" instead.
    To check out the original branch and stop rebasing, run "git
    rebase --abort".
    ```

12. You should notice the following output:

    ```
    CONFLICT (content): Merge conflict in pom.xml
    Resolved 'pom.xml' using previous resolution
    ```

13. As the merge conflict is the same in `pom.xml`, Git can solve the conflict in the file for you. This is very clear when you open the file and see there are no merge markers, as the resolution Git had recorded has been applied. Finish the merge by adding `pom.xml` and continue the rebase:

    ```
    $ git add pom.xml
    $ git rebase --continue
    Applying: Update maven-compiler-plugin to 2.5.2
    ```

14. Start Gitk to see that the commit has been rebased on top of the `origin/stable-3.2` branch:

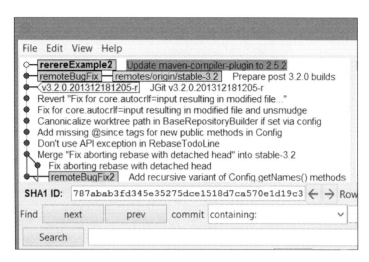

You can try the same scenario with merging and it would merge the file automatically for you.

There's more...

When you merge different branches often and you are not sure which branch a specific error fix is a part of, it is actually quite easy to find out.

1. You need to find a commit you are interested in getting this information for. Then, use the `--contains` flag for the `git branch` command:

```
$ git branch --contains 06ddee1
  anotherBugFix
  lastBugFix
  master
  newBugFix
  remoteBugFix
  remoteBugFix2
  remoteOldbugFix
* rerereExample2
```

2. The previous command lists all the branches that have the specific commit. If you leave out the `<commit>` option, Git will check HEAD. So, for instance, checking out the `rerereExample2` branch and executing the following command, you will see the commit is present only on that branch:

```
$ git checkout rerereExample2
Switched to branch 'rerereExample2'
$ git branch -a --contains
* rerereExample2
```

 The `-a` option indicates that you wish to check all the remote branches as well. If you leave this out, it will check only local branches.

However, as you can see, our commit is not on any remote branch as the commit has just been created locally and has not been pushed to any remotes yet.

 You can use tags, branch names, or commit hashes while using the `git branch -a --contains` command.

3. Let's try to see the branches where the `v2.3.0.201302130906` tag is present:

```
$ git branch -a --contains v2.3.0.201302130906
  anotherBugFix
  lastBugFix
  master
  newBugFix
  remoteBugFix
  remoteBugFix2
  remoteOldbugFix
  remotePartlyMerge
* rerereExample2
  remotes/origin/HEAD -> origin/master
  remotes/origin/master
  remotes/origin/stable-2.3
  remotes/origin/stable-3.0
  remotes/origin/stable-3.1
  remotes/origin/stable-3.2
```

That tag is in quite a lot of branches.

The difference between branches

Checking the difference between branches can show valuable information before merging.

A regular Git diff between two branches will show you all the information, but it can be rather exhausting to sit and look at; maybe you are only interested in one file. Thus, you don't need the long unified diff.

Getting ready

To start with, we decide on two branches, tags, or commits we want to see the diff between. Then, to list files that have changed between these branches, you can use the `--name-only` flag.

How to do it...

Perform the following steps to see the difference between the branches:

1. Diff the `origin/stable-3.1` with `origin/stable-3.2` branch:

    ```
    $ git diff --name-only origin/stable-3.1 origin/stable-3.2 org.
    eclipse.jgit/src/org/eclipse/jgit/transport/org.eclipse.jgit/src/
    org/eclipse/jgit/transport/BasePackFetch
    ```

    More output..

2. We are building the command in this pattern, that is, `git diff [options] <commit> <commit> <path>`. Then, we can diff what we care about while looking into the differences between branches. This is very useful if you are responsible for a subset of the source code, and you wish to diff that area only.

3. Let's try the same diff between branches, but this time we will diff the entire branches, not just a subdirectory; however, we only want to show the deleted or added files between the branches. This is done by using the `--diff-filter=DA` and `--name-status` options. The `--name-status` option will only show the filenames and the type of change. The `--diff-filter=DA` option will only show the deleted and added files:

    ```
    $ git diff --name-status --diff-filter=DA origin/stable-3.1
    origin/stable-3.2

    D org.eclipse.jgit.junit/src/org/eclipse/jgit/junit/Sam

    A org.eclipse.jgit.packaging/org.eclipse.jgit.target/jg
    ```

    More output..

4. This shows the files that have been added and deleted while moving from `origin/stable-3.1` to `origin/stable-3.2`:

5. If we switch the branches around like in the following command, we will get the opposite result.

```
$ git diff --name-status --diff-filter=DA origin/stable-3.2
origin/stable-3.1
A    org.eclipse.jgit.junit/src/org/eclipse/jgit/junit/Sam
D    org.eclipse.jgit.packaging/org.eclipse.jgit.target/jg
  More output..
```

Note that the indication letters A and D switched places because now we want to know what happens if we move from `origin/stable-3.2` to `origin/stable-3.1`.

There's more...

There are more options in the help files for Git. Just run `git merge --help` or `git branch --help` to see what other options you have. The option I have used and the examples shown are all examples that have given me the edge while working with Git as a release manager and Git mentor at Nokia.

4

Rebase Regularly and Interactively, and Other Use Cases

In this chapter, we will cover the following topics:

- ▶ Rebasing commits to another branch
- ▶ Continuing a rebase with merge conflicts
- ▶ Rebasing selective commits interactively
- ▶ Squashing commits using an interactive rebase
- ▶ Changing the author of commits using a rebase
- ▶ Auto-squashing commits

Introduction

Rebase is an incredibly strong feature of Git. Hopefully, you have used it before; if not, you might have heard about it. Rebasing is exactly what the word implies. So, if you have a certain commit A that is based on commit B, then rebasing A to C would result in commit A being based on commit C.

As you will see in the different examples in this chapter, it is not always as simple as that.

Rebasing commits to another branch

To start with, we are going to perform a very simple rebase where we will introduce a new file, commit this file, make a change to it, and then commit it again so that we end up with 2 new commits.

Getting ready

Before we start, we need a repository to work in. You can use a previous clone of `jgit`, but to get a close to identical output from the example, you can clone the `jgit` repository.

The `jgit` repository can be cloned as follows:

```
$ git clone https://git.eclipse.org/r/jgit/jgit chapter4
$ cd chapter4
```

How to do it...

We start by creating a local branch and then make two commits by performing the following steps; these are the commits that we want to rebase onto another branch:

1. Check out a new branch, `rebaseExample`, that tracks `origin/stable-3.1`:

   ```
   $ git checkout -b rebaseExample --track origin/stable-3.1
   Branch rebaseExample set up to track remote branch stable-  3.1
   from origin.
   Switched to a new branch 'rebaseExample'
   ```

2. Make two commits on the `rebaseExample` branch as follows:

   ```
   $ echo "My Fishtank

   Gravel, water, plants
   Fish, pump, skeleton" > fishtank.txt
   $ git add fishtank.txt
   $ git commit -m "My brand new fishtank"
   [rebaseExample 4b2c2ec] My brand new fishtank
    1 file changed, 4 insertions(+)
    create mode 100644 fishtank.txt
   $ echo "mosquitos" >> fishtank.txt
   $ git add fishtank.txt
   ```

```
$ git commit -m "Feeding my fish"
[rebaseExample 2132d88] Feeding my fish
 1 file changed, 1 insertion(+)
```

3. Then, we rebase the change on top of the `origin/stable-3.2` branch instead.

    ```
    $ git rebase origin/stable-3.2
    First, rewinding head to replay your work on top of it...
    Applying: My brand new fishtank
    Applying: Feed the fish
    ```

How it works

When you execute `git rebase`, Git starts by finding the common ancestor of the current HEAD branch and the branch you want to rebase to. When Git finds `merge-base`, it will find the commits that are not available on the branch you are rebasing onto. Git will simply try to apply those commits one by one.

Continuing a rebase with merge conflicts

When you rebase a commit or a branch on top of a different HEAD, you will eventually see a conflict.

If there is a conflict, you will be asked to solve the merge conflict and continue with the rebase using `git rebase --continue`.

How to do it

We will be creating a commit that adds the same `fishtank.txt` file on top of the `origin/stable-3.1` branch; then, we will try to rebase this on top of the `rebaseExample` branch we created in the *Rebasing commits to another branch* section:

1. Check out a branch named `rebaseExample2` that tracks `origin/stable-3.1`:

    ```
    $ git checkout -b rebaseExample2 --track origin/stable-3.1
    Checking out files: 100% (212/212), done.
    Branch rebaseExample2 set up to track remote branch stable-3.1
    from origin.
    Switched to a new branch 'rebaseExample2'
    ```

2. Make a commit on the branch.

```
$ echo "My Fishtank

Pirateship, Oister shell
Coconut shell
">fishtank.txt
$ git add fishtank.txt
$ git commit -m "My brand new fishtank"
[rebaseExample2 39811d6] My brand new fishtank
 1 file changed, 5 insertions(+)
 create mode 100644 fishtank.txt
```

3. Try to rebase the branch on top of the `rebaseExample` branch.

```
$ git rebase rebaseExample
First, rewinding head to replay your work on top of it...
Applying: My brand new fishtank
Using index info to reconstruct a base tree...
<stdin>:12: new blank line at EOF.
+
warning: 1 line adds whitespace errors.
Falling back to patching base and 3-way merge...
Auto-merging fishtank.txt
CONFLICT (add/add): Merge conflict in fishtank.txt
Failed to merge in the changes.
Patch failed at 0001 My brand new fishtank
The copy of the patch that failed is found in:
    c:/Users/Rasmus/repos/chapter4/.git/rebase-apply/patch

When you have resolved this problem, run "git rebase --continue".
If you prefer to skip this patch, run "git rebase --skip" instead.
To check out the original branch and stop rebasing, run "git
rebase --abort".
```

4. As predicted, we have a conflict. Solve the conflict in your preferred editor. Then, add the file to the index using `git add` and continue with the rebase.

```
$ git add fishtank.txt
$ git rebase --continue
Applying: My brand new fishtank
```

5. We can now check with `gitk` to see whether our change is rebased on top of the `rebaseExample` branch, as shown in the following screenshot:

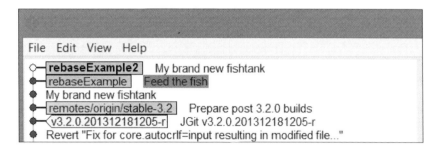

How it works

As we learned from the first example, Git will apply the commits that are not available on the branch you are rebasing to. In our example, it is only our commit, as we made it, that is available on the `rebaseExample2` branch.

There's more...

You might have noticed in the output of the failing rebase that you have two extra options for the commit.

When you have resolved this problem, run `git rebase --continue`. If you prefer to skip this patch, run `git rebase --skip` instead. To check out the original branch and stop rebasing, run `git rebase --abort`.

The first extra option we have is to totally ignore this patch by skipping it; you can do this using `git rebase --skip`. In our example, this will cause our branch to be fast-forwarded to the `rebaseExample` branch. So, both our branches will point to the same commit hash.

The second option is to abort the rebasing. If we choose to do this, then we will go back to the branch as it was prior to starting the rebase. This can be done using `git rebase --abort`.

Rebasing selective commits interactively

When you are working on a new feature and have branched from an old release into a feature branch, you might want to rebase this branch onto the latest release. When looking into the list of commits on the feature branch, you realize that some of the commits are not suitable for the new release. So, when you want to rebase the branch onto a new release, you will need to remove some commits. This can be achieved with interactive rebasing, where Git gives you the option to pick the commits you wish to rebase.

Getting ready

To get started with this example, you need to check the previously created branch, `rebaseExample`; if you don't have this branch, follow the steps from the *Rebasing a few commits* section and use the following command:

```
$ git checkout rebaseExample
Switched to branch 'rebaseExample'
Your branch is ahead of 'origin/stable-3.1' by 109 commits.
  (use "git push" to publish your local commits)
```

Notice that because we are tracking `origin/stable-3.1`, the Git checkout will tell us how far ahead we are in comparison with that branch.

How to do it

We will try to rebase our current branch, `rebaseExample`, on top of the `origin/stable-3.1` branch by performing the following steps. Remember that Git will apply the commits that are not available on the branch we are rebasing to; so, in this case, there will be a lot of commits:

1. Rebase the branch onto `origin/stable-3.1` by using the following command:

    ```
    $ git rebase --interactive origin/stable-3.1
    ```

2. What you will see now is a list of all the commits you will be rebasing onto the `origin/stable-3.1` branch. These commits are all the commits between the `origin/stable-3.1` and `rebaseExample` branches. The commits will be applied from top to bottom, so the commits will be listed in reverse order, at least compared to what you would normally see in Git. This actually makes good sense. The commits have the keyword `pick` to the left and then the abbreviated commit hash, and finally the title of the commit subject.

If you scroll down to the bottom, you will see a list like the following one:

```
pick 43405e6 My brand new fishtank
pick 08d0906 Feed the fish
# Rebase da6e87b..08d0906 onto da6e87b
#
# Commands:
#  p, pick = use commit
#  r, reword = use commit, but edit the commit message
#  e, edit = use commit, but stop for amending
#  s, squash = use commit, but meld into previous commit
#  f, fixup = like "squash", but discard this commit's log message
#  x, exec = run command (the rest of the line) using shell
#
# These lines can be re-ordered; they are executed from top to
bottom.
#
# If you remove a line here THAT COMMIT WILL BE LOST.
#
# However, if you remove everything, the rebase will be aborted.
#
# Note that empty commits are commented out
```

So, if we only want our fishtank commits to be based on top of the `origin/stable-3.1` branch, we should remove all the commits except for our two commits.

3. Remove all the lines except for the two commits at the bottom; for now, leave `pick` as the keyword. Save the file and close the editor, and you will get the following message from Git:

   Successfully rebased and updated refs/heads/rebaseExample.

4. Now, with `gitk`, try to check whether we accomplished what we predicted. The next screenshot shows our two fishtank commits on top of the `origin/stable-3.1` branch. The following screenshot is what we expected:

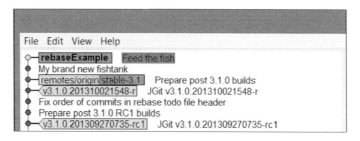

There's more...

The same thing could actually be achieved with a single small Git command. We have been rebasing commits from the `origin/stable-3.2` branch to the `rebaseExample` branch onto the `origin/stable-3.2` branch. This can also be achieved in the following manner:

```
$ git rebase --onto origin/stable-3.1 origin/stable-3.2 rebaseExample
First, rewinding head to replay your work on top of it...
Applying: My brand new fishtank
Applying: Feed the fish
```

The `--onto origin/stable-3.2` flag tells Git to rebase onto `origin/stable-3.2`, and it has to be from `origin/stable-3.1` to the `rebaseExample` branch. So, we end up having `rebaseExample` branch to the branch of the `origin/stable-3.1` and the like. The next diagram shows before the rebase example where we have our two commits on top of **origin/stable-3.2**, then after the rebase where our commits are on top of **origin/stable-3.1** as we wanted:

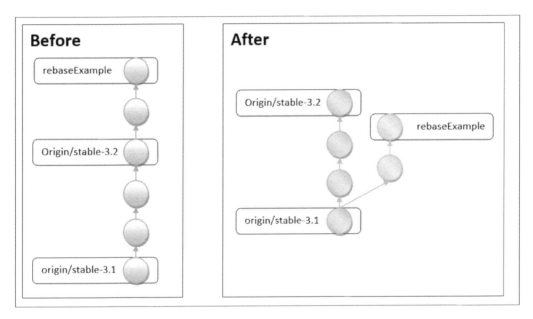

Squashing commits using an interactive rebase

When I work on a local branch, I prefer to commit in small increments with a few comments on what I did in the commits; however, as these commits do not build or pass any test requirements, I cannot submit them for review and verification one by one. I have to merge them in my branch, and still, cherry picking my fix would require me to cherry-pick twice the number of commits, which is not very handy.

What we can do is rebase and squash the commits into a single commit or at least a smaller number of commits.

Getting ready

To get started with this example, we need a new branch, namely `rebaseExample3`, that tracks `origin/stable-3.1`. Create the branch with the following command:

```
$ git checkout -b rebaseExample3 --track origin/stable-3.1
```

```
Branch rebaseExample3 set up to track remote branch stable-3.1 from origin.
```

```
Switched to a new branch 'rebaseExample3'
```

How to do it...

To really showcase this feature of Git, we will start by being six commits ahead of the `origin/stable-3.1` branch. This is to simulate the fact that we have just created six commits on top of the `rebaseExample3` branch; to do this, perform the following steps:

1. Find a commit that is between `origin/stable-3.1` and `origin/stable-3.2` and list the commits in reverse order. If you don't list them in reverse order, you can scroll down to the bottom of the output and find the commit we will use, as shown in the following snippet:

    ```
    $ git log origin/stable-3.1..origin/stable-3.2 --oneline --reverse

    8a51c44 Do not close ArchiveOutputStream on error

    3467e86 Revert "Close unfinished archive entries on error"

    f045a68 Added the git-describe implementation

    0be59ab Merge "Added the git-describe implementation"

    fdc80f7 Merge branch 'stable-3.1'

    7995d87 Prepare 3.2.0-SNAPSHOT builds

    5218f7b Propagate IOException where possible when getting refs.
    ```

2. Reset the `rebaseExample3` branch to the `5218f7b` commit; this will simulate that we have six commits on top of the `origin/stable-3.1` branch. This can be tested by running the status of Git as follows:

    ```
    $ git reset --hard 5218f7b
    HEAD is now at 5218f7b Propagate IOException where possible when getting refs.
    $ git status
    On branch rebaseExample3
    Your branch is ahead of 'origin/stable-3.1' by 6 commits.
      (use "git push" to publish your local commits)

    nothing to commit, working directory clean
    ```

3. Now we have these six commits on top of the `origin/stable-3.1` branch, and we want to squash these commits into two different commits instead of six commits. This can be done by simply running `git rebase --interactive`. Notice that we are not specifying which branch we want to rebase to since we have already set up a tracking branch when we created the branch using `--track`. To continue, let's execute the rebase command as follows:

    ```
    $ git rebase --interactive
    pick 8a51c44 Do not close ArchiveOutputStream on error
    pick f045a68 Added the git-describe implementation
    pick 7995d87 Prepare 3.2.0-SNAPSHOT builds
    pick 5218f7b Propagate IOException where possible when getting refs.
    ```

4. The editor will open, and you will see four commits and not six as you would expect. This is because the rebase in general refuses to take merge commits as part of the rebase scenario. You can use the `--preserve-merges` flag. As per the Help section of Git, this is not recommended.

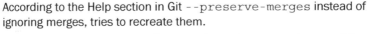

According to the Help section in Git `--preserve-merges` instead of ignoring merges, tries to recreate them.

The `--preserve-merges` flag uses the `--interactive` machinery internally, but combining it with the `--interactive` option explicitly is generally not a good idea unless you know what you are doing (see the BUGS in the following snippet).

5. Edit the file so it looks as follows:

```
pick 8a51c44 Do not close ArchiveOutputStream on error
squash f045a68 Added the git-describe implementation
pick 7995d87 Prepare 3.2.0-SNAPSHOT builds
squash 5218f7b Propagate IOException where possible when getting
refs.
```

6. Remember that commits are listed in reverse order as compared to the Git log. So, while squashing, we squash up into the commits we have marked with the pick. When you close the editor, Git will start the rebase from top to bottom. First, apply `8a51c44` and then squash `f045a68` into the commit `8a51c44`. This will open the commit message editor that contains both the commit messages. You can edit the commit messages, but for now, let us just close the editor to finish with the rebase and the squashing of these two commits. The editor will open one more time to complete the squashing of `5218f7b` into `7995d87`. Use `gitk` to verify the result.

   The following screenshot is as expected; now, we only have two commits on top of the `origin/stable3-1` branch:

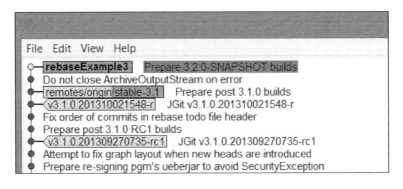

7. If you check the commit message of the `HEAD` commit, you will see that it has the information of two commits, as shown in the following command. This is because we decided not to change the commit message when we made the change:

```
$ git log -1
commit 9c96a651ff881c7d7c5a3974fa7a19a9c264d0a0
Author: Matthias Sohn <matthias.sohn@sap.com>
Date:   Thu Oct 3 17:40:22 2013 +0200


    Prepare 3.2.0-SNAPSHOT builds
```

```
      Change-Id: Iac6cf7a5bb6146ee3fe38abe8020fc3fc4217584
      Signed-off-by: Matthias Sohn <matthias.sohn@sap.com>


      Propagate IOException where possible when getting refs.


      Currently, Repository.getAllRefs() and Repository.getTags()
silently
      ignores an IOException and instead returns an empty map.
Repository
      is a public API and as such cannot be changed until the next
major
      revision change. Where possible, update the internal jgit APIs
to
      use the RefDatabase directly, since it propagates the error.


      Change-Id: I4e4537d8bd0fa772f388262684c5c4ca1929dc4c
```

There's more...

Now we have squashed two commits, but we could have used other keywords when editing the rebase's to-do list.

We will try the fixup functionality, which works like the squash functionality, by performing the following steps; the exception is that Git will select the commit message of the commits with the `pick` keyword:

1. Start by resetting back to our starting point.

    ```
    $ git reset --hard 5218f7b
    HEAD is now at 5218f7b Propagate IOException where possible when
    getting refs.
    $ git status
    On branch rebaseExample3
    Your branch is ahead of 'origin/stable-3.1' by 6 commits.
      (use "git push" to publish your local commits)


    nothing to commit, working directory clean
    ```

2. As you can see, we are back at the starting point, that is, we're six commits ahead of the `origin/stable-3.1` branch. Now, we can try the fixup functionality. Start the interactive rebase and change the file according to the following output. Notice that you can use `f` instead of `fixup`.

```
$ git rebase --interactive

pick 8a51c44 Do not close ArchiveOutputStream on error

f f045a68 Added the git-describe implementation

pick 7995d87 Prepare 3.2.0-SNAPSHOT builds

f 5218f7b Propagate IOException where possible when getting refs.
```

3. Once you close the editor, you will see rebase's progress through Git. As predicted, the commit message editor will not open; Git will just rebase the changes into two commits on top of the `orgin/stable-3.1` branch.

```
$ git rebase --interactive

[detached HEAD 70b4eb7] Do not close ArchiveOutputStream on error

 Author: Jonathan Nieder <jrn@google.com>

 6 files changed, 537 insertions(+), 2 deletions(-)

 create mode 100644 org.eclipse.jgit.test/tst/org/eclipse/jgit/
api/DescribeComma

ndTest.java

 create mode 100644 org.eclipse.jgit/src/org/eclipse/jgit/api/
DescribeCommand.ja

va

[detached HEAD c5bc5cc] Prepare 3.2.0-SNAPSHOT builds

 Author: Matthias Sohn <matthias.sohn@sap.com>

 67 files changed, 422 insertions(+), 372 deletions(-)

 rewrite org.eclipse.jgit.http.server/META-INF/MANIFEST.MF (61%)

 rewrite org.eclipse.jgit.java7.test/META-INF/MANIFEST.MF (66%)

 rewrite org.eclipse.jgit.junit/META-INF/MANIFEST.MF (73%)

 rewrite org.eclipse.jgit.pgm.test/META-INF/MANIFEST.MF (61%)

 rewrite org.eclipse.jgit.pgm/META-INF/MANIFEST.MF (63%)

 rewrite org.eclipse.jgit.test/META-INF/MANIFEST.MF (77%)

 rewrite org.eclipse.jgit.ui/META-INF/MANIFEST.MF (67%)

 rewrite org.eclipse.jgit/META-INF/MANIFEST.MF (64%)

Successfully rebased and updated refs/heads/rebaseExample3.
```

4. Another difference is that the commit message from the two commits we marked with fixup has disappeared. So, if you compare this with the previous example, it is very clear what the difference is; it is shown in the following command:

```
commit c5bc5cc9e0956575cc3c30c3be4aecab19980e4d
Author: Matthias Sohn <matthias.sohn@sap.com>
Date:    Thu Oct 3 17:40:22 2013 +0200


    Prepare 3.2.0-SNAPSHOT builds


    Change-Id: Iac6cf7a5bb6146ee3fe38abe8020fc3fc4217584

    Signed-off-by: Matthias Sohn matthias.sohn@sap.com
```

5. Finally, we can also confirm that we still have the same source code, but with different commits. This can be done by comparing this commit with the commit we created via `9c96a65`, using the following command:

```
$ git diff  9c96a65
```

As predicted, there is no output from `git diff`, so we still have the same source code.

This check can also be performed on the previous example.

Changing the author of commits using a rebase

When I start working on a new project, I often forget to set my author name and author e-mail address for the specified project; therefore, I often have commits in my local branch that have been committed with the wrong username and/or e-mail ID. Unfortunately, I can't use the same account everywhere as some work with regards to my cooperate account still needs to be done; however, for most other parts, I can use my private account.

Getting ready

Before we begin this exercise, we need a branch, as always with Git. Name the branch `resetAuthorRebase` and make it track `origin/master`. Use the following command to achieve this:

```
$ git checkout -b resetAuthorRebase -t origin/master
Branch resetAuthorRebase set up to track remote branch master from origin.
Switched to a new branch 'resetAuthorRebase'
```

How to do it...

Now, we want to change the author of all the commits from `origin/stable-3.2` to our `HEAD`, which is `master`. This is just an example; you will rarely have to change the author of commits that have already been published to a remote repository.

You can change the author of the `HEAD` commit by using `git commit --amend --reset-author`; however, this will only change the author of `HEAD` and leave the rest of the commits as they were. We will start by changing the author of the `HEAD` commit and then verifying why that is wrong by performing the following steps:

1. Change the author of the `HEAD` commit as follows:

   ```
   $ git commit --amend --reset-author

   [resetAuthorRebase b0b2836] Update Kepler target platform to use
   Kepler SR2 orbi

   t R-build

    1 file changed, 1 insertion(+), 1 deletion(-)
   ```

2. Verify that you have changed it with the Git log command:

   ```
   $ git log --format='format:%h %an <%ae>' origin/stable-3.2..HEAD

   b0b2836 Rasmus Voss <rasmus.voss@live.dk>

   b9a0621 Matthias Sohn <matthias.sohn@sap.com>

   ba15d82 Matthias Sohn matthias.sohn@sap.com
   ```

3. We will list all the commits from `origin/stable-3.2` to `HEAD` and we will define a format with `%h` as the abbreviated commit hash, `%an` for the author's name, and `%ae` for the author's e-mail address. From the output, you can see that I am now the author of the `HEAD` commit, but what we really wanted was to change the author of all the commits. To do this, we will rebase onto the `origin/stable-3.2` branch; then, for each commit, we will stop to amend and reset the author. Git can do most of that work with `--exec option` for the `git` rebase, as follows:

   ```
   git rebase --interactive --exec "git commit --amend --reset-
   author" origin/stable-3.2

   pick b14a939 Prepare 3.3.0-SNAPSHOT builds

   exec git commit --amend --reset-author

   pick f2abbd0 archive: Prepend a specified prefix to all entry
   filenames

   exec git commit --amend --reset-author
   ```

4. As you can see, Git has opened the rebase's to-do list for you, and between every commit, you have the `exec` keyword and the command we specified on the command line. You can have more `exec` lines between commits if you have a use case for them. Closing the editor will start the rebase.

5. As you will see, this process is not very good as the commit message editor opens every time and you have to close the editor to allow Git to continue with the rebase. To stop the rebase, clear the commit message editor and Git will return to the command line; then, you can use `git rebase --abort` as follows:

```
Executing: git commit --amend --reset-author
Aborting commit due to empty commit message.
Execution failed: git commit --amend --reset-author
You can fix the problem, and then run


        git rebase --continue
$ git rebase --abort
```

To achieve what we really want, you can add the `--reuse-message` option for `git commit`; this will reuse the commit message for the commit you will specify. We want to use the message of HEAD as we are going to amend it to the HEAD commit. So, try again as shown in the following command:

```
git rebase --interactive --exec "git commit --amend --reset-author
--reuse-message=HEAD" origin/stable-3.2
Executing: git commit --amend --reset-author --reuse-message=HEAD
[detached HEAD 0cd3e87] Prepare 3.3.0-SNAPSHOT builds
 51 files changed, 291 insertions(+), 291 deletions(-)
 rewrite org.eclipse.jgit.java7.test/META-INF/MANIFEST.MF (62%)
 rewrite org.eclipse.jgit.junit/META-INF/MANIFEST.MF (73%)
 rewrite org.eclipse.jgit.pgm.test/META-INF/MANIFEST.MF (61%)
 rewrite org.eclipse.jgit.test/META-INF/MANIFEST.MF (76%)
 rewrite org.eclipse.jgit.ui/META-INF/MANIFEST.MF (67%)
Executing: git commit --amend --reset-author --reuse-message=HEAD
[detached HEAD faaf25e] archive: Prepend a specified prefix to all
entry filenam
es
 5 files changed, 115 insertions(+), 1 deletion(-)
Executing: git commit --amend --reset-author --reuse-message=HEAD
[detached HEAD cfd743e] [CLI] Add option --millis / -m to debug-
show-dir-cache c
Ommand
Successfully rebased and updated refs/heads/resetAuthorRebase.
```

6. Git provides an output indicating that the action was a success; however, to verify, you can execute the previous Git log command and you should see the e-mail address has changed on all the commits, as shown in the following command:

```
$ git log --format='format:%h %an <%ae>' origin/stable-3.2..HEAD
9b10ff9 Rasmus Voss <rasmus.voss@live.dk>
d8f0ada Rasmus Voss <rasmus.voss@live.dk>
53df2b7 Rasmus Voss rasmus.voss@live.dk
```

How it works...

It works as you would expect! There is one thing to remember: when using the `exec` option, Git will check the work area for unstaged and staged changes. Consider the following command line:

```
exec echo rainy_day > weather_main.txt
exec echo sunny_day > weather_california.txt
```

If you have a line as illustrated in the preceding command, the first `exec` would be executed and you will then have an unstaged change in your work area. Git would complain and you have to solve that before continuing with the next exec. So, if you want to do something like this, you must create a single exec line that executes all the things you want. Besides this, the rebase functionality is fairly simple, as it just tries to apply the changes in the order that is specified in the rebase's to-do list. Git will only apply the changes specified in the list, so if you remove some of them, they will not be applied. This is a way to clean up a feature branch for unwanted commits, for instance, commits that enable you to debug.

Auto-squashing commits

When I work with Git, I often create a lot of commits for a single bug fix, but when making the delivery to the remote repository, I prefer and recommend to deliver the bug fix as one commit. This can be achieved with an interactive rebase, but since this should be a common workflow, Git has a built-in feature called autosquash that will help you squash the commits together.

Getting ready

Before we begin with this exercise, we will create a branch from `origin/master` so we are ready to add commits to our fix.

Let's start with something like this:

```
$ git checkout -b readme_update_developer --track origin/master
Branch readme_update_developer set up to track remote branch master from
origin.
Switched to a new branch 'readme_update_developer'
```

How to do it...

After checking the branch, we will create the first commit that we want to squash other commits to. We need to use the abbreviated commit hash from this commit to automatically create other commits that will squash to this commit by performing the following steps:

1. Start by echoing some text into README.md:

   ```
   $ echo "More information for developers" >> README.md
   ```

2. This will append more information to README.md for developers; verify that the file has changed using the git status as follows:

   ```
   $ git status
   On branch readme_update_developer
   Your branch is up-to-date with 'origin/master'.

   Changes not staged for commit:
     (use "git add <file>..." to update what will be committed)
     (use "git checkout -- <file>..." to discard changes in working
   directory)

           modified:   README.md

   no changes added to commit (use "git add" and/or "git commit -a")
   ```

3. Now, we want to add and commit this; we can do this with the commit command with the -a flag, which will add any unstaged changes to the commit, as shown in the following command:

   ```
   $ git commit -a -m "Updating information for developers"
   [readme_update_developer d539645] Updating information for
   developers
    1 file changed, 1 insertion(+)
   ```

4. After you create the commit, remember the abbreviated commit hash; I have highlighted it in bold in the command output. The abbreviation will be different in your environment, and you must have your own abbreviation once you finish the exercise.

5. To continue, we will add three commits to the branch, and we would like to squash two of these with the first commit, as shown in the following command:

```
$ echo "even More information for developers" >> README.md
$ git commit -a --squash=d539645 --no-edit
[readme_update_developer d62922d] squash! Updating information for developers
 1 file changed, 1 insertion(+)
```

6. This is the first commit. Notice why we needed to store the abbreviated hash of the first commit; we used it with the --squash option for git commit. This option will create the commit with the subject of the commit specified. It will also add "squash!" to the start of the subject. This is to indicate that Git should squash this commit when performing a rebase. Now, create the second commit, as shown in the following command:

```
$ echo "even More information for developers" >> README.md
$ git commit -a --squash=d539645 --no-edit
[readme_update_developer 7d6194d] squash! Updating information for developers
 1 file changed, 1 insertion(+)
```

7. We have added two commits that we would like to squash with the first commit. When committing, I also used the --no-edit option; this will skip the opening of the commit's message editor. If you leave the flag out, the editor will open as it usually does when committing. The difference is that the commit subject has already been set, and you only need to write the commit message. Now, we will create the last commit; we don't want to squash this commit:

```
$ echo "Adding configuration information" >> README.md
$ git commit -a -m "Updating information on configuration"
[readme_update_developer fd07857] Updating information on configuration
 1 file changed, 1 insertion(+)
```

8. Now, we add the final commit that does not have anything to do with the first three commits we added. This is why we did not use the --squash option. We can now squash the commits together using git rebase -i:

```
$ git rebase -i
```

9. You will get the rebase's to-do list up in the configured commit editor. What we would have expected was to have Git configure a squash for the commits we wanted to squash, as shown in the following command:

```
pick d539645 Updating information for developers
pick d62922d squash! Updating information for developers
pick 7d6194d squash! Updating information for developers
pick fd07857 Updating information on configuration
```

10. What you can see is that Git inserted squash to the subject of two of the commits, but besides this, we did not get what we had expected. Git requires that you specify --autosquash to the git rebase -i command. Close the editor and Git will just perform the rebase and will give the following output:

```
Successfully rebased and updated
refs/heads/readme_update_developer.
```

11. Let's try again with --autosquash and see what happens with the rebase's to-do list:

```
$ git rebase -i --autosquash
pick d539645 Updating information for developers
squash d62922d squash! Updating information for developers
squash 7d6194d squash! Updating information for developers
pick fd07857 Updating information on configuration
```

12. Now the rebase's to-do list looks much more like what we expected it to look like. Git has preconfigured the to-do list to show which commits it will squash and which commits it will keep.

13. Closing the to-do list now will start the rebase, and we don't want that. This is because if you clear the to-do list and close the editor, the rebase will be aborted, which is what we want now. The output will be as follows:

```
Nothing to do
```

14. What we really want to do is just run git rebase -i and Git will use --autosquash as a default. This can be achieved with git config rebase. autosquash true; try it and then run git rebase -i:

```
$ git config rebase.autosquash true
$ git rebase -i
```

15. The rebase's to-do list pops up, and we have the expected result as follows:

```
pick d539645 Updating information for developers
squash d62922d squash! Updating information for developers
squash 7d6194d squash! Updating information for developers
pick fd07857 Updating information on configuration
```

16. Now close the editor and allow the rebase to start. The editor opens and you can change the commit message for the combined message as shown in the following command:

```
# This is a combination of 3 commits.

# The first commit's message is:

Updating information for developers


# This is the 2nd commit message:


squash! Updating information for developers


# This is the 3rd commit message:


squash! Updating information for developers
```

17. Modify the message and close the editor; Git continues with the rebase and completes with the following message:

```
[detached HEAD baadd53] Updating information for developers
 1 file changed, 3 insertions(+)
Successfully rebased and updated refs/heads/readme_update_
developer.
Verify the commit log with git log -3
$ git log -3
commit 6d83d44645e330d0081d3679aca49cd9bc20c891
Author: Rasmus Voss <rasmus.voss@schneider-electric.com>
Date:   Wed May 21 10:52:03 2014 +0200


    Updating information on configuration


commit baadd53018df2f6f3cdf88d024c3b9db16e526cf
Author: Rasmus Voss <rasmus.voss@schneider-electric.com>
Date:   Wed May 21 10:25:43 2014 +0200


    Updating information for developers
```

```
commit 6d724dcd3355f09e3450e417cf173fcafaee9e08
Author: Shawn Pearce <spearce@spearce.org>
Date:    Sat Apr 26 10:40:30 2014 -0700
```

18. As expected, we now have two commits on top of the `origin/master` commit.

Hopefully, this can assist you when you are just committing away but want to deliver the code as one commit.

There's more...

If you want to avoid opening the commit message editor like in step 17 of the *Auto-squashing commits* recipe, you can use `--fixup= d539645`. This will instead use the commit message from the first commit and totally disregard any message written in the commits.

5

Storing Additional Information in Your Repository

In this chapter, we will cover the following topics:

- ► Adding your first Git note
- ► Separating notes by category
- ► Retrieving notes from the remote repository
- ► Pushing Git notes to a remote repository
- ► Tagging commits in the repository

Introduction

Git is powerful in many ways. One of the most powerful features of Git is that it has immutable history. This is powerful because nobody can squeeze something into the history of Git without it being noticed by the people who have cloned the repository. This also causes some challenges for developers as some developers would like to change the commit messages after a commit has been released. This is a feature that is possible in many other version control systems but because of the immutable history with Git, it has Git notes, which is essentially an extra `refs/notes/commits` reference in Git. Here, you add additional information to the commits that can be listed when running a `git log` command. You can also release the notes into a remote repository so that people can fetch the notes.

Adding your first Git note

We will add some extra information to the already released code. If we were doing it in the actual commits, we would see the commit hashes change.

Getting ready

Before we start, we need a repository to work in; you can use the previous clone of `jgit`, but to get an output from the example that's almost identical, you can clone the `jgit` repository as follows:

```
$ git clone https://git.eclipse.org/r/jgit/jgit chapter5
$ cd chapter5
```

How to do it...

We start by creating a local branch `notesMessage` tracking `origin/stable-3.2`. Then, we will try and change the commit message and see that the commit hash changes:

1. Checkout the branch `notesMessage` tracking `origin/stable-3.2`:

   ```
   $ git checkout -b notesMessage   --track origin/stable-3.2
   Branch notesMessage set up to track remote branch stable-3.2 from
   origin.
   Switched to a new branch 'notesMessage'
   ```

2. List the commit hash of HEAD of your branch:

   ```
   $ git log -1
   commit f839d383e6fbbda26729db7fd57fc917fa47db44
   Author: Matthias Sohn <matthias.sohn@sap.com>
   Date:   Wed Dec 18 21:16:13 2013 +0100

       Prepare post 3.2.0 builds

       Change-Id: Ie2bfdee0c492e3d61d92acb04c5bef641f5f132f
       Signed-off-by: Matthias Sohn <matthias.sohn@sap.com>
   ```

3. Change the commit message by amending the commit using `git commit --amend`. Add a line above the `Change-Id:` line with "Update MANIFEST files":

   ```
   $ git commit --amend
   ```

4. Now, we list the commit again and see that the commit hash has changed:

```
$ git log -1
commit 5ccc9c90d29badb1bd860d29860715e0becd3d7b
Author: Matthias Sohn <matthias.sohn@sap.com>
Date:    Wed Dec 18 21:16:13 2013 +0100

    Prepare post 3.2.0 builds

    Update MANIFEST files
    Change-Id: Ie2bfdee0c492e3d61d92acb04c5bef641f5f132f
    Signed-off-by: Matthias Sohn matthias.sohn@sap.com
```

5. Notice that the commit parts have changed from
    `f839d383e6fbbda26729db7fd57fc917fa47db44` to
    `5ccc9c90d29badb1bd860d29860715e0becd3d7b`, as the commit is derived from
    the content in the commit, the parents of the commit, and the commit message. So,
    the commit hash will change when updating the commit message. Since we have
    changed the content of the HEAD commit, we are no longer based on the HEAD commit
    of the `origin/stable-3.2` branch. This becomes visible in `gitk` and `git status`:

```
$ git status
On branch notesMessage
Your branch and 'origin/stable-3.2' have diverged,
and have 1 and 1 different commit each, respectively.
  (use "git pull" to merge the remote branch into yours)

nothing to commit, working directory clean
```

6. As you can see from the output, our branch has diverged from `origin/stable-3.2`;
    this is also visible from Gitk. Notice that I specified which branches and commits I want
    to see with `gitk`. In this case, I want to see `origin/stable-3.2` and HEAD:

```
$ gitk origin/stable-3.2 HEAD
```

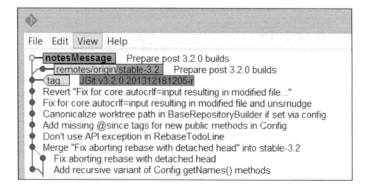

7. To prevent the this result, we can add a note to the commit message. Let's start by resetting the branch to `origin/stable-3.2` and then adding a note to the commit:

```
$ git reset --hard origin/stable-3.2
HEAD is now at f839d38 Prepare post 3.2.0 builds
```

8. Now, add the same message as the previous one but just as a note:

```
$ git notes add -m "Update MANIFEST files"
```

9. We have added the note directly from the command line without invoking the editor by using the `-m` flag and then a message. The log will now be visible when running `git log`:

```
$ git log -1

commit f839d383e6fbbda26729db7fd57fc917fa47db44
Author: Matthias Sohn <matthias.sohn@sap.com>
Date:   Wed Dec 18 21:16:13 2013 +0100

    Prepare post 3.2.0 builds

    Change-Id: Ie2bfdee0c492e3d61d92acb04c5bef641f5f132f
    Signed-off-by: Matthias Sohn <matthias.sohn@sap.com>

Notes:
    Update MANIFEST files
```

10. As you can see from the log output, we have a `Notes:` section with our note. Although it does not add the note directly in the commit message as the `--amend` option does, we still have our important addition to the commit message. We can verify with `git status` that we have no longer diverged:

```
$ git status
On branch notesMessage
Your branch is up-to-date with 'origin/stable-3.2'.

nothing to commit, working directory clean
```

There's more...

So, you have your notes for your commit and now you want to add to them. You will perhaps expect that you just add the note again with more information. This is not the case. You have the option to append, edit, or force the note to be created:

1. Start by trying to add the note again with additional information:

   ```
   $ git notes add -m "Update MANIFESTS files for next version"
   error: Cannot add notes. Found existing notes for object
   f839d383e6fbbda26729db7
   fd57fc917fa47db44. Use '-f' to overwrite existing notes
   ```

2. As predicted, we cannot add the note but we can do it with the -f flag:

   ```
   $ git notes add -f -m "Update MANIFESTS files for next version"
   Overwriting existing notes for object
   f839d383e6fbbda26729db7fd57fc917fa47db44
   ```

3. Git overwrites the existing notes due to the -f flag. You can also use --force, which is the same. Verify it with git log:

   ```
   $ git log -1
   commit f839d383e6fbbda26729db7fd57fc917fa47db44
   Author: Matthias Sohn <matthias.sohn@sap.com>
   Date:   Wed Dec 18 21:16:13 2013 +0100


       Prepare post 3.2.0 builds


       Change-Id: Ie2bfdee0c492e3d61d92acb04c5bef641f5f132f
       Signed-off-by: Matthias Sohn <matthias.sohn@sap.com>


   Notes:
       Update MANIFESTS files for next version
   ```

4. You can also append a current note with git notes append:

   ```
   $ git notes append -m "Verified by Rasmus Voss"
   ```

5. There is no output from this unless something goes wrong, but you can verify this by using `git log` again. To keep the output to a minimum, we are using `--oneline`. This will show a minimum output of the commit. But to show the note, we have to add `--notes`, which will show the notes for the commits in the output:

```
$ git log -1 --notes --oneline
f839d38 Prepare post 3.2.0 builds
Notes:
    Update MANIFESTS files for next version

    Verified by Rasmus Voss
```

6. As we can see from the output, we have the line appended to the note. If you try to use the `edit` option, you will see that you can only use this with the `-m` flag. This makes good sense as you should edit the note and not overwrite or append an already created note:

```
$ git notes edit -m "Rasmus Voss"
The -m/-F/-c/-C options have been deprecated for the 'edit'
subcommand.
Please use 'git notes add -f -m/-F/-c/-C' instead.
```

7. As you can see, Git rejects doing and mentions other ways of doing it.

 The `git notes add` and `git notes edit` commands without any arguments will do exactly the same, that is, open the configured editor and allow you to write a note to the commit.

Separating notes by category

As we saw in the previous example, we can add notes to the commits, but in some cases, it makes sense to store the information sorted by categories, such as `featureImplemented`, `defect`, and `alsoCherryPick`. As briefly explained at the beginning of the chapter, notes are stored in `refs/notes/commits` but we can add multiple references so that we can easily sort and list the different scopes of the notes.

Getting ready

To start this example, we need a new branch that tracks the `origin/stable-3.1` branch; we name the branch `notesReferences`, and create and checkout the branch with the following command:

```
$ git checkout -b notesReferences --track origin/stable-3.1
Branch notesReferences set up to track remote branch stable-3.1 from origin.
Switched to a new branch 'notesReferences'
```

How to do it...

Imagine a situation where we have corrected a defect and did everything we could to ensure the quality of the commit before releasing it. Nonetheless, we had to make another fix for the same defect.

So, we want to add a note to the reference `refs/notes/alsoCherryPick`, which should indicate that if you cherry pick this commit, you should also cherry pick the other commits as they fix the same defect.

In this example, we will find a commit and add some extra information to the commit in multiple notes' reference specifications:

1. Start by listing the top ten commits on the branch so we have something to copy and paste from:

```
$ git log -10 --oneline
da6e87b Prepare post 3.1.0 builds
16ca725 JGit v3.1.0.201310021548-r
c6aba99 Fix order of commits in rebase todo file header
5a2a222 Prepare post 3.1.0 RC1 builds
6f0681e JGit v3.1.0.201309270735-rc1
a065a06 Attempt to fix graph layout when new heads are introduced
b4f07df Prepare re-signing pgm's ueberjar to avoid SecurityException
aa4bbc6 Use full branch name when getting ref in BranchTrackingStatus
570bba5 Ignore bitmap indexes that do not match the pack checksum
801aac5 Merge branch 'stable-3.0'
```

2. Now, to add a note for the `b4f07df` commit in the ref `alsoCherryPick`, we must use the `--ref` option for `git notes`. This has to be specified before the add option:

```
$ git notes --ref alsoCherryPick add -m "570bba5" b4f07df
```

3. No output means success when adding notes. Now that we have a note, we should be able to list it with a single `git log -1` command. However, this is not the case. You actually need to specify that you want to list the notes from the specific ref. This can be done with the `--notes=alsoCherryPick` option for `git log`:

```
$ git log -1 b4f07df357fccdff891df2a4fa5c5bd9e83b4a4a
--notes=alsoCherryPick

commit b4f07df357fccdff891df2a4fa5c5bd9e83b4a4a

Author: Matthias Sohn <matthias.sohn@sap.com>

Date:    Tue Sep 24 09:11:47 2013 +0200


    Prepare re-signing pgm's ueberjar to avoid SecurityException
More output...
    Change-Id: Ia302e68a4b2a9399cb18025274574e31d3d3e407

    Signed-off-by: Matthias Sohn <matthias.sohn@sap.com>


Notes (alsoCherryPick):
    570bba5
```

4. As you can see from the output, Git shows the `alsoCherryPick` notes. The reason for not showing is that Git defaults to adding notes into `refs/notes/commits`. It would be nice if you could just show the `alsoCherryPick` notes' reference by default. This can be done by configuring Git as follows:

```
$ git config notes.displayRef "refs/notes/alsoCherryPick"
```

5. By configuring this option, you are telling Git to always list these notes. But what about the default notes? Have we overwritten the configuration to list the default `refs/notes/commits` notes? We can check this with `git log -1` to see if we still have the test note displayed:

```
$ git log -1

commit da6e87bc373c54c1cda8ed563f41f65df52bacbf

Author: Matthias Sohn <matthias.sohn@sap.com>

Date:    Thu Oct 3 17:22:08 2013 +0200


    Prepare post 3.1.0 builds
```

```
Change-Id: I306a3d40c6ddb88a16d17f09a60e3d19b0716962

Signed-off-by: Matthias Sohn <matthias.sohn@sap.com>


Notes:

    test note
```

6. No, we did not overwrite the setting to list notes in the default refs. Knowing that we can have as many `notes.displayRef` configurations as we want, we should add all the refs we want to use in our repo. In some situations, it is even better to just add `refs/notes/*`. This will configure Git to show all the notes:

```
$ git config notes.displayRef 'refs/notes/*'
```

7. If we add another note in `refs/notes/defect` now, we should be able to list it without specifying which notes' reference we want to list when using `git log`. We are adding to the commit that already has a note in the `alsoCherryPick` reference:

```
$ git notes --ref defect add -m "Bug:24435"
b4f07df357fccdff891df2a4fa5c5bd9e83b4a4a
```

8. Now, list the commit with `git log`:

```
$ git log -1 b4f07df357fccdff891df2a4fa5c5bd9e83b4a4a

commit b4f07df357fccdff891df2a4fa5c5bd9e83b4a4a

Author: Matthias Sohn <matthias.sohn@sap.com>

Date:    Tue Sep 24 09:11:47 2013 +0200


    Prepare re-signing pgm's ueberjar to avoid SecurityException
    See http://dev.eclipse.org/mhonarc/lists/jgit-dev/msg02277.
html


    Change-Id: Ia302e68a4b2a9399cb18025274574e31d3d3e407

    Signed-off-by: Matthias Sohn <matthias.sohn@sap.com>


Notes (alsoCherryPick):
    570bba5


Notes (defect):
    Bug:24435
```

9. Git shows both notes, which is what we would expect.

How it works...

I have been writing about the `refs/notes/alsoCherryPick` reference and so on. As you know, we refer to the remote branches as references such as `refs/remotes/origin/stable-3.2`, but the local branches are also references such as `refs/heads/develop for instance.`

Since you can create a branch that starts at a specific reference, you should be able to create a branch that starts at the `refs/notes/alsoCherrypick` reference:

1. Create a branch that starts from `refs/notes/alsoCherryPick`. Also, checkout the branch:

   ```
   $ git checkout -b myNotes notes/alsoCherryPick
   Switched to a new branch 'myNotes'
   ```

2. The `myNotes` branch now points to `HEAD` on `refs/notes/alsoCherryPick`. Listing the files on the branch will show a file with the commit hash of the commit we have added the notes to:

   ```
   $ ls
   b4f07df357fccdff891df2a4fa5c5bd9e83b4a4a
   ```

3. Showing the file content will show the text we used as note text:

   ```
   $ cat b4f07df357fccdff891df2a4fa5c5bd9e83b4a4a
   570bba5
   ```

4. As you can see, the abbreviated commit hash `570bba5` we added as a note for `b4f07df357fccdff891df2a4fa5c5bd9e83b4a4a` is in the file. If we had a longer message, that message would also be shown here.

Retrieving notes from the remote repository

So far, we have been creating notes in our own local repository, which is okay. But if we want to share those notes, we have to be sure to be able to push them. We would also like to be able to retrieve other people's notes from the remote repository. Unfortunately, this is not so plain and simple.

Getting ready

Before we can start, we need another clone from the local clone we already have. This is to show the push and fetch mechanism of Git with `git notes`:

1. Start by checking out the master branch:

   ```
   $ git checkout master
   ```

```
Checking out files: 100% (1529/1529), done.
Switched to branch 'master'
Your branch is up-to-date with 'origin/master'.
```

2. Now, create local branches of all the `stable-3.x` branches:

    ```
    $ git branch stable-3.0 origin/stable-3.0
    Branch stable-3.0 set up to track remote branch stable-3.0 from origin.
    $ git branch stable-3.1 origin/stable-3.1
    Branch stable-3.1 set up to track remote branch stable-3.1 from origin.
    $ git branch stable-3.2 origin/stable-3.2
    Branch stable-3.2 set up to track remote branch stable-3.2 from origin.
    ```

3. We are checking out all these branches because we want to clone this repository and by default all the `refs/heads/*` branches will be cloned. So, when we clone the `chapter5` directory, you will see that we only get the branches we see if you execute `git branch`:

    ```
    $ git branch
    * master
      myNotes
      notesMessage
      notesReference
      stable-3.0
      stable-3.1
      stable-3.2
    ```

4. Now, go one directory up so you can create your new clone from the `chapter5` directory:

    ```
    cd ..
    $ git clone ./chapter5 shareNotes
    Cloning into 'shareNotes'...
    done.
    ```

5. Now, enter the `shareNotes` directory and run `git branch -a` to see that the only remote branches we have are the branches we had checked out as local branches in the `chapter5` directory. After this, we are ready to fetch some notes:

    ```
    cd shareNotes
    $ git branch -a
    ```

```
* master
  remotes/origin/HEAD -> origin/master
  remotes/origin/master
  remotes/origin/myNotes
  remotes/origin/notesMessage
  remotes/origin/notesReference
  remotes/origin/stable-3.0
  remotes/origin/stable-3.1
  remotes/origin/stable-3.2
```

6. As predicted, the list matches the Git branch output from the `chapter5` directory.

How to do it...

We have now prepared the setup to push and fetch notes. The challenge is that Git is not a default setup to retrieve and push notes, so you won't usually see other people's notes:

1. We start by showing that we did not receive the notes during the clone:

```
$ git log -1 b4f07df357fccdff891df2a4fa5c5bd9e83b4a4a
--notes=alsoCherryPick
warning: notes ref refs/notes/alsoCherryPick is invalid
commit b4f07df357fccdff891df2a4fa5c5bd9e83b4a4a
Author: Matthias Sohn <matthias.sohn@sap.com>
Date:   Tue Sep 24 09:11:47 2013 +0200

    Prepare re-signing pgm's ueberjar to avoid SecurityException
```

2. As expected, the output does not show the note. In the `chapter5` directory, we will see the note. To enable the notes to be fetched, we need to create a new fetch rule configuration; it needs to be similar to the fetch rule for `refs/heads`. Take a look at the configuration from `git config`:

```
$ git config --get remote.origin.fetch
+refs/heads/*:refs/remotes/origin/*
```

3. This shows that we are fetching `refs/heads` into the `refs/remotes/origin` reference, but what we also want to do is fetch `refs/notes/*` into `refs/notes/*`:

```
$ git config --add remote.origin.fetch '+refs/notes/*:refs/
notes/*'
```

4. You should now have it configured. If you leave out the `--add` option from your command, you will overwrite your current settings. Verify that the rule now exists:

```
$ git config --get-all  remote.origin.fetch
+refs/heads/*:refs/remotes/origin/*
+refs/notes/*:refs/notes/*
```

5. Now, try and fetch the notes:

```
$ git fetch
From c:/Users/Rasmus/repos/./chapter5
 * branch              master        -> FETCH_HEAD
 * [new ref]           refs/notes/alsoCherryPick -> refs/notes/
alsoCherryPick
 * [new ref]           refs/notes/commits -> refs/notes/commits
 * [new ref]           refs/notes/defect -> refs/notes/defect
 * [new ref]           refs/notes/defects -> refs/notes/defects
```

6. As the Git output indicates, we have received some new refs. So, let us check whether we have the note on the commit now:

```
$ git log -1 b4f07df357fccdff891df2a4fa5c5bd9e83b4a4a
--notes=alsoCherryPick
commit b4f07df357fccdff891df2a4fa5c5bd9e83b4a4a
Author: Matthias Sohn <matthias.sohn@sap.com>
Date:   Tue Sep 24 09:11:47 2013 +0200

    Prepare re-signing pgm's ueberjar to avoid SecurityException
More output...
    Signed-off-by: Matthias Sohn <matthias.sohn@sap.com>
Notes (alsoCherryPick):
    570bba5
```

7. We now have the notes in our repository, which is what we expected.

How it works...

We fetched the notes. The reason why it works is because of the way we fetched. By default, Git is configured to fetch `refs/heads/*` into `refs/remotes/origin/*`. This way, we can easily keep track of what is remote and what is local. The branches in our local repo are in `refs/heads/*`. These branches are also listed when you execute `git branch`.

For notes, we need to fetch `refs/notes/*` into `refs/notes/*` since we want to get the notes from the server and use them with the `git show`, `git log`, and `git notes` Git commands.

Pushing notes to a remote repository

We have tried and succeeded in retrieving the notes from the remote repository, but what about your notes? How can you push them to the server? This has to be done with the push command just as with any other references, such as branches and commits, when you want to publish them to a remote repository.

How to do it...

Before we can push the notes from the shareNotes repository, we have to create a note to be pushed, as the notes we have now are all available on the remote repository. The remote repository in this case is the chapter5 directory:

1. I have found a commit I would like to add a note to, and I want to add the note in the verified reference:

   ```
   $ git notes --ref verified add -m "Verified by rasmus.voss@live.
   dk" 871ee53b52a
   ```

2. Now that we have added the note, we can list it with the git log command:

   ```
   $ git log --notes=verified -1 871ee53b52a
   commit 871ee53b52a7e7f6a0fe600a054ec78f8e4bff5a
   Author: Robin Rosenberg <robin.rosenberg@dewire.com>
   Date:   Sun Feb 2 23:26:34 2014 +0100

       Reset internal state canonical length in WorkingTreeIterator
   when moving

       Bug: 426514
       Change-Id: Ifb75a4fa12291aeeece3dda129a65f0c1fd5e0eb
       Signed-off-by: Matthias Sohn <matthias.sohn@sap.com>

   Notes (verified):
       Verified by rasmus.voss@live.dk
   ```

3. As expected, we can see the note. If you cannot see the note, you probably missed --notes=verified for the git log command, since we have not configured verified as notes.displayRef. To push the note, we must use the git push command, because the default push rule in Git is to push branches to refs/heads/<branchname>. So, if we just try to push the note to the remote, nothing happens:

   ```
   $ git push
   Everything up-to-date
   ```

4. You will probably see a warning about `git push.default` not being configured; you can safely ignore this for these examples. The important part is that Git shows that everything is up-to-date. But we know we have created a Git note for a commit. So to push these notes, we need to push our note references to the remote notes references. This can be done as follows:

```
$ git push origin refs/notes/*
Counting objects: 15, done.
Delta compression using up to 4 threads.
Compressing objects: 100% (4/4), done.
Writing objects: 100% (5/5), 583 bytes | 0 bytes/s, done.
Total 5 (delta 0), reused 0 (delta 0)
To c:/Users/Rasmus/repos/./chapter5/
 * [new branch]      refs/notes/verified -> refs/notes/verified
```

5. Now something happened; we have a new branch on the remote named `refs/notes/verified`. This is because we have pushed the notes to the remote. What we can do to verify it is go to the `chapter5` directory and check if the `871ee53b52a` commit has a Git note:

```
$ cd ../chapter5/
$ git log --notes=verified -1 871ee53b52a
commit 871ee53b52a7e7f6a0fe600a054ec78f8e4bff5a
Author: Robin Rosenberg <robin.rosenberg@dewire.com>
Date:   Sun Feb 2 23:26:34 2014 +0100


    Reset internal state canonical length in WorkingTreeIterator
when moving


    Bug: 426514
    Change-Id: Ifb75a4fa12291aeeece3dda129a65f0c1fd5e0eb
    Signed-off-by: Matthias Sohn <matthias.sohn@sap.com>


Notes (verified):
    Verified by rasmus.voss@live.dk
```

6. As predicted, we can see the note in this directory.

There's more...

Since Git notes do not work as normal branches, it can be a little difficult to push them back and forth to a repository when you are trying to collaborate on them. Since you cannot just fetch and merge the Git notes branches as easily with other branches, a clear recommendation is to build some tools to add these notes so you only have one server adding the notes.

A very simple but value adding note could be the Jenkins build and test information that published notes about which tests have passed on a commit hash; this is very valid when you have to reopen a defect. You can then actually see in the repository which test has been executed on the commit hash.

Tagging commits in the repository

If you are releasing software with Git, you are bound to deal with tags as the tag describes the different software releases in the repository. There are two types of tags, a lightweight tag and an annotated tag. The lightweight tag is very similar to a branch, since it is just a named reference like `refs/tags/version123`, which points to the commit hash of the commit you are tagging; whereas if it were a branch, it would be `refs/heads/version123`. The difference is the branch moves forward when you work and commit to it. The tag should always point to the same commit hash.

Getting ready

Before we start, you must go to the `chapter5` directory, where we made the original clone for this chapter.

We should start by tagging the commit that is ten commits behind `origin/stable-2.3` and is not a merge. In order to find that commit, we will use the `git log` command.

For the `git log` command, we are using the `--no-merges` option, which will show commits that only have one parent. The `--oneline` option we have used before tells Git to limit the output to one line per commit.

Find the commit as follows:

```
$ git log -11 --no-merges --oneline origin/stable-2.3

49ec6c1 Prepare 2.3.2-SNAPSHOT builds

63dcece JGit v2.3.1.201302201838-r

3b41fcb Accept Change-Id even if footer contains not well-formed entries

5d7b722 Fix false positives in hashing used by PathFilterGroup
```

```
9a5f4b4 Prepare post 2.3.0.201302130906 builds

19d6cad JGit v2.3.0.201302130906

3f8ac55 Replace explicit version by property where possible

1c4ee41 Add better documentation to DirCacheCheckout

e9cf705 Prepare post 2.3rc1 builds

ea060dd JGit v2.3.0.201302060400-rc1

60d538f Add getConflictingNames to RefDatabase
```

How to do it...

Now that we have found the `60d538f` commit, we should make it a lightweight tag:

1. Use the `git tag` command to give a meaningful release name:

   ```
   $ git tag 'v2.3.0.201302061315rc1' ea060dd
   ```

2. Since there is no output, it is a success; to see whether the tag is available, use the `git tag` command:

   ```
   $ git tag -l "v2.3.0.2*"
   v2.3.0.201302061315rc1
   v2.3.0.201302130906
   ```

3. We are using the `git tag` command with `-l` as a flag, since we want to list the tags and not tag the current HEAD. Some repositories have a lot of tags, so to prevent the list from being too long, you can specify which tags you want to list and use a * wildcard as I have used. Our tag is available, but all it really says is that we have a tag in the repository with the name `v2.3.0.201302061315rc1`, and if you are using `git show v2.3.0.201302061315rc1`, you will see that the output is the same as `git show ea060dd`:

   ```
   $ git show v2.3.0.201302061315rc1
   commit ea060dd8e74ab588ca55a4fb3ff15dd17343aa88
   Author: Matthias Sohn <matthias.sohn@sap.com>
   Date:   Wed Feb 6 13:15:01 2013 +0100

       JGit v2.3.0.201302060400-rc1

       Change-Id: Id1f1d174375f7399cee4c2eb23368d4dbb4c384a
       Signed-off-by: Matthias Sohn <matthias.sohn@sap.com>
   ```

```
diff --git a/org.eclipse.jgit.ant.test/META-INF/MANIFEST.MF b/org.
eclipse.jgit.a
```

```
$ git show ea060dd
commit ea060dd8e74ab588ca55a4fb3ff15dd17343aa88
Author: Matthias Sohn <matthias.sohn@sap.com>
Date:    Wed Feb 6 13:15:01 2013 +0100

     JGit v2.3.0.201302060400-rc1

     Change-Id: Id1f1d174375f7399cee4c2eb23368d4dbb4c384a
     Signed-off-by: Matthias Sohn <matthias.sohn@sap.com>

diff --git a/org.eclipse.jgit.ant.test/META-INF/MANIFEST.MF b/org.
eclipse.jgit.a
```

4. There will also be a lot of file diff information in the output but it is exactly the same output. So, in order to add more information, we should use an annotated tag. An annotated tag is a tag where you have to add some information to the tag. To create an annotated tag, we use the `--annotate` tag for the `git tag` command:

```
git tag --annotate -m "Release Maturity rate 97%"
'v2.3.0.201409022257rc2' 1c4ee41
```

5. The `-m` flag is the same as `--message`, as I wanted to give the tag a message. If you leave out the `-m` flag, Git will open the configured editor and you can write a full release note into the annotation of the tag. We can check the tag information with `git show`:

```
$ git show 'v2.3.0.201409022257rc2'
tag v2.3.0.201409022257rc2
Tagger: Rasmus Voss <rasmus.voss@live.dk>
Date:    Sun Feb 9 22:58:28 2014 +0100

Release Maturity rate 97%

commit 1c4ee41dc093266c19d4452879afe5c0f7f387f4
Author: Christian Halstrick christian.halstrick@sap.com
```

6. We can actually see the tag name and information we added with the `-m` flag. With the lightweight tag, we don't see anything about the tag from the output. We actually don't even see the tag name when using Git show on a lightweight tag.

There's more...

Tags are very powerful as they can add valuable information to the repository, and since tags should be considered official releases in the repository, we should be very careful with them.

Naturally, you can push the tags to a remote area, and contributors to the repository would fetch those tags. This is where you have to be careful. With a legacy version control system, you can go back in time and just change the release, and since these legacy systems are all based on a centralized server where you have to be connected in order to work, changing a release is not that bad, since not so many people use the release or have even downloaded the release. But it is different in Git. If you change a tag that you have already pushed to point to another commit hash, then those developers who have already fetched the tag will not get the new tag unless the delete the tag locally.

1. To prove the dangers of not getting new tag, we will try to delete a tag and recreate it to point to another commit hash:

    ```
    $ git tag -d v1.3.0.201202121842-rc4
    Deleted tag 'v1.3.0.201202121842-rc4' (was d1e8804)
    ```

2. Now that we have deleted the tag, we are ready to recreate the tag again to point to HEAD:

    ```
    $ git tag -a -m "Local created tag" v1.3.0.201202121842-rc4
    ```

3. We have recreated the tag and it points to HEAD because we did not specify a commit hash at the end of the command. Now, execute `git fetch` to see whether you can get the tag overwritten from the remote repository:

    ```
    $ git fetch
    ```

4. Since there is no output, the tag was probably not overwritten. Let us verify with `git show`:

    ```
    $ git show v1.3.0.201202121842-rc4
    tag v1.3.0.201202121842-rc4
    Tagger: Rasmus Voss <rasmus.voss@live.dk>
    Date:   Sun Feb 9 23:17:18 2014 +0100

    Local created tag

    commit 1c4ee41dc093266c19d4452879afe5c0f7f387f4
    ```

5. As you can see from the output, it is still our locally created tag. To get the tag from the remote again, we need to delete the local tag and do a Git fetch. To delete a tag, you need to apply the -d flag:

    ```
    $ git tag -d v1.3.0.201202121842-rc4
    Deleted tag 'v1.3.0.201202121842-rc4' (was 28be24b)
    ```

```
$ git fetch

From https://git.eclipse.org/r/jgit/jgit

* [new tag]          v1.3.0.201202121842-rc4 ->
v1.3.0.201202121842-rc4
```

6. As you can see, Git has fetched the tag from the server again. We can verify with `git show`:

```
$ git show v1.3.0.201202121842-rc4

tag v1.3.0.201202121842-rc4

Tagger: Matthias Sohn <matthias.sohn@sap.com>

Date:    Mon Feb 13 00:57:56 2012 +0100


JGit 1.3.0.201202121842-rc4

-----BEGIN PGP SIGNATURE-----

Version: GnuPG/MacGPG2 v2.0.14 (Darwin)


iF4EABEIAAYFAk84UhMACgkQWwXM3hQMKHbwewD/VD62MWCVfLCYUIEz20C4Iywx

40Ol5TedaLFwIOS55HcA/ipDh6NWFvJdWK3Enm2krjegUNmd9zXT+0pNjtlJ+Pyi

=LRoe

-----END PGP SIGNATURE-----


commit 53917539f822afa12caaa55db8f57c29570532f3
```

7. So, as you can see, we have the correct tag again, but it should also be a warning that once you push a tag to a remote repository, you should never change it, since the developers who are fetching from the repository may never know unless they clone again or delete the tags locally and fetch them again.

In this chapter, we learned how you can tag your commits and add notes to them. This is a powerful method to store additional information after the commit has been committed and published to a shared repository. But before you actually publish your commit, you have the chance to add the most valuable information for a commit. The commit message is where you must specify what you are doing and sometimes why you are doing it.

If you are solving a bug, you should list the bug ID; if you are using a special method to solve the problem, it is recommended that you describe why you have used this awesome technique to solve the problem. So when people look back on your commits, they can also learn a few things on why different decisions were made.

6

Extracting Data from the Repository

In this chapter, we will cover the following topics:

- ▶ Extracting the top contributor
- ▶ Finding bottlenecks in the source tree
- ▶ Grepping the commit messages
- ▶ The contents of the releases

Introduction

Whether you work in big or small organizations, safeguarding and maintaining data is always important and it keeps track of a fair amount for you, it is just a matter of extracting the data. Some of the data is included in the system by you or any other developer when you fill in the commit message with proper information; for instance, details of the bug you are fixing from the bug tracking system.

The data is not only valid for management, but can also be used to add more time to refactor the `.c` files, where almost all bugs are fixed.

Extracting the top contributor

Git has a few built-in stats you can get instantaneously. The `git log` command has different options, such as `--numstat`, that will show the number of files added and lines deleted for each file since each commit. However, for finding the top committer in the repository, we can just use the `git shortlog` command.

Getting ready

As with all the examples throughout the book, we are using the `jgit` repository; you can either clone it or go to one of the clones you might already have.

Clone the `jgit` repository as follows:

```
$ git clone https://git.eclipse.org/r/jgit/jgit chapter6
$ cd chapter6
```

How to do it...

The `shortlog` Git command is very simple and does not leave a lot of options or flags to use with it. It can show the log but in a boiled-down version, and then it can summarize it for us:

1. Start by showing the last five commits with `shortlog`. We can use `-5` to limit the amount of output:

   ```
   $ git shortlog -5
   Jonathan Nieder (1):
           Update commons-compress to 1.6

   Matthias Sohn (2):
           Update com.jcraft.jsch to 0.1.50 in Kepler target platform
           Update target platforms to use latest orbit build

   SATO taichi (1):
           Add git checkout --orphan implementation

   Stefan Lay (1):
           Fix fast forward rebase with rebase.autostash=true
   ```

2. As you can see, the output is very different from the `git log` output. You can try it for yourself with `git log -5`. The numbers in parentheses are the number of commits by that committer. Below the name and number are the commit titles of the commits. Note that no commit hashes are shown. To find the top committer with just those five commits is easy, but when you try running `git shortlog` without `-5`, it is hard to find that person. To sort and find the top committer, we can use the `-n` or `--numbered` option to sort the output. The top committer is on top:

   ```
   $ git shortlog -5 --numbered
   Matthias Sohn (2):
   ```

```
      Update com.jcraft.jsch to 0.1.50 in Kepler target platform
      Update target platforms to use latest orbit build


Jonathan Nieder (1):
      Update commons-compress to 1.6


SATO taichi (1):
      Add git checkout --orphan implementation


Stefan Lay (1):
      Fix fast forward rebase with rebase.autostash=true
```

3. As you can see, the output is nicely sorted. If we don't care about the commit subjects, we can use -s or --summary to only show the commit count for each developer:

    ```
    $ git shortlog -5 --numbered --summary
        2   Matthias Sohn
        1   Jonathan Nieder
        1   SATO taichi
        1   Stefan Lay
    ```

4. Finally, we have what we want, except we don't have the e-mail addresses of the committers; this option is also available with -e or --email. This will also show the e-mail addresses of the committers in the list. This time, we will try it on the entire repository. Currently, we have only listed it for the HEAD commit. To list it for the repository, we need to add --all at the end of the command so as to execute the command for all branches:

    ```
    $ git shortlog  --numbered --summary --email --all
        765   Shawn O. Pearce <spearce@spearce.org>
        399   Matthias Sohn <matthias.sohn@sap.com>
        360   Robin Rosenberg <robin.rosenberg@dewire.com>
        181   Chris Aniszczyk <caniszczyk@gmail.com>
        172   Shawn Pearce <spearce@spearce.org>
        160   Christian Halstrick <christian.halstrick@sap.com>
        114   Robin Stocker robin@nibor.org
    ```

5. So, this is the list now; we know who contributed with the most commits, but this picture can be a little skewed as the top committer may just happen to be the creator of the project and may not actively contribute to the repository. So, to list the top committers for the last six months, we can add `--since="6 months ago"` to the `git shortlog` command:

```
$ git shortlog  --numbered --summary --email --all --since="6
months ago"
    73  Matthias Sohn <matthias.sohn@sap.com>

    15  Robin Stocker <robin@nibor.org>

    14  Robin Rosenberg <robin.rosenberg@dewire.com>

    13  Shawn Pearce <sop@google.com>

    12  Stefan Lay <stefan.lay@sap.com>

     8  Christian Halstrick <christian.halstrick@sap.com>

     7  Colby Ranger cranger@google.com
```

6. As you can see, the picture has changed since the start of the repository.

> You can use "n weeks ago", "n days ago", "n months ago", "n hours ago", and so on for specifying time periods. You can also use specific dates such as "1 october 2013".

You can also list the top committer for a specific month using the `--until` option, where you can specify the date you wish to list the commit until. This can be done as follows:

```
$ git shortlog  --numbered --summary --email --all --since="30
september" --until="1 november 2013"
    15  Matthias Sohn <matthias.sohn@sap.com>

     4  Kaloyan Raev <kaloyan.r@zend.com>

     4  Robin Rosenberg <robin.rosenberg@dewire.com>

     3  Colby Ranger <cranger@google.com>

     2  Robin Stocker <robin@nibor.org>

     1  Christian Halstrick <christian.halstrick@sap.com>

     1  Michael Nelson <michael.nelson@tasktop.com>

     1  Rüdiger Herrmann <ruediger.herrmann@gmx.de>

     1  Tobias Pfeifer <to.pfeifer@web.de>

     1 Tomasz Zarna tomasz.zarna@tasktop.com
```

7. As you can see, we get another list, and it seems like Matthias is the main contributor, at least compared to the initial result. These types of data can also be used to visualize the shift of responsibility in a repository by collecting the data for each month since the repository's initialization.

There's more...

While working with code, it is often useful to know who to go to when you need to perform a fix in the software, especially in an area where you are inexperienced. So, it would be nice to figure out who is the code owner of the file or the files you are changing. The obvious reason is to get some input on the code, but also to know who to go to for a code review. You can again use `git shortlog` to figure this out. You can use the command on the files as well:

1. To do this, we simply add the file to the end of the `git shortlog` command:

   ```
   $ git shortlog  --numbered --summary --email ./pom.xml
       86  Matthias Sohn <matthias.sohn@sap.com>
       21  Shawn O. Pearce <spearce@spearce.org>
        4  Chris Aniszczyk <caniszczyk@gmail.com>
        4  Jonathan Nieder <jrn@google.com>
        3  Igor Fedorenko <igor@ifedorenko.com>
        3  Kevin Sawicki <kevin@github.com>
        2  Colby Ranger cranger@google.com
   ```

2. As for `pom.xml`, we also have a top committer. As all the options you have for `git log` are available for `shortlog`, we can also do this on a directory.

   ```
   $ git shortlog  --numbered --summary --email ./org.eclipse.jgit.
   console/
       57  Matthias Sohn <matthias.sohn@sap.com>
       11  Shawn O. Pearce <spearce@spearce.org>
        9  Robin Rosenberg <robin.rosenberg@dewire.com>
        2  Chris Aniszczyk <caniszczyk@gmail.com>
        1  Robin Stocker robin@nibor.org
   ```

3. As you can see, it is fairly simple to get some indication on who to go to for the different files or directories in Git.

Finding bottlenecks in the source tree

Often, the development teams know where the bottleneck in the source tree is, but it can be challenging to convince the management that you need resources to rewrite some code. However, with Git, it is fairly simple to extract that type of data from the repository.

Getting ready

Start by checking out the `stable-3.1` release:

```
$ git checkout stable-3.1
Branch stable-3.1 set up to track remote branch stable-3.1 from origin.
Switched to a new branch 'stable-3.1'
```

How to do it...

We want to start by listing some stats for one commit, and then we can extend the examples to larger chunks of commits:

1. The first option we will be using is –dirstat for git log:

    ```
    $ git log -1 --dirstat
    commit da6e87bc373c54c1cda8ed563f41f65df52bacbf
    Author: Matthias Sohn <matthias.sohn@sap.com>
    Date:    Thu Oct 3 17:22:08 2013 +0200

            Prepare post 3.1.0 builds

            Change-Id: I306a3d40c6ddb88a16d17f09a60e3d19b0716962
            Signed-off-by: Matthias Sohn <matthias.sohn@sap.com>

        5.0% org.eclipse.jgit.http.server/META-INF/
        6.9% org.eclipse.jgit.http.test/META-INF/
        3.3% org.eclipse.jgit.java7.test/META-INF/
        4.3% org.eclipse.jgit.junit.http/META-INF/
        6.6% org.eclipse.jgit.junit/META-INF/
        5.5% org.eclipse.jgit.packaging/
    ```

```
 5.9% org.eclipse.jgit.pgm.test/META-INF/

13.7% org.eclipse.jgit.pgm/META-INF/

15.4% org.eclipse.jgit.test/META-INF/

 3.7% org.eclipse.jgit.ui/META-INF/

13.1% org.eclipse.jgit/META-INF/
```

2. The `--dirstat` option shows which directories have changed in the commit and how much they have changed compared to each other. The default setting is to count the number of lines added to or removed from the commit. So, rearranging the code potentially does not count for any change as the line count might be the same. You can compensate for this slightly by using `--dirstat=lines`. This option will look at each file line by line and see whether they have changed compared to the previous version:

```
$ git log -1 --dirstat=lines

commit da6e87bc373c54c1cda8ed563f41f65df52bacbf

Author: Matthias Sohn <matthias.sohn@sap.com>

Date:    Thu Oct 3 17:22:08 2013 +0200


    Prepare post 3.1.0 builds


    Change-Id: I306a3d40c6ddb88a16d17f09a60e3d19b0716962

    Signed-off-by: Matthias Sohn <matthias.sohn@sap.com>


 4.8% org.eclipse.jgit.http.server/META-INF/

 6.5% org.eclipse.jgit.http.test/META-INF/

 3.2% org.eclipse.jgit.java7.test/META-INF/

 4.0% org.eclipse.jgit.junit.http/META-INF/

 6.1% org.eclipse.jgit.junit/META-INF/

 6.9% org.eclipse.jgit.packaging/

 5.7% org.eclipse.jgit.pgm.test/META-INF/

13.0% org.eclipse.jgit.pgm/META-INF/

14.6% org.eclipse.jgit.test/META-INF/

 3.6% org.eclipse.jgit.ui/META-INF/

13.8% org.eclipse.jgit/META-INF/
```

3. This also gives a slightly different result. If you would like to limit the output to only show directories with a certain percentage or higher, we can limit the output as follows:

```
$ git log -1 --dirstat=lines,10
commit da6e87bc373c54c1cda8ed563f41f65df52bacbf
Author: Matthias Sohn <matthias.sohn@sap.com>
Date:   Thu Oct 3 17:22:08 2013 +0200

    Prepare post 3.1.0 builds

    Change-Id: I306a3d40c6ddb88a16d17f09a60e3d19b0716962
    Signed-off-by: Matthias Sohn <matthias.sohn@sap.com>

  13.0% org.eclipse.jgit.pgm/META-INF/
  14.6% org.eclipse.jgit.test/META-INF/
  13.8% org.eclipse.jgit/META-INF/
```

4. By adding `10` to the `--dirstat=lines` command, we are asking Git to only show the directories that have 10 percent or higher changes; you can use any number you like here. By default, Git does not count the changes in the subdirectories, but only the files in the directory. So, in this diagram, only changes in `File A1` are counted as changes. For the `Dir A1` directory and the `File B1` file, it is counted as a change in `Dir A2`:

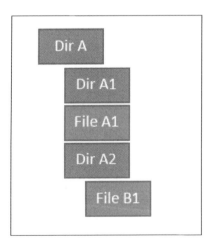

5. To cumulate this, we can add `cumulative` to the `--dirstat=lines,10` command, and this will cumulate the changes and calculate a percentage. Be aware that the percentage can go beyond 100 due to the way it is calculated:

```
$ git log -1 --dirstat=files,10,cumulative

commit da6e87bc373c54c1cda8ed563f41f65df52bacbf

Author: Matthias Sohn <matthias.sohn@sap.com>

Date:    Thu Oct 3 17:22:08 2013 +0200


    Prepare post 3.1.0 builds


    Change-Id: I306a3d40c6ddb88a16d17f09a60e3d19b0716962

    Signed-off-by: Matthias Sohn <matthias.sohn@sap.com>


  31.3% org.eclipse.jgit.packaging/
```

6. As you can see, the output is slightly different from what we have seen earlier. By using `git log --dirstat`, you can get some information about what goes on in the repository. Obviously, you can also do this for all the commits between two releases or two commit hashes. Let's try this, but instead of using `git log`, we will be using `git diff`, as Git will show the accumulated diff between the two releases, and `git log` will show the dirstat for each commit between the releases:

```
$ git diff  origin/stable-3.1..origin/stable-3.2 --dirstat
   4.0% org.eclipse.jgit.packaging/org.eclipse.jgit.target/
   3.9% org.eclipse.jgit.pgm.test/tst/org/eclipse/jgit/pgm/
   4.1% org.eclipse.jgit.pgm/
  20.7% org.eclipse.jgit.test/tst/org/eclipse/jgit/api/
  21.3% org.eclipse.jgit.test/tst/org/eclipse/jgit/internal/
storage/file/
   5.2% org.eclipse.jgit.test/tst/org/eclipse/jgit/
  14.5% org.eclipse.jgit/src/org/eclipse/jgit/api/
   6.5% org.eclipse.jgit/src/org/eclipse/jgit/lib/
   3.9% org.eclipse.jgit/src/org/eclipse/jgit/transport/
   4.6% org.eclipse.jgit/src/org/eclipse/jgit/
```

7. So, between the `origin/stable-3.1` and `origin/stable-3.2` branches, we can see which directories have the highest percentage of changes. We can then dig a little deeper using `--stat` or `--numstat` for the directory, and again use `git diff`. We will also use `--relative="org.eclipse.jgit.test/tst/org/eclipse/"`, which will show the relative path of the files from `org.eclipse.jgit.test/tst/org/eclipse/`. This will look better in the console. Feel free to try this without using the following option:

```
$ git diff --pretty  origin/stable-3.1..origin/stable-3.2
--numstat  --relative
="org.eclipse.jgit.test/tst/org/eclipse/jgit/internal/"  org.
eclipse.jgit.test/
tst/org/eclipse/jgit/internal/
4          2          storage/file/FileRepositoryBuilderTest.java
8          1          storage/file/FileSnapshotTest.java
0          741        storage/file/GCTest.java
162        0          storage/file/GcBasicPackingTest.java
119        0          storage/file/GcBranchPrunedTest.java
119        0          storage/file/GcConcurrentTest.java
85         0          storage/file/GcDirCacheSavesObjectsTest.jav
104        0          storage/file/GcKeepFilesTest.java
180        0          storage/file/GcPackRefsTest.java
120        0          storage/file/GcPruneNonReferencedTest.java
146        0          storage/file/GcReflogTest.java
78         0          storage/file/GcTagTest.java
113        0          storage/file/GcTestCase.java
```

8. The first number is the number of lines added, and the second number is the lines removed from the files between the two branches.

There's more...

We have used `git log`, `git diff`, and `git shortlog` to find information about the repository, but there are so many options for those commands on how to find bottlenecks in the source code.

If we want to find the files with the most commits, and these are not necessarily the files with the most line additions or deletions, we can use `git log`:

1. We can use `git log` between the `origin/stable-3.1` and `origin/stable-3.2` branches and list all the files changed in each commit. Then, we just need to sort and accumulate the result with some bash tools:

   ```
   $ git log origin/stable-3.1..origin/stable-3.2 --format=format:
   --name-only
   ```

   ```
   org.eclipse.jgit.ant.test/META-INF/MANIFEST.MF

   org.eclipse.jgit.ant.test/pom.xml
   ```

2. First, we are just executing the command without the use of the bash tools. You can see from the extensive output that you only see file names and nothing else. This is due to the options used. The `--format=format:` option tells Git to not display any commit-message-related information, and `--name-only` tells Git to list the files for each commit. Now all we have to do is count them:

   ```
   $ git log origin/stable-3.1..origin/stable-3.2 --format=format:
   --name-only | sed '/^$/d'  | sort | uniq -c | sort -r | head -10
       12 se.jgit/src/org/eclipse/jgit/api/RebaseCommand.java
       12 est/tst/org/eclipse/jgit/api/RebaseCommandTest.java
        9 org.eclipse.jgit/META-INF/MANIFEST.MF
        7 org.eclipse.jgit.pgm.test/META-INF/MANIFEST.MF
        7 org.eclipse.jgit.packaging/pom.xml
        6 pom.xml
        6 pse.jgit/src/org/eclipse/jgit/api/RebaseResult.java
        6 org.eclipse.jgit.test/META-INF/MANIFEST.MF
        6 org/eclipse/jgit/pgm/internal/CLIText.properties
        6 org.eclipse.jgit.pgm/META-INF/MANIFEST.MF
   ```

3. Now we have a list of the top ten files between the two releases, but before we proceed further, let's just go through what we did. We got the list of files, and we used `sed '/^$/d'` to remove empty lines from the output. After this, we used `sort` to sort the list of files. Then, we used `uniq -c`, which counts the occurrences of each item in the files and adds the number from the output. Finally, we sorted in reverse order using `sort -r` and displayed only the top ten results using `head 10`. To proceed from here, we should list all the commits between the branches that are changing the top file:

   ```
   $ git log origin/stable-3.1..origin/stable-3.2 org.eclipse.jgit/
   src/org/eclipse
   ```

   ```
   /jgit/api/RebaseCommand.java
   ```

```
commit e90438c0e867bd105334b75df3a6d640ef8dab01

Author: Stefan Lay <stefan.lay@sap.com>

Date:    Tue Dec 10 15:54:48 2013 +0100


    Fix aborting rebase with detached head


    Bug: 423670

    Change-Id: Ia6052867f85d4974c4f60ee5a6c820501e8d2427


commit f86a488e32906593903acb31a93a82bed8d87915
```

4. By adding the file to the end of the `git log` command, we will see the commits between the two branches. Now all we have to do is to grep commits that have the bug, so we can tell our manager the number of bugs we fixed in this file.

Grepping the commit messages

Now we know how to list and sort files that we make frequent changes to and vice versa, but we are also interested in finding out the bugs we are fixing, the features we are implementing, and perhaps who is signing the code. All this information is usually available in the commit message. Some companies have a policy that you need to have a referral to a bug, a feature, or some other reference in the commit message. By having this information in the commit message, it is a lot easier to produce a nice release note as well.

Getting ready

As we will mostly be grepping the Git database in these examples, we really don't need to check something out or be at a specific commit for this example. So, if you are still lurking around in the `chapter6` folder, we can continue.

How to do it...

Let's see how many commits in the repository are referring to a bug:

1. First of all, we need to know the pattern for bugs referred to in the commit messages. I did this by looking in the commits, and the pattern for Jgit is to use `Bug: 6` `digits`; so, to find all of these commits, we use the `--grep` option for `git log`, and we can grep for `"[Bb] [Uu] [gG]: [0-9]\+"`:

```
$ git log --all --grep="^[bB] [uU] [gG]: [0-9]"

commit 3db6e05e52b24e16fbe93376d3fd8935e5f4fc9b

Author: Stefan Lay <stefan.lay@sap.com>
```

```
Date:    Wed Jan 15 13:23:49 2014 +0100
```

```
         Fix fast forward rebase with rebase.autostash=true
```

```
         The folder .git/rebase-merge was not removed in this case. The
         repository was then still in rebase state, but neither abort
nor
         continue worked.
```

```
         Bug: 425742
         Change-Id: I43cea6c9e5f3cef9d6b15643722fddecb40632d9
```

2. You should get a lot of commits as output, but you should notice all the commits have a referral to a bug ID. So what was the grep doing? The `^[Bb] [Uu] [gG] :` part matches any combination of lowercase and uppercase bugs. The `^` character means from the beginning of the line. The `:` character is matching `:`. Then, we have `[0-9] \+`, which will match any number between zero and nine, and the `\+` part means one or more occurrences. But enough with regular expressions for grep. We have a lot of output (which is valuable), but for now, we just want to count the commits. We can do this by piping it to `wc -l` (wordcount `-l` is to count the lines):

    ```
    $ git log --all --oneline --grep="^[bB] [uU] [gG] : [0-9]\+" | wc -l
        366
    ```

3. Before piping it to `wc`, remember to use `--oneline` to limit the output to one line for each commit. As you can see, when I was writing this, Jgit has reference to 366 bugs that have all been fixed and released into the repository. If you are used to using regular expressions in another scripting or programming language, you will see that using `--grep` does not support everything. You can enable a more extensive regular expression support using the `--extended-regexp` option for `git log`; however, the pattern still has to be used with `--grep`:

    ```
    $ git log --all --oneline  --extended-regexp --grep="^[bB] [uU]
    [gG] : [0-9]{6}"
    3db6e05 Fix fast forward rebase with rebase.autostash=true
    c6194c7 Update com.jcraft.jsch to 0.1.50 in Kepler target platform
    1def0a1 Fix for core.autocrlf=input resulting in modified file and
    unsmudge
    0ce61ca Canonicalize worktree path in BaseRepositoryBuilder if set
    via config
    e90438c Fix aborting rebase with detached head
    2e0d178 Add recursive variant of Config.getNames() methods
    ```

4. I have used it in the preceding example, and you can see we are getting the same commits. I have used a slightly different expression, and have now added {6} instead of \+ the {6}, which searches for six occurrences of the associated pattern; in our case, it is six digits as it is next to the [0-9] pattern. We can verify by counting the lines or commits again with wc -l:

```
$ git log --all --oneline  --extended-regexp --grep="^[bB] [uU]
[gG]: [0-9]{6}" | wc -l
    366
```

5. We get the same number. To shrink the regular expression even more, we can use --regexp-ignore-case, which will ignore the case for the pattern:

```
$ git log --all --oneline  --regexp-ignore-case --extended-regexp
--grep="^bug: [0-9]{6}"
3db6e05 Fix fast forward rebase with rebase.autostash=true
c6194c7 Update com.jcraft.jsch to 0.1.50 in Kepler target platform
1def0a1 Fix for core.autocrlf=input resulting in modified file and
unsmudge
0ce61ca Canonicalize worktree path in BaseRepositoryBuilder if set
via config
e90438c Fix aborting rebase with detached head
2e0d178 Add recursive variant of Config.getNames() methods
```

6. Now we have the exact same output, and we no longer have [bB] [uU] [Gg] but just bug.

Now you know how to grep the commit messages for information, and you can grep for anything in the commit message and list all the commits where the regular expression matches.

The contents of the releases

While extracting information from Git, one of the natural things to do is to generate release notes. To generate a release note, you need all the valid information from the repository between this release and the previous release.

We can utilize some of the methods we have used earlier to generate the data we want.

How to do it...

We start by listing the commits between two tags, `v2.3.1.201302201838-r` and `v3.0.0.201305080800-m7`, and then we build on that information:

1. By using `git log` with `v3.0.0.201305080800-m7..` `v3.0.0.201305080800-m7`, we will get the commits between the tags:

   `$ git log --oneline v2.3.1.201302201838-r..v3.0.0.201305080800-m7`

   `00108d0 JGit v3.0.0.201305080800-m7`

   `e27993f Add missing @since tags`

   `d7cc6eb Move org.eclipse.jgit.pgm's resource bundle to internal package`

   `75e1bdb Merge "URIish: Allow multiple slashes in paths"`

   `b032623 Remove unused repository field from RevWalk`

   `a626f9f Merge "Require a DiffConfig when creating a FollowFilter"`

2. As we have a lot of commits between these two tags, let's count them using `wc -l`:

   `$ git log --oneline v2.3.1.201302201838-r..v3.0.0.201305080800-m7 | wc -l`

   `   211`

3. There are 211 commits between the tags. Now, we will show the most modified files between the releases:

   `$ git log  v2.3.1.201302201838-r..v3.0.0.201305080800-m7 --format=format: --name-only | sed '/^$/d'  | sort | uniq -c | sort -r | head -10`

   `   11 org.eclipse.jgit/src/org/eclipse/jgit/internal/st`

   `   10 org.eclipse.jgit/src/org/eclipse/jgit/internal/sto`

   `   10 org.eclipse.jgit.pgm/resources/org/eclipse/jgit/p`

   `    9 org.eclipse.jgit.test/META-INF/MANIFEST.MF`

   `    8 pom.xml`

   `    8 org.eclipse.jgit/src/org/eclipse/jgit/storage/pac`

   `    8 org.eclipse.jgit/src/org/eclipse/jgit/internal/sto`

   `    8 org.eclipse.jgit.pgm/src/org/eclipse/jgit/pgm/CLI`

   `    7 org.eclipse.jgit/src/org/eclipse/jgit/storage/dfs/D`

   `    7 org.eclipse.jgit/src/org/eclipse/jgit/storage/dfs/D`

4. This information is valid as we now have an overview of where the majority of the changes are. Then, we can find the commit that refers to bugs so we can list the bug IDs:

```
$ git log --format=format:%h --regexp-ignore-case  --extended-
regexp --grep="bug: [0-9]{6}"  v2.3.1.201302201838-r..
v3.0.0.201305080800-m7 | xargs -n1 git log -1 | grep --ignore-case
-E "commit [0-9a-f]{40}|bug:"

commit e8f720335f86198d4dc99af10ffb6f52e40ba06f

    Bug: 406722

commit f448d62d29acc996a97ffbbdec955d14fde5c254

    Bug: 388095

commit 68b378a4b5e08b80c35e6ad91df25b1034c379a3

    Bug: 388095

commit 8bd1e86bb74da17f18272a7f2e8b6857c800a2cc

    Bug: 405558

commit 37f0e324b5e82f55371ef8adc195d35f7a196c58

    Bug: 406722

commit 1080cc5a0d67012c0ef08d9468fbbc9d90b0c238

    Bug: 403697

commit 7a42b7fb95ecd2c132b2588e5ede0f1251772b30

    Bug: 403282

commit 78fca8a099bd2efc88eb44a0b491dd8aecc222b0

    Bug: 405672

commit 4c638be79fde7c34ca0fcaad13d7c4f1d9c5ddd2

    Bug: 405672
```

5. So, what we have here is a nice list of the bugs being fixed and their corresponding commit hashes.

How it works...

We are using some bash tools to get this list of fixed bugs. I will briefly explain what they are doing in this section:

- The `xargs -n1 git log -1` part will execute `git log -1` on each commit coming from the first `git log` command, `git log --format=format:%h --regexp-ignore-case --extended-regexp --grep="bug: [0-9]{6}"` `v2.3.1.201302201838-r..v3.0.0.201305080800-m7`.

- The `grep --ignore-case -E "commit [0-9a-f]{40}|bug:"` grep will ignore the case in the regular expression and `-E` will enable an extended regular expression. You might see that a lot of these options for the tool grep are the same options we have for `git log`. The regular expression is matching commit and 40 characters with the `[0-9a-f]` range or `bug:`. The | character means or. Remember we are in the out from `git log -1`.

All of this information we have extracted is the basis for a good, solid release note, with information on what has changed from one release to another.

The next natural step would be to look into the bug tracking system and also list the titles for each error being fixed in the commits. However, that is not something we will go through here as it all depends on the system you are using.

7

Enhancing Your Daily Work with Git Hooks, Aliases, and Scripts

In this chapter, we will cover the following topics:

- ▸ Using a branch description in the commit message
- ▸ Creating a dynamic commit message
- ▸ Using external information in the commit message
- ▸ Preventing the push of specific commits
- ▸ Configuring and using Git aliases
- ▸ Configuring and using Git scripts
- ▸ Setting up and using a commit template

Introduction

In order to function in a corporate environment, there should be certain prerequisites to the code that is produced. It should be able to compile and pass specific sets of unit tests. There should also be certain documentation in the commit messages, such as references to a bug fix ID or an instance. Most of these are just scripts that are executed, so why not put these items in to the process? In this chapter, you will see some examples of how to transfer data from one location to the commit message before you see the message. You will also learn how you can verify whether you are pushing your code to the right location. Finally, you will see how you can add scripts to Git.

A hook in Git is a script that will be executed on different events, such as pushing, committing, or rebasing. These scripts, if they exit with a non-zero value, cancel the current Git operation. You can find these hook scripts in the `.git/hooks` folder in any Git clone. If they have the `.sample` file extension, then they are not active.

Using a branch description in the commit message

In *Chapter 3, Branching, Merging, and Options*, we mentioned that you can set a description to your branch, and this information can be retrieved from a script using the `git config --get branch.<branchname> description` command. In this example, we will take this information and use it for the commit message.

We will be using the prepare-commit-msg hook. The prepare-commit-msg hook is executed every time you want to commit, and the hook can be set to anything you wish to check for before you actually see the commit message editor.

Getting ready

We need a clone and a branch to get started on this exercise, so we will clone `jgit` again to the `chapter7.5` folder:

```
$ git clone https://git.eclipse.org/r/jgit/jgit chapter7.5
Cloning into 'chapter7.5'...
remote: Counting objects: 2170, done
remote: Finding sources: 100% (364/364)
remote: Total 45977 (delta 87), reused 45906 (delta 87)
Receiving objects: 100% (45977/45977), 10.60 MiB | 1.74 MiB/s, done.
Resolving deltas: 100% (24651/24651), done.
Checking connectivity... done.
Checking out files: 100% (1577/1577), done.
```

Checkout a local `descriptioInCommit` branch that tracks the `origin/stable-3.2` branch:

```
$ cd chapter7.5
$ git checkout -b descriptioInCommit  --track origin/stable-3.2
Branch descriptioInCommit set up to track remote branch stable-3.2 from origin.
Switched to a new branch 'descriptioInCommit'
```

How to do it...

We will start by setting the description for our local branch. Then, we will create the hook that can extract this information and put it in the commit message.

We have our local `descriptioInCommit` branch for which we need to set a description. We will use the `--edit-description` Git branch to add a description to our local branch. This opens the description editor, and you can type in a message by performing the following steps:

1. When you execute the command, the description editor will open and you can type in a message:

   ```
   $ git branch  --edit-description descriptioInCommit
   ```

2. Now, type in the following message:

   ```
   Remote agent not connection to server


   When the remote agent is trying to connect
   it will fail as network services are not up
   and running when remote agent tries the first time
   ```

3. You should write your branch description just as you write your commit messages. It makes more sense only then to reuse the description in the commit. Now, we will verify whether we have a message with the following description:

   ```
   $ git config --get branch.descriptioInCommit.description
   Remote agent not connection to server


   When the remote agent is trying to connect
   it will fail as network services are not up
   and running when remote agent tries the first time
   ```

4. As expected, we have the desired output. Now, we can continue with creating the hook that will take the description and use it.

   Next, we will check if we have a description for the hook, and if we do, we will use that description as the commit message.

5. First, we will ensure that we can get the information into the commit message at our desired position. There are many ways to do this, and I have settled on the following one: open the prepare-commit-msg hook file and type in the following script:

   ```bash
   #!/bin/bash
   BRANCH=$(git branch | grep '\*'| sed 's/\*//g'|  sed 's/ //g')
   DESCRIPTION=$(git config --get branch.${BRANCH}.description)
   ```

```
echo $BRANCH
#echo "$DESCRIPTION"
if [ -z "$DESCRIPTION" ]; then
  echo "No desc for branch using default template"
else
  # using tr to convert newlines to #
   # else sed will have a problem.
  DESCRIPTION=$(echo "$DESCRIPTION" | tr -s '\n' '#')
   # replacing # with \n
  DESCRIPTION=$(echo "$DESCRIPTION" | sed 's/#/\\n/g')
  # replacing the first \n with \n\n
  DESCRIPTION=$(echo "$DESCRIPTION" | sed 's/\\n/\\n\\n/')

  echo "$DESCRIPTION"
  using
  sed -i "1 i$DESCRIPTION" $1
fi
```

6. Now, we can try to create a commit and see whether the message is being displayed as predicted. Use `git commit --allow-empty` to generate an empty commit but also to trigger the prepare-commit-msg hook:

```
$ git commit --allow-empty
```

7. You should get the message editor with our branch description as the commit message as follows:

```
Remote agent not connection to server

When the remote agent is trying to connect
it will fail as network services are not up
and running when remote agent tries the first time

# Please enter the commit message for your changes. Lines starting
# with '#' will be ignored, and an empty message aborts the commit.
# On branch descriptioInCommit
# Your branch is up-to-date with 'origin/stable-3.2'.
#
```

```
# Untracked files:
#        hen the remote agent is trying to connect
#
```

8. This is as we expected. Save the commit message and close the editor.
   Try using the `git log -1` command to verify whether we have the following
   message in our commit:

```
$ git log -1
commit 92447c6aac2f6d675f8aa4cb88e5abdfa46c90b0
Author: Rasmus Voss <rasmus.voss@live.dk>
Date:   Sat Mar 15 00:19:35 2014 +0100

    Remote agent not connection to server

    When the remote agent is trying to connect
    it will fail as network services are not up
    and running when remote agent tries the first time
```

9. You should get something similar to a commit message that is the same as
   our branch description. However, what about an empty branch description?
   How will our hook handle that? We can try again with a new branch named
   `noDescriptionBranch`, use `git checkout` to create it, and check it,
   as shown in the following command:

```
$ git checkout -b noDescriptionBranch
Switched to a new branch 'noDescriptionBranch'
```

10. Now, we will make yet another empty commit to see whether the commit
    message will be as follows:

```
$ git commit --allow-empty
```

11. You should get the commit message editor with the default commit message text
    as follows:

```
# Please enter the commit message for your changes. Lines starting
# with '#' will be ignored, and an empty message aborts the
commit.
# On branch noDescriptionBranch
# Untracked files:
#        hen the remote agent is trying to connect
#
```

This is all as we expected. This script can be combined with the next exercise that will take
content from a defect system as well.

Creating a dynamic commit message template

Developers can be encouraged to do the right thing, or developers can be forced to do the right thing; however, in the end, developers need to spend time coding. So, if a good commit message is required, we can use the prepare-commit-msg hook to assist the developer.

In this example, we will create a commit message for developers that contains information about the state of the work area. It will also insert some information from a web page; this could just as well be defect information from Bugzilla for instance.

Getting ready

To start with this exercise, we will not be cloning a repository, but we will be creating one. For doing this, we will be using `git init`, as shown in the following code. You can use `git init <directory>` to create a new repository somewhere, or you can also go to a directory and execute `git init`, and Git will create a repository for you.

```
$ git init chapter7
Initialized empty Git repository in c:/Users/Rasmus/repos/chapter7/.git/
$ cd chapter7
```

How to do it...

We have our `chapter7` directory where we just initialized our repository. In this directory, the hooks are already available. Just look into the `.git/hooks` directory. We will be using the prepare-commit-msg hook. Perform the following steps:

1. Start by looking into the folder with the following hooks:

```
$ ls .git/hooks/
applypatch-msg.sample      pre-applypatch.sample
pre-rebase.sample          commit-msg.sample
pre-commit.sample          prepare-commit-msg.sample
post-update.sample         pre-push.sample
update.sample
```

2. As you can see, there are plenty of hooks in each of the hook files. There is an example script and a small explanation to what the hook does and when it is executed. To enable `prepare-commit-msg`, rename the file as shown in the following code:

    ```
    $ cd .git/hooks/
    $ mv prepare-commit-msg.sample prepare-commit-msg
    $ cd ../..
    ```

3. Open the `prepare-commit-msg` file in you preferred editor; I prefer gVim.

4. You can read the information in the file, but for our examples, we will clear the file so that we can include the script.

5. Now include the following command in the file:

    ```
    #!/bin/bash
    echo "I refuse to commit"
    exit 1
    ```

6. Save the file.

7. Finally, try to commit something or nothing. Usually, you cannot make a commit that is empty, but with the `--allow-empty` option, you can create an empty commit as follows:

    ```
    $ git commit --allow-empty
    I refuse to commit
    ```

8. As you can see, we get the message we put in the `prepare-commit-msg` script file. You can check whether we don't have a commit by using `git log -1` as follows:

    ```
    $ git log -1
    fatal: bad default revision 'HEAD'
    ```

    There is no commit, and we get an error message that we have not seen before. The message has to be there because there is no commit so far in this repository. Before we make further changes to the script, we should know that the prepare commit message hook takes some arguments depending on the situation. The first argument is always `.git/COMMIT_EDITMSG`, and the second argument can be merge, commit, squash, or template, depending on the situation. We can use these in the script.

9. Change the script so that we can reject amending commits as follows:

```
#!/bin/bash
if [ "$2" == "commit" ]; then
  echo "Not allowed to amend"
  exit 1
fi
```

10. Now that we have changed the script, let's create a commit and try to amend it as follows:

```
$ echo "alot of fish" > fishtank.txt
$ git add fishtank.txt
$ git commit -m "All my fishes are belong to us"
[master (root-commit) f605886] All my fishes are belong to us
 1 file changed, 1 insertion(+)
 create mode 100644 fishtank.txt
```

11. Now that we have a commit, let's try to amend it using `git commit --amend`:

```
$ git commit --amend
Not allowed to amend
```

12. As we expected, we were not allowed to amend the commit. If we wish to extract some information, for instance, from a bug handling system, we will have to put this information in to the file before opening the editor. So, again, we will change the script as follows:

```
#!/bin/bash
if [ "$2" == "commit" ]; then
  echo "Not allowed to amend"
  exit 1
fi
MESSAGE=$(curl http://whatthecommit.com | grep "<p>" | sed
's/<p>//')
sed -i -r "s/# Please/$MESSAGE\n&/" $1:
```

13. This script downloads a commit message from `http://www.whatthecommit.com/` and inserts it into the commit message; so, every time you commit, you will get a new message from the web page. Let's give it a try by using the following command:

```
$ echo "gravel, plants, and food" >>fishtank.txt
$ git add fishtank.txt
$ git commit
```

14. When the commit message editor opens, you should see a message from `whatthecommit.com`. Close the editor, and using `git log -1`, verify whether we have the commit as follows:

```
git log -1
commit c087f75665bf516af2fe30ef7d8ed1b775bcb97d
Author: Rasmus Voss <rasmus.voss@live.dk>
Date:   Wed Mar 5 21:12:13 2014 +0100


    640K ought to be enough for anybody
```

15. As expected, we have succeeded with the commit. Obviously, this is not the best message to have for the committer. However, what I have done for my current employer is listed the bugs assigned to the developer as follows in the commit message:

```
# You have the following artifacts assigned
# Remove the # to add the artifact ID to the commit message

#[artf23456] Error 02 when using update handler on wlan
#[artf43567] Enable Unicode characters for usernames
#[artf23451] Use stars instead of & when keying pword
```

16. This way, the developer can easily select the correct bug ID, or the artefact ID from team Forge in this case, using the correct format for the other systems that will look into the commit messages.

There's more...

You can extend the functionalities of the prepare commit message hook very easily, but you should bear in mind that the waiting time for fetching some information should be worth the benefits. One thing that is usually easy to check is a dirty work area.

Here, we need to use the `git status` command in the prepare commit message hook, and we need to predict whether we will have modified files after the commit:

1. To check this, we need to have something staged for committing and some unstaged changes as follows:

```
$ git status
On branch master
nothing to commit, working directory clean
```

2. Now, modify the `fishtank.txt` file:

   ```
   $ echo "saltwater" >>fishtank.txt
   ```

3. Use `git status --porcelain` to check the work area:

   ```
   $ git status --porcelain
    M fishtank.txt
   ```

4. Add the file to the staging area using `git add`:

   ```
   $ git add fishtank.txt
   ```

5. Now try `git status -porcelain`:

   ```
   $ git status --porcelain
   M  fishtank.txt
   ```

6. What you should note is the space before M the first time we use the `--porcelain` option for `git status`. The `porcelain` option provides a machine-friendly output that shows the state of the files for git status. The first character is the status in the staging area, whereas the second character is the status in the work area. So, MM `fishtank.txt` would mean the file is modified in the work area and in the staging area. So, if you modify `fishtank.txt` again, the following is the result you can expect:

   ```
   $ echo "sharks and oysters" >> fishtank.txt
   $ git status --porcelain
   MM fishtank.txt
   ```

7. As expected, the output from `git status` is MM `fishtank.txt`. We can use this in the hook to tell whether the work area will have uncommitted changes after we commit. Add the following command to the `prepare-commit-msg` file:

   ```
   for file in $(git status --porcelain)
   do
       if [ ${file:1:1} ]; then
          DIRTY=1
       fi
   done
   if [ "${DIRTY}" ]; then
       sed -i -r "s/# Please/You have a dirty workarea are you sure you
   wish to commit \?\n&/" $1
   fi
   ```

8. First, we list all the files that have changed with `git status --porcelain`. Then, for each of these, we check whether there is a second character. If this is true, we will have a dirty work area after the commit. In the end, we just insert the message in the commit message so that it is available for the developer to see. Let's try and commit the change by using the following command:

   ```
   $ git commit
   ```

9. Note that you have a message like the following one. The first line might be different as we still have the message from `http://www.whatthecommit.com/`:

   ```
   somebody keeps erasing my changes.

   You have a dirty workarea are you sure you wish to commit ?

   # Please enter the commit message for your changes. Lines starting
   # with '#' will be ignored, and an empty message aborts the
   commit.
   # On branch master
   # Changes to be committed:
   #         modified:    fishtank.txt
   #
   # Changes not staged for commit:
   #         modified:    fishtank.txt
   #
   ```

10. Saving the file and closing the editor will create the commit. Verify with `git log -1` as follows:

    ```
    $ git log -1
    commit 70cad5f7a2c3f6a8a4781da9c7bb21b87886b462
    Author: Rasmus Voss <rasmus.voss@schneider-electric.com>
    Date:    Thu Mar 6 08:25:21 2014 +0100


            somebody keeps erasing my changes.

            You have a dirty workarea are you sure you wish to commit ?
    ```

11. We have the information we expected. The text about the dirty work area is in the commit message .To clean up nicely before the next exercise, we should reset our work area to HEAD as follows:

    ```
    $ git reset --hard HEAD
    HEAD is now at 70cad5f somebody keeps erasing my changes.
    ```

Now, it is just a matter of finding out what suits you. Is there any information you would like to check before you commit and potentially push the code to a remote? I can think of the following options:

- ▶ Style checks in code
- ▶ Pylint to check your Python scripts
- ▶ Check for files that you are not allowed to add to Git

There are several other items, probably one for every organization or development team in the world. However, this clearly is one way of taking tedious manual work away from the developer so that he or she can focus on coding.

Using external information in the commit message

The commit hook is executed when you close the commit message editor. It can, among other things, be used to manipulate the commit message or review the commit message by machine to check whether it has a specific format.

In this recipe, we will be manipulating and checking the content of a commit message.

Getting ready

To start this exercise, we just need to create a branch and check it out. We need to disable the current prepare-commit-msg hook; we can do this by simply renaming it. Now, we can start working on the commit-msg hook by using the following command:

```
git checkout -b commit-msg-example

Switched to a new branch 'commit-msg-example'

$ mv .git/hooks/prepare-commit-msg .git/hooks/prepare-commit-msg.example
```

How to do it...

What we want to do in the first example is to check whether the defect information is correct. There is no need to release a commit that refers to a defect that does not exist:

1. We will start by testing the commit-msg hook. First, make a copy of the current hook, then we will force the hook to exit with a non-zero value that will abort the creation of the commit:

   ```
   $ cp .git/hooks/commit-msg.sample .git/hooks/commit-msg
   ```

2. Now, open the file in your preferred editor and add the following lines to the file:

```
#!/bin/bash
echo "you are not allowed to commit"
exit 1
```

3. Now, we will try to make a commit and see what happens as follows:

```
$ echo "Frogs, scallops, and coco shell" >> fishtank.txt
$ git add fishtank.txt
$ git commit
```

4. The editor will open and you can write a small commit message. Then, close the editor. You should see the you are not allowed to commit message, and if you check with git log -1, you will see that you don't have a commit with the message you just used, as follows:

```
you are not allowed to commit
$ git log -1
commit 70cad5f7a2c3f6a8a4781da9c7bb21b87886b462
Author: Rasmus Voss <rasmus.voss@schneider-electric.com>
Date:   Thu Mar 6 08:25:21 2014 +0100

    somebody keeps erasing my changes.
    You have a dirty workarea are you sure you wish to commit ?
```

5. As you can see, the commit message hook is executed after you close the message editor, whereas the prepare-commit-msg hook is executed before the message editor. To validate, if we have a proper reference to the hook in our commit message, we will be checking whether a specific error is available for the Jenkins-CI project. Replace the lines in the commit-msg hook so that it looks like the following command:

```
#!/bin/bash
JIRA_ID=$(cat $1 | grep jenkins | sed 's/jenkins //g')
ISSUE_INFO=$(curl https://issues.jenkins-ci.org/browse/JENKINS-
${JIRA_ID} | grep "The issue you are trying to view does not
exist.")
if [ "${ISSUE_INFO}" ]; then
  echo "Jenkins issue ${JIRA_ID} does not exist"
  echo "Please try again"
  exit 1
else
```

```
    TITLE=$(curl https://issues.jenkins-ci.org/browse/JENKINS-$JIRA_
ID} | grep -E "<title>.*<\/title>")
    echo "Jenkins issue ${JIRA_ID}"
    echo "${TITLE}"
    exit 0
fi
```

6. We are using Curl to retrieve the web page, and we are using grep to find a line with `The issue you are trying to view does not exist`; if we find this text, we know that the ID does not exist. Now we should create a commit and see what happens if we put in the wrong ID, `jenkins 384895`, or an ID that exists as `jenkins 3157`. To check this, we will create a commit as follows:

```
$ echo "more water" >> fishtank.txt
$ git add fishtank.txt
$ git commit
```

7. In the commit message, write something such as `Feature cascading...` as a commit message subject. Then, in the body of the commit message, insert `jenkins 384895`. This is the important part as the hook will use that number to look it up on the Jenkins issue tracker:

```
Feature: Cascading...


jenkins 384895
```

8. You should end up with the following output:

```
Jenkins issue 384895 does not exist
Please try again
```

9. This is what we expected. Now, verify with `git status` whether the change has not been committed:

```
$ git status
On branch commit-msg-example
Changes to be committed:
    (use "git reset HEAD <file>..." to unstage)

        modified:   fishtank.txt
```

10. Now we will try to commit again; this time, we will be using the correct JIRA ID:

```
$ git commit
```

11. Key in a commit message like the previous one; this time make sure the Jenkins issue ID is one that exists. You can use 3157:

```
Feature: Cascading...


jenkins 3157
```

12. Saving the commit message should result in an output as follows. We can clean it some more by removing the title HTML tags:

```
<title>[#JENKINS-3157] Feature request: cascading project settings
- Jenkins JIRA</title>

[commit-msg-example 3d39ca3] Feature: Cascading...

1 file changed, 2 insertions(+)
```

13. As you can see, we can get information to output. We could also add this information to the commit message itself. Then, we can change and insert this as the `else` clause in the script:

```
TITLE=$(curl https://issues.jenkins-ci.org/browse/JENKINS-${JIRA_
ID} | grep -E "<title>.*<\/title>")

TITLE=$(echo ${TITLE} | sed 's/^<title>//' |sed 's/<\/title>$//')

echo "${TITLE}" >> $1

echo "Jenkins issue ${JIRA_ID}"

echo "${TITLE}"

   exit 0
```

14. To test, we will create a commit again, and in the message, we need to specify the JIRA ID that exists:

```
$ echo "Shrimps and mosquitos" >> fishtank.txt

$ git add fishtank.txt

$ git commit
```

After saving the commit message editor you will get an output similar like this.

```
Jenkins issue 3157

[#JENKINS-3157] Feat

[commit-msg-example 6fa2cb4] More cascading

1 file changed, 1 insertion(+)
```

15. To verify whether we got the information in the message, we will use `git log -1` again:

```
$ git log -1
commit 6fa2cb47989e12b05cd2689aa92244cb244426fc
Author: Rasmus Voss <rasmus.voss@schneider-electric.com>
Date:   Thu Mar 6 09:46:18 2014 +0100

    More cascading

    jenkins 3157
    [#JENKINS-3157] Feature request: cascading project settings -
Jenkins JIRA
```

As expected, we have the information at the end of the commit. In these examples, we are just discarding the commit message if the JIRA ID does not exist; this is a little harsh on the developer. So, you can combine this with the prepare-commit-msg hook. So, if commit-msg halts the commit process, then save the message temporarily so that the prepare-commit-msg hook can use that message when the developer tries again.

Preventing the push of specific commits

The pre-push hooks are triggered whenever you use the push command and the script execution happens before the push; so, we can prevent a push if we find a reason to reject the push. One reason could be you have a commit that has the `nopush` text in the commit message.

Getting ready

To use the Git pre-push, we need to have a remote repository for which we will be cloning `jgit` again as follows:

```
$ git clone https://git.eclipse.org/r/jgit/jgit chapter7.1
Cloning into 'chapter7.1'...
remote: Counting objects: 2429, done
remote: Finding sources: 100% (534/534)
remote: Total 45639 (delta 145), reused 45578 (delta 145)
Receiving objects: 100% (45639/45639), 10.44 MiB | 2.07 MiB/s, done.
Resolving deltas: 100% (24528/24528), done.
Checking connectivity... done.
Checking out files: 100% (1576/1576), done.
```

How to do it...

We want to be able to push to a remote, but unfortunately, Git will try to authenticate through HTTPS for the `jgit` repository before the hooks are executed. Because of this, we will create a local clone from the `chapter7.1` directory. This will make our remote a local folder.

```
$ git clone --branch master ./chapter7.1/ chapter7.2

Cloning into ' chapter7.2'...

done.

Checking out files: 100% (1576/1576), done.

$ cd chapter7.2
```

We are cloning the `chapter7.1` directory in a folder named `chapter7.2`, and checking the master branch when the clone has finished. Now, we can go back to the `chapter7.1` directory and continue with the exercise.

What we now want to do is to create a commit with a commit message that has `nopush` as part of it. By adding this word to the commit message, the code in the hook will automatically stop the push. We will be doing this on top of a branch. So, to start with, you should check out a `prepushHook` branch that tracks the `origin/master` branch and then creates a commit. We will try to push it for the remote when we have the pre-push commit in place, as follows:

1. Start by creating a new branch named `prepushHook` that tracks `origin/master`:

    ```
    $ git checkout -b prepushHook  --track origin/master

    Branch prepushHook set up to track remote branch master from
    origin.

    Switched to a new branch 'prepushHook'
    ```

2. Now, we reset back in time; it is not so important how far back we do this. So, I have just selected a random commit as follows:

    ```
    $ git reset --hard 2e0d178

    HEAD is now at 2e0d178 Add recursive variant of Config.getNames()
    methods
    ```

3. Now we can create a commit. We will do a simple inline replace with `sed` and then add `pom.xml` and commit it:

    ```
    $ sed -i -r 's/2.9.1/3.0.0/g' pom.xml

    $ git add pom.xml

    $ git commit -m "Please nopush"

    [prepushHook 69d571e] Please nopush

    1 file changed, 1 insertion(+), 1 deletion(-)
    ```

4. To verify whether we have the commit with the text, run `git log -1`:

```
$ git log -1
commit 1269d14fe0c32971ea33c95126a69ba6c0d52bbf
Author: Rasmus Voss <rasmus.voss@live.dk>
Date:    Thu Mar 6 23:07:54 2014 +0100

        Please nopush
```

5. We have what we want in the commit message. Now, we just need to prep the hook. We will start by copying the sample hook to the real name so that it will be executed on push:

```
cp .git/hooks/pre-push.sample .git/hooks/pre-push
```

6. Edit the hook so that it has the code as shown in the following snippet:

```
#!/bin/bash
echo "You are not allowed to push"
exit 1
```

7. Now, we are ready to push. We will be pushing our current branch HEAD to the master branch in the remote:

```
$ git push origin HEAD:refs/heads/master
You are not allowed to push
error: failed to push some refs to '../chapter7.1/'
```

8. As expected, the hook is being executed, and the push is being denied by the hook. Now we can implement the check we want. We want to exit if we have the word nopush in any commit message. We can use `git log --grep` to search for commits with the keyword nopush in the commit message, as shown in the following command:

```
$ git log --grep "nopush"
commit 51201284a618c2def690c9358a07c1c27bba22d5
Author: Rasmus Voss <rasmus.voss@live.dk>
Date:    Thu Mar 6 23:07:54 2014 +0100

        Please nopush
```

9. We have our newly created commit with the keyword `nopush`. Now, we will make a simple check for this in the hook and edit the pre-push hook so that it has the following text:

```
#!/bin/bash
COMMITS=$(git log --grep "nopush")
if [ "$COMMITS" ]; then
    echo "You have commit(s) with nopush message"
    echo "aborting push"
    exit 1
fi
```

10. Now we can try to push again to see what the result will be. We will try to push our HEAD to the master branch on the remote `origin`:

```
$ git push origin HEAD:refs/heads/master
You have commit(s) with nopush message
aborting push
error: failed to push some refs to 'c:/Users/Rasmus/repos/./
chapter7.1/'
```

As expected, we are not allowed to push as we have the `nopush` message in the commit.

There's more...

Having a hook that can prevent you from pushing commits that you don't want to push is very handy. You can specify any keywords you want. Words such as `reword`, `temp`, `nopush`, `temporary`, or `hack` can all be things you want to stop, but sometimes you want to get them through anyway.

What you can do is have a small checker that will check for specific words and then list the commits and ask if you want to push anyway.

If you change the script to the following snippet, the hook will try to find commits with the keyword `nopush` and list them. If you wish to push them anyway, then you can find an answer to the question and Git will push anyway.

```
#!/bin/bash
COMMITS=$(git log --grep "nopush" --format=format:%H)
if [ $COMMITS ]; then
        exitmaybe=1
```

```
fi
if [ $exitmaybe -eq 1 ]; then
while true
do
  'clear'
  for commit in "$COMMITS"
  do
    echo "$commit has no push in the message"
  done
  echo "Are you sure you want to push the commit(s) "
  read REPLY <&1
  case $REPLY in
    [Yy]* ) break;;
    [Nn]* ) exit 1;;
    * ) echo "Please answer yes or no.";;
  esac
done
fi
```

Try it with the `git push` command again as shown in the following snippet:

```
$ git push origin HEAD:refs/heads/master
Commit 70fea355bac0c65fd51f4874d75e65b4a29ad763 has nopush in message
Are you sure you want to push the commit(s)
```

Type n and press enter. Then, expect the push to be aborted with the following message:

```
error: failed to push some refs to 'c:/Users/Rasmus/repos/./chapter7.1/'
```

As predicted, it will not push. However, on the other hand, if you press y, Git will push to the remote. Try it now using the following command:

```
$ git push origin HEAD:refs/heads/master
054c5f78fdc82141e9d73e6b6955c38ff79c8b2e has no push in the message
Are you sure you want to push the commit(s)
y
To c:/Users/Rasmus/repos/./chapter7.1/
 ! [rejected]          HEAD -> master (non-fast-forward)
```

```
error: failed to push some refs to 'c:/Users/Rasmus/repos/./chapter7.1/'
hint: Updates were rejected because a pushed branch tip is behind its
remote
hint: counterpart. Check out this branch and integrate the remote changes
hint: (e.g. 'git pull ...') before pushing again.
hint: See the 'Note about fast-forwards' in 'git push --help' for
details.
```

As predicted, the push will be tried, but as you can see from the output, we are rejected by the remote. This is because we diverged, and the push was not working at the tip of the master branch.

So, with this hook, you can make your life a little easier by having the hook prevent you from accidentally pushing something you are not interested in getting pushed. This example also considers commits that have been released; so, if you select a different keyword, then other commits, not only the locally created ones, will be taken into consideration by the script.

Configuring and using Git aliases

Git aliases, like Unix aliases, are short commands that can be configured on a global level or for each repository. It is a simple way of renaming some Git commands to short abbreviations, for example, `git checkout` could be `git co` and so on.

How to do it...

It is very simple and straightforward to create an alias. You simply need to configure it with `git config`.

What we will do is check a branch and then create its aliases one by one and execute them to view their output by performing the following steps:

1. So, we will start by checking a branch named `gitAlias` that tracks the `origin/stable-3.2` branch:

   ```
   $ git checkout -b gitAlias --track origin/stable-3.2
   Branch gitAlias set up to track remote branch stable-3.2 from
   origin.
   Switched to a new branch 'gitAlias'
   ```

2. After this, we can start creating some aliases. We will start with the following one that will simply just amend your commit:

   ```
   $ git config alias.amm 'commit --amend'
   ```

3. Executing this alias will open the commit message editor with the following message from the HEAD commit:

```
$ git amm
Prepare post 3.2.0 builds


Change-Id: Ie2bfdee0c492e3d61d92acb04c5bef641f5f132f
Signed-off-by: Matthias Sohn matthias.sohn@sap.com
```

4. As you can see, it can be very simple to speed up the process of your daily workflow with Git aliases. The following command will just work on the last 10 commits using --oneline as an option for git log:

```
$ git config alias.lline 'log --oneline -10'
```

5. Using the alias will give you the following output:

```
$ git lline
314a19a Prepare post 3.2.0 builds
699900c JGit v3.2.0.201312181205-r
0ff691c Revert "Fix for core.autocrlf=input resulting in mo
1def0a1 Fix for core.autocrlf=input resulting in modified f
0ce61ca Canonicalize worktree path in BaseRepositoryBuilder
be7942f Add missing @since tags for new public methods ig
ea04d23 Don't use API exception in RebaseTodoLine
3a063a0 Merge "Fix aborting rebase with detached head" into
e90438c Fix aborting rebase with detached head
2e0d178 Add recursive variant of Config.getNames() methods
```

6. You can also perform a simple checkout. Thus, instead of using the Git checkout, you can just as well use git co <branch>. Configure it as follows:

```
$ git config alias.co checkout
```

7. You will see that the aliases take arguments just as the regular Git command does. Let's try the alias using the following command:

```
$ git co master
Switched to branch 'master'
Your branch is up-to-date with 'origin/master'.
$ git co gitAlias
Switched to branch 'gitAlias'
Your branch and 'origin/stable-3.2' have diverged,
and have 1 and 1 different commit each, respectively.
  (use "git pull" to merge the remote branch into yours)
```

8. The command works as expected. You may wonder why we diverged after checking out the `gitAlias` branch again. Then, we diverged when we amended the HEAD commit. This is because the next alias is creating a commit with everything that has not been committed in the work area, except for the untracked files:

    ```
    $ git config alias.ca 'commit -a -m "Quick commit"'
    ```

9. Before we can test the alias, we should create a file and modify it to show what it actually does. So, create a file as shown in the following command:

    ```
    $ echo "Sharks" > aquarium
    $ echo "New HEADERTEXT" >pom.xml
    ```

10. To verify what you want, run `git status`:

    ```
    Changes not staged for commit:
        (use "git add <file>..." to update what will be committed)
        (use "git checkout -- <file>..." to discard changes in working
    directory)

            modified:    pom.xml


    Untracked files:
        (use "git add <file>..." to include in what will be committed)

            aquarium


    no changes added to commit (use "git add" and/or "git commit -a")
    ```

11. Now we can test the alias using the following command:

    ```
    $ git ca
    [gitAlias ef9739d] Quick commit
     1 file changed, 1 insertion(+), 606 deletions(-)
     rewrite pom.xml (100%)
    ```

12. To verify whether the `aquarium` file was not a part of the commit, use `git status`:

    ```
    Untracked files:
        (use "git add <file>..." to include in what will be committed)


            aquarium


    nothing added to commit but untracked files present (use "git add"
    to track)
    ```

13. You can also use `git log -1 --name-status` to see the commit we just created:

```
$ git log -1
commit ef9739d0bffe354c75b82f3b785780f5e3832776
Author: Rasmus Voss <rasmus.voss@live.dk>
Date:   Thu Mar 13 00:01:49 2014 +0100

        Quick commit
```

14. The output is just as we expected. The next alias is a little different as it will count the number of commits in the repository, and this can be done with the `wc` (wordcount) tool. However, since this is not a built-in Git tool, we have to use the exclamation mark and also specify Git:

```
$ git config alias.count '!git log --all --oneline | wc -l'
```

15. Let's try it with the following command:

```
$ git count
   3008
```

16. So, currently, I have 3008 commits in the repository. This also means you can execute external tools as if they were Git tools just by creating a Git alias; for instance, if you are using Windows, you can create an alias as follows:

```
$ git config alias.wa '!explorer .'
```

17. This alias will open up an explorer window at the path you are currently at. The next one shows what changed in the HEAD commit. It executes this with the `--name-status` option for `git log`:

```
$ git config alias.gl1 'log -1 --name-status'
```

18. Now try it using the following command:

```
$ git gl1
commit ef9739d0bffe354c75b82f3b785780f5e3832776
Author: Rasmus Voss <rasmus.voss@live.dk>
Date:   Thu Mar 13 00:01:49 2014 +0100

        Quick commit


M       pom.xml
```

19. As you can see, it simply lists the commit and the files including what happened to the files in the commit. As the aliases take arguments, we can actually reuse this functionality to list the information for another branch. Let's try it with the following command:

```
$ git gll origin/stable-2.1
commit 54c4eb69acf700fdf80304e9d0827d3ea13cbc6d
Author: Matthias Sohn <matthias.sohn@sap.com>
Date:    Wed Sep 19 09:00:33 2012 +0200

        Prepare for 2.1 maintenance changes

        Change-Id: I436f36a7c6dc86916eb4cde038b27f9fb183465a
        Signed-off-by: Matthias Sohn <matthias.sohn@sap.com>

M       org.eclipse.jgit.ant.test/META-INF/MANIFEST.MF
M       org.eclipse.jgit.ant.test/pom.xml
M       org.eclipse.jgit.ant/META-INF/MANIFEST.MF
M       org.eclipse.jgit.ant/pom.xml
M       org.eclipse.jgit.console/META-INF/MANIFEST.MF
M       org.eclipse.jgit.console/pom.xml
M       org.eclipse.jgit.http.server/META-INF/MANIFEST.MF
M       org.eclipse.jgit.http.server/pom.xml
```

As you can see, we get the expected output. So, for instance, if you have been using a specific set of options for `git diff`, then you can just as well make it an alias to use it with ease.

How it works...

It is as simple as inserting text in the `config` file. So, you can try and open the `.git/config` configuration file, or you can list the configuration with `git config -list`:

```
$ git config --list  | grep alias
alias.amm=commit --amend
alias.lline=log --oneline -10
alias.co=checkout
alias.ca=commit -a -m "Quick commit"
alias.count=!git log --all --oneline | wc -l
```

This alias feature is very strong, and the idea behind it is that you should use it to shorten those long one-liners that you use otherwise. You can also use this feature to cut down those one-liners to small aliases so that you can use the command frequently and with more precision. If you have it as an alias, you will run it the same way every time, where keying a long command is bound to fail once in a while.

Configuring and using Git scripts

Yes, we have aliases, and aliases do what they do best—take small one-liners and convert them into small useful Git commands. However, when it comes to larger scripts that are also a part of your process, and you would like to incorporate them into Git, you can simply name the script `git-scriptname`, and then use it as `git scriptname`.

How to do it...

There are a few things to remember. The script has to be in your path so that Git can use the script. Besides this, only imagination sets the boundary:

1. Open your favorite editor and insert the following lines in the file:

```
#!/bin/bash
NUMBEROFCOMMITS=$(git log --all --oneline | wc -l)
while :
  WHICHCOMMIT=$(( ( RANDOM % ${NUMBEROFCOMMITS} ) + 1 ))
  COMMITSUBJECT=$(git log --oneline --all -${WHICHCOMMIT} | tail
-n1)
  COMMITSUBJECT_=$(echo $COMMITSUBJECT | cut -b0-60)
do
  if [ $RANDOM -lt 14000 ]; then
    printf "\e[1m%-60s \e[32m%-10s\e[m\n" "${COMMITSUBJECT_}" '
PASSED'
  elif [ $RANDOM -gt 15000 ]; then
    printf "\e[1m%-60s \e[31m%-10s\e[m\n" "${COMMITSUBJECT_}" '
FAILED'
  fi
Done
```

2. Save the file with the name `git-likeaboss`. This is a very simple script that will list random commit subjects with either passed or failed as the result. It will not stop until you press *Ctrl + c*.

```
$ git likeaboss
5ec4977 Create a MergeResult for deleted/modified    PASSED
fcc3349 Add reflog message to TagCommand             PASSED
```

```
591998c Do not allow non-ff-rebase if there are ed    PASSED
0d7dd66 Make sure not to overwrite untracked notfil    PASSED
5218f7b Propagate IOException where possible where    FAILED
f5fe2dc Teach PackWriter how to reuse an existing s    FAILED
```

3. Note you can also tab complete these commands, and Git will take them into consideration when you slightly misspell commands as follows:

```
$ git likeboss
git: 'likeboss' is not a git command. See 'git --help'.


Did you mean this?
        likeaboss
```

I know this script in itself is not so useful in a day-to-day environment, but I hope you get the point I am trying to make. All scripts revolve around the software delivery chain and you can just as well name them Git as they are part of Git. This makes it much easier to remember which scripts you have are available for your job.

 Both Git aliases and Git scripts will show up as Git commands while using tab completion. Type in `git <tab> <tab>` to see the list of possible Git commands.

Setting up and using a commit template

In this chapter, we have been using dynamic templates, but Git also has the option of a static commit template, which essentially is just a text file configured as a template. Using the template is very easy and straightforward.

Getting ready

First of all, we need a template. This has to be a text file whose location you should know. Create a file with the following content:

```
#subject no more than 74 characters please


#BugFix id in the following formats
#artf [123456]
#PCP [AN12354365478]
#Bug: 123456
```

```
#Descriptive text about what you have done
#Also why you have chosen to do in that way as
#this will make it easier for reviewers and other
#developers.
```

This is my take on a simple commit message template. You might find that there are other templates out there that prefer to have the bug in the title or at the bottom of the commit message. The reason for having this at the top is that people often tend not to read the important parts of the text! The important part here is the formatting of the references to systems outside Git. If we get these references correct, we can automatically update the defect system as well. Save the files as `~/committemplate`.

How to do it...

We will configure our newly created template, and then we will make a commit that will utilize the template.

To configure the template, we need to use `git config commit.template <pathtofile>` to set l,t, and as soon as it is set, we can try to create a commit and see how it works:

1. Start by configuring the template as follows:

   ```
   $ git config commit.template  ~/committemplate
   ```

2. Now list the `config` file to see that it has been set:

   ```
   $ git config --list | grep template
   commit.template=c:/Users/Rasmus/committemplate
   ```

3. As we predicted, the configuration was a success. The template, just as any other configuration, can be set at a global level using `git config --global`, or it can be set at a local repository level by leaving out the `--global` option. We configured our commit template for this repository only. Let's try and make a commit:

   ```
   $ git commit --allow-empty
   ```

4. Now the commit message editor should open, and you should see our template in the commit message editor:

   ```
   #subject no more than 74 characters please


   #BugFix id in the following formats
   #artf [123456]
   #PCP [AN12354365478]
   #Bug: 123456
   ```

```
#Descriptive text about what you have done
#Also why you have chosen to do in that way as
#this will make it easier for reviewers and other
#developers.
```

It is really as simple as that.

So, in this chapter, we have seen how we can prevent pushing when we have special words in our commit messages. We have also seen how you can dynamically create a commit message with valid information for you or another developer when you are committing. We have also seen how we can build functionality into your own Git by adding small scripts or aliases that all are executed using the Git way. I hope this information will help you to work smarter instead of harder.

8

Recovering from Mistakes

In this chapter, we will cover the following topics:

- ▶ Undo – remove a commit completely
- ▶ Undo – remove a commit and retain the changes to files
- ▶ Undo – remove a commit and retain the changes in the staging area
- ▶ Undo – working with a dirty area
- ▶ Redo – recreate the latest commit with new changes
- ▶ Revert – undo the changes introduced by a commit
- ▶ Reverting a merge
- ▶ Viewing past Git actions with git reflog
- ▶ Finding lost changes with git fsck

Introduction

It is possible to correct mistakes made in Git the with `git push` context (without exposing them if the mistake is found before sharing or publishing the change). If the mistake is already pushed, it is still possible to undo the changes made to the commit that introduced the mistake.

We'll also look at the `reflog` command and how we can use that and `git fsck` to recover lost information.

There is no `git undo` command in core Git. One of the reasons being ambiguity on what needs to be undone, for example, the last commit, the added file, and so on. If you want to undo the last commit, how should that be done? Should the changes introduced to the files by the commit be deleted? For instance, just roll back to the last known good commit, or should they be kept so that could be changed for a better commit or should the commit message simply be reworded?. In this chapter, we'll explore the possibilities to undo a commit in several ways depending on what we want to achieve. We'll explore four ways to undo a commit:

> ▸ Undo everything; just remove the last commit like it never happened

> ▸ Undo the commit and unstage the files; this takes us back to where we were before we started to add the files

> ▸ Undo the commit, but keep the files in the index or staging area so we can just perform some minor modifications and then complete the commit

> ▸ Undo the commit with the dirty work area

The undo and redo commands in this chapter are performed on commits that are already published in the example repository. You should usually *not* perform the undo and redo commands on commits that are already published in a public repository, as you will be rewriting history. However, in the following recipes, we'll use an example repository and execute the operations on published commits so that everyone can have the same experience.

Undo – remove a commit completely

In this example, we'll learn how we can undo a commit as if it had never happened. We'll learn how we can use the `reset` command to effectively discard the commit and thereby reset our branch to the desired state.

Getting ready

In this example, we'll use the example of the `hello world` repository, clone the repository, and change your working directory to the cloned one:

```
$ git clone https://github.com/dvaske/hello_world_cookbook.git
$ cd hello_world_cookbook
```

How to do it...

First, we'll try to undo the latest commit in the repository as though it never happened:

1. We'll make sure our working directory is clean, no files are in the modified state, and nothing is added to the index:

   ```
   $ git status
   On branch master
   Your branch is up-to-date with 'origin/master'.

   nothing to commit, working directory clean
   ```

2. Also, check what is in our working tree:

   ```
   $ ls
   HelloWorld.java Makefile      hello_world.c
   ```

3. If all works well, we'll check the log to see the history of the repository. We'll use the `--oneline` switch to limit the output:

   ```
   $ git log --oneline
   3061dc6 Adds Java version of 'hello world'
   9c7532f Fixes compiler warnings
   5b5d692 Initial commit, K&R hello world
   ```

4. The most recent commit is the `3061dc6 Adds Java version of 'hello world'` commit. We will now undo the commit as though it never happened and the history won't show it:

   ```
   $ git reset --hard HEAD^
   HEAD is now at 9c7532f Fixes compiler warnings
   ```

5. Check the log, status, and filesystem so that you can see what actually happened:

   ```
   $ git log --oneline
   9c7532f Fixes compiler warnings
   5b5d692 Initial commit, K&R hello world
   $ git status
   On branch master
   ```

```
Your branch is behind 'origin/master' by 1 commit, and can be
fast-forwarded.

  (use "git pull" to update your local branch)


nothing to commit, working directory clean
$ ls
hello_world.c
```

6. The commit is now gone along with all the changes it introduced (`Makefile` and `HelloWorld.java`).

In the last output of `git status`, you can see that our `master` branch is one behind `origin/master`. This is similar to what we mentioned at the beginning of the chapter because we are removing and undoing commits that are already published. Also, as mentioned, you should *only* perform the undo and redo (`git reset`) operations on commits that are not shared yet. Here, we only show it on the published commits to make the example easy to reproduce.

How it works...

Effectively, we are just changing the pointer of the `master` branch to point to the previous commit HEAD, which means the first parent of HEAD. Now the branch will point to `9c7532f`, instead of the commit we removed, `35b29ae`. This is shown in the following figure:

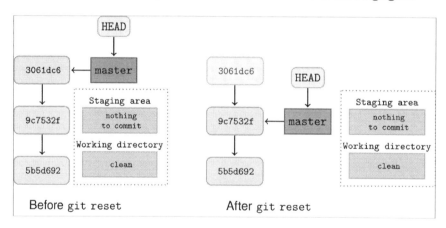

The figure also shows that the original `3061dc6` commit is still present in the repository, but new commits on the `master` branch will start from `9c7532f`; the `3061dc6` commit is called a **dangling** commit.

 You should only do this undo operation to commits you haven't shared (pushed) yet, as when you create new commits after undo or reset, those commits form a new history that will diverge from the original history of the repository.

When the `reset` command is executed, Git looks at the commit pointed to by HEAD and finds the parent commit from this. The current branch, `master`, and the HEAD pointer are then reset to the parent commit and so are the staging area and working tree.

Undo – remove a commit and retain the changes to files

Instead of performing the hard reset and thereby losing all the changes the commit introduced, the reset can be performed so that the changes are retained in the working directory.

Getting ready

We'll again use the example of the `hello world` repository. Make a fresh clone of the repository, or reset the `master` branch if you have already cloned one.

You can make a fresh clone as follows:

```
$ git clone https://github.com/dvaske/hello_world_cookbook.git
$ cd hello_world_cookbook
```

You can reset the existing clone as follows:

```
$ cd hello_world_cookbook
$ git checkout master
$ git reset --hard origin master
HEAD is now at 3061dc6 Adds Java version of 'hello world'
```

How to do it...

1. First, we'll check whether we have made no changes to files in the working tree (just for the clarity of the example) and the history of the repository:

```
$ git status
On branch master
Your branch is up-to-date with 'origin/master'.

nothing to commit, working directory clean

$ git log --oneline
3061dc6 Adds Java version of 'hello world'
9c7532f Fixes compiler warnings
5b5d692 Initial commit, K&R hello world
```

2. Now, we'll undo the commit and retain the changes introduced in the working tree:

```
$ git reset --mixed HEAD^

$ git log --oneline
9c7532f Fixes compiler warnings
5b5d692 Initial commit, K&R hello world

$ git status
On branch master
Your branch is behind 'origin/master' by 1 commit, and can be
fast-forwarded.
    (use "git pull" to update your local branch)

Untracked files:
    (use "git add <file>..." to include in what will be committed)

        HelloWorld.java
        Makefile

nothing added to commit but untracked files present (use "git add"
to track)
```

We can see that our commit is undone, but the changes to the file are preserved in the working tree, so more work can be done in order to create a proper commit.

How it works...

From the parent commit pointed to by the commit at HEAD, Git resets the branch pointer and HEAD to point to the parent commit. The staging area is reset, but the working tree is kept as it was before the reset, so the files affected by the undone commit will be in the modified state. The following figure depicts this:

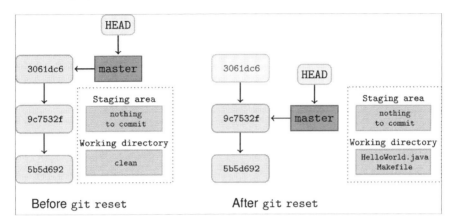

The `--mixed` option is the default behavior of `git reset`, so it can be omitted:

git reset HEAD^

Undo – remove a commit and retain the changes in the staging area

Of course, it is also possible to undo the commit, but keep the changes to the files in the index or the staging area so that you are ready to recreate the commit with, for example, some minor modifications.

Getting ready

We'll still use the example of the `hello world` repository. Make a fresh clone of the repository, or reset the `master` branch if you have already cloned one.

Create a fresh clone as follows:

```
$ git clone https://github.com/dvaske/hello_world_cookbook.git
$ cd hello_world_cookbook
```

We can reset the existing clone as follows:

```
$ cd hello_world_cookbook
$ git checkout master
$ git reset --hard origin master
HEAD is now at 3061dc6 Adds Java version of 'hello world'
```

How to do it...

1. Check whether we have no files in the modified state and check the log:

```
$ git status
On branch master
Your branch is up-to-date with 'origin/master'.

nothing to commit, working directory clean

$ git log --oneline
3061dc6 Adds Java version of 'hello world'
9c7532f Fixes compiler warnings
5b5d692 Initial commit, K&R hello world
```

2. Now, we can undo the commit, while retaining the changes in the index:

```
$ git reset --soft HEAD^

$ git log --oneline
9c7532f Fixes compiler warnings
5b5d692 Initial commit, K&R hello world

$ git status
On branch master
Your branch is behind 'origin/master' by 1 commit, and can be
fast-forwarded.
  (use "git pull" to update your local branch)

Changes to be committed:
  (use "git reset HEAD <file>..." to unstage)

    new file:   HelloWorld.java
    new file:   Makefile
```

You can now do minor (or major) changes to the files you need, add them to the staging area, and create a new commit.

How it works...

Again, Git will reset the branch pointer and HEAD to point to the previous commit. However, with the --soft option, the index and working directories are not reset, that is, they have the same state just as they had before we created the now undone commit.

The following figure shows the Git state before and after the undo:

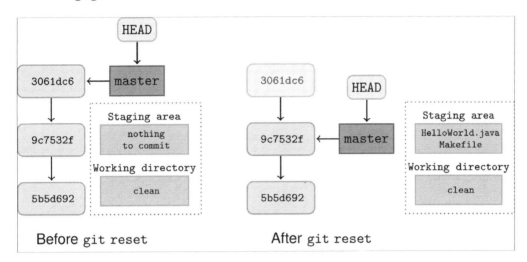

Undo – working with a dirty area

In the previous examples, we assumed that the working tree was clean, that is, no tracked files are in the modified state. However, this is not always the case, and if a *hard reset* is done, the changes to the modified files will be lost. Fortunately, Git provides a smart way to quickly put stuff away so that it can be retrieved later using the git stash command.

Getting ready

Again, we'll use the example of the hello world repository. Make a fresh clone of the repository, or reset the master branch if you have already cloned.

We can create the fresh clone as follows:

```
$ git clone https://github.com/dvaske/hello_world_cookbook.git
$ cd hello_world_cookbook
```

We can reset the existing clone as follows:

```
$ cd hello_world_cookbook
$ git checkout master
$ git reset --hard origin master
HEAD is now at 3061dc6 Adds Java version of 'hello world'
```

We'll also need to have some files in the working condition, so we'll change `hello_world.c` to the following:

```
#include <stdio.h>

void say_hello(void) {
  printf("hello, world\n");
}

int main(void){
  say_hello();
  return 0;
}
```

How to do it...

In order not to accidently delete any changes you have in your working tree when you are about to undo a commit, you can have a look at the current state of your working directory with `git status` (as we already saw). If you have changes and you want to keep them, you can stash them away before undoing the commit and retrieve them afterwards. Git provides a `stash` command that can put unfinished changes away so it is easy to make quick context switches without losing work. The `stash` functionality is described further in *Chapter 12, Tips and Tricks*. For now, you can think of the `stash` command like a stack where you can put your changes away and pop them later.

With the `hello_world.c` file in the working directory modified to the preceding state, we can try to do a hard reset on the HEAD commit, keeping our changes to the file by stashing them away before the reset and applying them back later:

1. First, check the history:

   ```
   $ git log --oneline
   3061dc6 Adds Java version of 'hello world'
   9c7532f Fixes compiler warnings
   5b5d692 Initial commit, K&R hello world
   ```

2. Then, check the status:

```
$ git status
On branch master
Your branch is up-to-date with 'origin/master'.

Changes not staged for commit:
  (use "git add <file>..." to update what will be committed)
  (use "git checkout -- <file>..." to discard changes in working
directory)

  modified:    hello_world.c

no changes added to commit (use "git add" and/or "git commit -a")
```

3. As expected, `hello_world.c` was in the modified state; so, stash it away, check the status, and perform the reset:

```
$ git stash
aved working directory and index state WIP on master: 3061dc6 Adds
Java version of 'hello world'
HEAD is now at 3061dc6 Adds Java version of 'hello world'

$ git status
On branch master
Your branch is up-to-date with 'origin/master'.

nothing to commit, working directory clean

$ git reset --hard HEAD^
HEAD is now at 9c7532f Fixes compiler warnings
$ git log --oneline
9c7532f Fixes compiler warnings
5b5d692 Initial commit, K&R hello world
```

4. The reset is done, and we got rid of the commit we wanted. Let's resurrect the changes we stashed away and check the file:

```
$ git stash pop
On branch master
```

```
Your branch is behind 'origin/master' by 1 commit, and can be
fast-forwarded.
  (use "git pull" to update your local branch)

Changes not staged for commit:
  (use "git add <file>..." to update what will be committed)
  (use "git checkout -- <file>..." to discard changes in working
directory)

modified:    hello_world.c

no changes added to commit (use "git add" and/or "git commit -a")
Dropped refs/stash@{0} (e56b68a1f5a0f72afcfd064ec13eefcda7a175ca)

$ cat hello_world.c
#include <stdio.h>

void say_hello(void) {
  printf("hello, world\n");
}

int main(void){
  say_hello();
  return 0;
}
```

So, the file is back to the state before the reset, and we got rid of the unwanted commit.

How it works...

The `reset` command works as explained in the previous examples, but combined with the `stash` command, it forms a very useful tool that corrects mistakes even though you have already starting working on something else. The `stash` command works by saving the current state of your working directory and the staging area. Then, it reverts your working directory to a clean state.

See also

▶ Refer to *Chapter 12, Tips and Tricks*, for more details on the `git stash` command

Redo – recreate the latest commit with new changes

As with undo, redo can mean a lot of things. In this context, redoing a commit will mean creating almost the same commit again with the same parent(s) as the previous commit, but with different content and/or different commit messages. This is quite useful if you've just created a commit but perhaps have forgotten to add a necessary file to the staging area before you committed, or if you need to reword the commit message.

Getting ready

Again, we'll use the `hello world` repository. Make a fresh clone of the repository, or reset the `master` branch if you have already cloned.

We can create a fresh clone as follows:

```
$ git clone https://github.com/dvaske/hello_world_cookbook.git
$ cd hello_world_cookbook
```

We can reset an existing clone as follows:

```
$ cd hello_world_cookbook
$ git checkout master
$ git reset --hard origin master
HEAD is now at 3061dc6 Adds Java version of 'hello world'
```

How to do it...

Let's pretend we need to redo the latest commit because we need to reword the commit message to include a reference to the issue tracker.

1. Let's first take a look at the latest commit and make sure the working directory is clean:

    ```
    $ git log -1
    commit 3061dc6cf7aeb2f8cb3dee651290bfea85cb4392
    Author: Aske Olsson <aske.olsson@switch-gears.dk>
    Date:   Sun Mar 9 14:12:45 2014 +0100

        Adds Java version of 'hello world'

        Also includes a makefile
    ```

```
$ git status

On branch master

Your branch is up-to-date with 'origin/master'.


nothing to commit, working directory clean
```

2. Now, we can redo the commit and update the commit message with the `git commit --amend` command. This will bring up the default editor, and we can add a reference to the issue tracker in the commit message (`Fixes: RD-31415`):

```
$ git commit --amend

Adds Java version of 'hello world'


Also includes a makefile


Fixes: RD-31415

# Please enter the commit message for your changes. Lines starting

# with '#' will be ignored, and an empty message aborts the
commit.

#

# Author:    Aske Olsson <aske.olsson@switch-gears.dk>

#

# On branch master

# Your branch is up-to-date with 'origin/master'.

#

# Changes to be committed:

#       new file:    HelloWorld.java

#       new file:    Makefile

#

~

~

[master 75a41a2] Adds Java version of 'hello world'

 Author: Aske Olsson <aske.olsson@switch-gears.dk>

 2 files changed, 19 insertions(+)

 create mode 100644 HelloWorld.java

 create mode 100644 Makefile
```

3. Now let's check the log again to see whether everything worked:

    ```
    $ git log -1
    commit 75a41a2f550325234a2f5f3ba41d35867910c09c
    Author: Aske Olsson <aske.olsson@switch-gears.dk>
    Date:    Sun Mar 9 14:12:45 2014 +0100


        Adds Java version of 'hello world'


        Also includes a makefile


        Fixes: RD-31415
    ```

4. We can see that the commit message has changed, but we can't verify from the log output that the parent of the commit is the same as in the original commit, and so on, as we saw in the first commit we did. To check this, we can use the `git cat-file` command we learned about in *Chapter 1, Navigating Git*. First, let's see how the original commit looked:

    ```
    $ git cat-file -p 3061dc6
    tree d3abe70c50450a4d6d70f391fcbda1a4609d151f
    parent 9c7532f5e788b8805ffd419fcf2a071c78493b23
    author Aske Olsson <aske.olsson@switch-gears.dk> 1394370765 +0100
    committer Aske Olsson <aske@schantz.com> 1394569447 +0100
    Adds Java version of 'hello world'


    Also includes a makefile
    ```

    The parent commit is b8c39bb35c4c0b00b6cfb4e0f27354279fb28866 and the root tree is d3abe70c50450a4d6d70f391fcbda1a4609d151f.

5. Let's check the data from the new commit:

    ```
    $ git cat-file -p HEAD
    tree d3abe70c50450a4d6d70f391fcbda1a4609d151f
    parent 9c7532f5e788b8805ffd419fcf2a071c78493b23
    author Aske Olsson <aske.olsson@switch-gears.dk> 1394370765 +0100
    committer Aske Olsson <aske@schantz.com> 1394655225 +0100


    Adds Java version of 'hello world'
    ```

```
Also includes a makefile
```

```
Fixes: RD-31415
```

The parent is the same, that is, `9c7532f5e788b8805ffd419fcf2a071c78493b23` and the root tree is also the same, that is, `d3abe70c50450a4d6d70f391fcbda1a4609d151f`. This is what we expected as we only changed the commit message. If we had added some changes to the staging area and executed `git commit --amend`, we would have included those changes in the commit and the root-tree SHA1 ID would have been different, but the parent commit ID still the same.

How it works...

The `--amend` option to `git commit` is roughly equivalent to performing `git reset --soft HEAD^`, followed by fixing the files needed and adding those to the staging area. Then, we will run `git commit` reusing the commit message from the previous commit (`git commit -c ORIG_HEAD`).

There is more...

We can also use the `--amend` method to add missing files to our latest commit. Let's say you needed to add the `README.md` file to your latest commit in order to get the documentation up to date, but you have already created the commit though you have not pushed it yet.

You then add the file to the index as you would while starting to craft a new commit. You can check with `git status` that only the `README.md` file is added:

```
$ git add README.md
$ git status
On branch master
Your branch and 'origin/master' have diverged,
and have 1 and 1 different commit each, respectively.
  (use "git pull" to merge the remote branch into yours)


Changes to be committed:
  (use "git reset HEAD <file>..." to unstage)


    new file:   README.md
```

Now you can amend the latest commit with `git commit --amend`. The command will include files in the index in the new commit and you can, as with the last example, reword the commit message if needed. It is not needed in this example, so we'll pass the `--no-edit` option to the command:

```
$ git commit --amend --no-edit
[master f09457e] Adds Java version of 'hello world'
 Author: Aske Olsson <aske.olsson@switch-gears.dk>
 3 files changed, 20 insertions(+)
 create mode 100644 HelloWorld.java
 create mode 100644 Makefile
 create mode 100644 README.md
```

You can see from the output of the commit command that three files were changed and `README.md` was one of them.

> You can also reset the author information (name, e-mail, and timestamp) with the `commit --amend` command. Just pass along the `--reset-author` option and Git will create a new timestamp and read author information from the configuration or environment, instead of the using the information from the old commit object.

Revert – undo the changes introduced by a commit

Revert can be used to undo a commit in history that has already been published (pushed), whereas this can't be done with the `amend` or `reset` options without rewriting history.

Revert works by applying the anti-patch introduced by the commit in question. A revert will, by default, create a new commit in history with a commit message that describes which commit has been reverted.

Getting ready

Again, we'll use the `hello world` repository. Make a fresh clone of the repository, or reset the `master` branch if you have already cloned.

We can create a fresh clone as follows:

```
$ git clone https://github.com/dvaske/hello_world_cookbook.git
$ cd hello_world_cookbook
```

We can reset the existing clone as follows:

```
$ cd hello_world_cookbook
$ git checkout master
$ git reset --hard origin master
HEAD is now at 3061dc6 Adds Java version of 'hello world'
```

How to do it...

1. First, we'll list the commits in the repository:

    ```
    $ git log --oneline
    3061dc6 Adds Java version of 'hello world'
    9c7532f Fixes compiler warnings
    5b5d692 Initial commit, K&R hello world
    ```

2. We'll revert the second commit, b8c39bb:

    ```
    $ git revert 9c7532f
    Revert "Fixes compiler wanings"

    This reverts commit 9c7532f5e788b8805ffd419fcf2a071c78493b23.

    # Please enter the commit message for your changes. Lines starting
    # with '#' will be ignored, and an empty message aborts the
    commit.
    # On branch master
    # Your branch is up-to-date with 'origin/master'.
    #
    # Changes to be committed:
    #       modified:   hello_world.c
    #
    ~
    ~
    ~
    "~/aske/packt/repos/hello_world_cookbook/.git/COMMIT_EDITMSG" 12L,
    359C
    [master 9b94515] Revert "Fixes compiler warnings"
     1 file changed, 1 insertion(+), 5 deletions(-)
    ```

3. When we check the log, we can see that a new commit has been made:

    ```
    $ git log --oneline
    9b94515 Revert "Fixes compiler warnings"
    3061dc6 Adds Java version of 'hello world'
    ```

```
9c7532f Fixes compiler warnings
5b5d692 Initial commit, K&R hello world
```

We can take a closer look at the two commits with `git show` if we want a closer investigation of what happened.

How it works...

Git revert applies the anti-patch of the commit in question to the current HEAD pointer. It will generate a new commit with the "anti-patch" and a commit message that describes the reverted commit(s).

There's more...

It's possible to revert more than one commit in a single revert, for example, `git revert master~6..master~2` will revert the commits from the sixth commit from the bottom in `master` to the third commit from the bottom in `master` (both included).

It is also possible not to create a commit while reverting; passing the `-n` option to `git revert` will apply the needed patched but only to the working tree and the staging area.

Reverting a merge

Merge commits are a special case when it comes to revert. In order to be able to revert a merge commit, you'll have to specify which parent side of the merge you want to keep. However, when you revert a merge commit, you should keep in mind that though reverting will undo the changes to files, it doesn't undo history. This means that when you revert a merge commit, you declare that you will not have any of the changes introduced by the merge in the target branch. The effect of this is that the subsequent merges from the other branch will only bring in changes of commits that are not ancestors of the reverted merge commit.

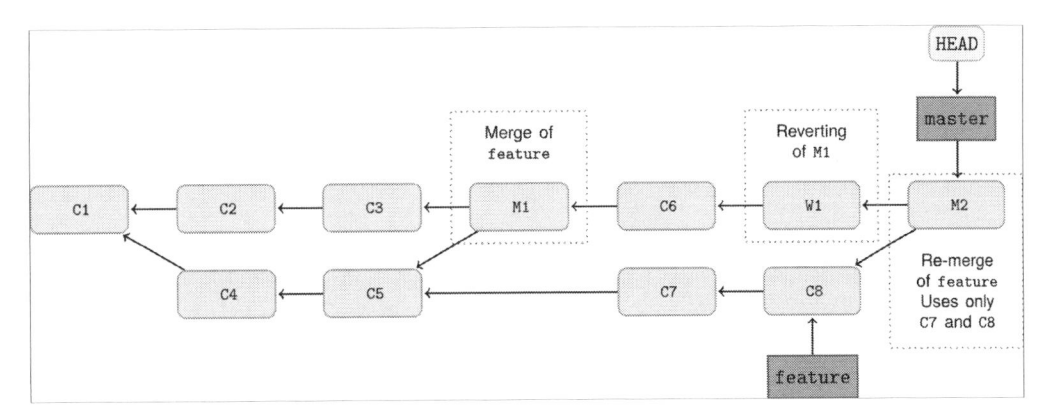

In this example, we will learn how to revert a merge commit, and we'll learn how we can merge the branch again, getting all the changes merged by reverting the reverted merge commit.

Getting ready

Again, we'll use the `hello world` repository. Make a fresh clone of the repository, or reset the `master` branch if you have already cloned.

We can create a fresh clone as follows:

```
$ git clone https://github.com/dvaske/hello_world_cookbook.git
$ cd hello_world_cookbook
```

We can reset the existing clone as follows:

```
$ cd hello_world_cookbook
$ git checkout master
$ git reset --hard origin master
HEAD is now at 3061dc6 Adds Java version of 'hello world'
```

In this example, we also need to use some of the other branches in the repository, so we need to create them locally:

```
$ git branch -f feature/p-lang origin/feature/p-lang
Branch feature/p-lang set up to track remote branch feature/p-lang from origin.
$ git checkout develop
Switched to branch 'develop'
Your branch is up-to-date with 'origin/develop'.
$ git reset --hard origin/develop
HEAD is now at a95abc6 Adds Groovy hello world
```

How to do it...

On the `develop` branch, we have just checked out that there is a merge commit that introduces "hello world" programs from languages that start with P. Unfortunately, the Perl version doesn't run:

```
$ perl hello_world.pl
Can't find string terminator '"' anywhere before EOF at hello_world.pl
line 3.
```

The following steps will help you revert a merge:

1. Let's take a look at history, the latest five commits, and find the merge commit:

```
$ git log --oneline --graph -5
* a95abc6 Adds Groovy hello world
*   5ae3beb Merge branch 'feature/p-lang' into develop
|\
| * 7b29bc3 php version added
| * 9944417 Adds perl hello_world script
* | ed9af38 Hello world shell script
|/
```

The commit we are looking for is 5ae3beb Merge branch 'feature/p-lang' into develop; this adds the commits for "hello world" in Perl and PHP to the develop branch. We would like the fix of the Perl version to happen on the feature branch, and then merge it to develop when ready. In order to keep develop stable, we need to revert the merge commit that introduced the faulty Perl version. Before we perform the merge, let's just have a look at the contents of HEAD:

```
$ git ls-tree --abbrev HEAD
100644 blob 28f40d8    helloWorld.groovy
100644 blob 881ef55    hello_world.c
100644 blob 5dd01c1    hello_world.php
100755 blob ae06973    hello_world.pl
100755 blob f3d7a14    hello_world.py
100755 blob 9f3f770    hello_world.sh
```

2. Revert the merge, keeping the history of the first parent:

```
$ git revert -m 1 5ae3beb
[develop e043b95] Revert "Merge branch 'feature/p-lang' into develop"
 2 files changed, 4 deletions(-)
 delete mode 100644 hello_world.php
 delete mode 100755 hello_world.pl
```

3. Let's have a look at the contents of our new HEAD state:

```
$ git ls-tree --abbrev HEAD
100644 blob 28f40d8    helloWorld.groovy
100644 blob 881ef55    hello_world.c
100755 blob f3d7a14    hello_world.py
100755 blob 9f3f770    hello_world.sh
```

The Perl and PHP files introduced in the merge are gone, so the revert did its job.

How it works...

The `revert` command will take the patches introduced by the commit you want to revert and apply the reverse/anti patch to the working tree. If all goes well, that is, there are no conflicts, a new commit will be made. While reverting a merge commit, only the changes introduced in the mainline (the `-m` option) will be kept, and all the changes introduced in the other side of the merge will be reverted.

There is more...

Though it is easy to revert a merge commit, you might run into issues if you later want to the branch again because the issues on the merge have not been fixed. When revert of the merge commit is performed, you actually tell Git that you do not want any of the changes that the other branch introduced in this branch. So, when you try to merge in the branch again, you will only get the changes from the commits that are not ancestors of the reverted merge commit.

We will see this in action by trying to merge the `feature/p-lang` branch with the `develop` branch again:

```
$ git merge --no-edit feature/p-lang
CONFLICT (modify/delete): hello_world.pl deleted in HEAD and modified in
feature/p-lang. Version feature/p-lang of hello_world.pl left in tree.
Automatic merge failed; fix conflicts and then commit the result.
```

We can solve the conflict just by adding `hello_world.pl`:

```
$ git add hello_world.pl
$ git commit
[develop 2804731] Merge branch 'feature/p-lang' into develop
```

Let's check the tree if everything seems right:

```
$ git ls-tree --abbrev HEAD
100644 blob 28f40d8    helloWorld.groovy
100644 blob 881ef55    hello_world.c
100755 blob 6611b8e    hello_world.pl
100755 blob f3d7a14    hello_world.py
100755 blob 9f3f770    hello_world.sh
```

The `hello_world.php` file is missing, but this makes sense as the change that introduced it was reverted in the reverted merge commit.

To perform a proper re-merge, we first have to revert the reverting merge commit; this can seem a bit weird, but it is the way to get the changes from before the revert back into our tree. Then, we can perform another merge of the branch, and we'll end up with all the changes introduced by the branch we're merging in. However, we first we have to discard the merge commit we just made with a hard reset:

```
$ git reset --hard HEAD^
HEAD is now at c46deed Revert "Merge branch 'feature/p-lang' into
develop"
```

Now, we can revert the reverting merge and re-merge the branch:

```
$ git revert HEAD
[develop 9950c9e] Revert "Revert "Merge branch 'feature/p-lang' into
develop""
 2 files changed, 4 insertions(+)
 create mode 100644 hello_world.php
 create mode 100755 hello_world.pl


$ git merge feature/p-lang
Merge made by the 'recursive' strategy.
 hello_world.pl | 2 +-
 1 file changed, 1 insertion(+), 1 deletion(-)
```

Let's check the tree for the Perl and PHP files, and see whether the Perl file has been fixed:

```
$ git ls-tree --abbrev HEAD
100644 blob 28f40d8    helloWorld.groovy
100644 blob 881ef55    hello_world.c
100644 blob 5dd01c1    hello_world.php
100755 blob 6611b8e    hello_world.pl
100755 blob f3d7a14    hello_world.py
100755 blob 9f3f770    hello_world.sh


$ perl hello_world.pl
Hello, world!
```

See also

For more information on reverting merges, refer to the following articles:

- ▸ The *How To Revert a Faulty Merge* article at `https://www.kernel.org/pub/software/scm/git/docs/howto/revert-a-faulty-merge.html`
- ▸ The *Undoing Merges* article at `http://git-scm.com/blog/2010/03/02/undoing-merges.html`

Viewing past Git actions with git reflog

The `reflog` command stores information on updates to the tip of the branches in Git, where the normal `git log` command shows the ancestry chain from HEAD, and the `reflog` command shows what HEAD has pointed to in the repository. This is your history in the repository that tells how you have moved between branches, created your commits and resets, and so on. Basically, anything that makes HEAD point to something new is recorded in the `reflog`. This means that by going through `reflog` command, you can find *lost* commits that none of your branches nor other commits point to. This makes the `reflog` command a good starting point for trying to find a lost commit.

Getting ready

Again, we'll use the `hello world` repository. If you make a fresh clone, make sure to run the scripts for this chapter so that there will be some entries in the `reflog` command. The scripts can be found on the book's homepage. If you just reset the `master` branch to `origin/master` after performing the recipes in this chapter, everything is ready.

We can create a fresh clone as follows:

```
$ git clone https://github.com/dvaske/hello_world_cookbook.git
$ cd hello_world_cookbook
```

We can reset an existing clone as follows:

```
$ cd hello_world_cookbook
$ git checkout master
$ git reset --hard origin master
HEAD is now at 3061dc6 Adds Java version of 'hello world'
```

How to do it...

1. Let's try to run the `reflog` command and limit ourselves to just the latest seven entries:

```
$ git reflog -7
3061dc6 HEAD@{0}: checkout: moving from develop to master
d557284 HEAD@{1}: merge feature/p-lang: Merge made by the
'recursive' strategy.
9950c9e HEAD@{2}: revert: Revert "Revert "Merge branch 'feature/p-
lang' into develop""
c46deed HEAD@{3}: reset: moving to HEAD^
2804731 HEAD@{4}: commit (merge): Merge branch 'feature/p-lang'
into develop
c46deed HEAD@{5}: revert: Revert "Merge branch 'feature/p-lang'
into develop"
a95abc6 HEAD@{6}: checkout: moving from master to develop
```

 In your repository, the commits will have different SHA-1 hashes due to the fact that the commits generated in the examples will have slightly different content, specifically your user name and e-mail address, but the order should be approximately the same.

We can see the movements we did in the last example by reverting, committing, and resetting. We can see the merge commit, `2804731`, that we abandoned. It didn't merge in all the changes we wanted it to due to the previous merge and its revert.

2. We can take a closer look at the commit with `git show`:

```
$ git show 2804731
commit 2804731c3abc4824cdab66dc7567bed4cddde0d3
Merge: c46deed 32fa2cd
Author: Aske Olsson <aske@schantz.com>
Date:   Thu Mar 13 23:20:21 2014 +0100


    Merge branch 'feature/p-lang' into develop


    Conflicts:
        hello_world.pl
```

Indeed, this was the commit we chose to abandon in the previous example. We can also look at the tree of the commit, just as we did in the previous example, and check whether they are the same:

```
git ls-tree --abbrev 2804731
100644 blob 28f40d8     helloWorld.groovy
100644 blob 881ef55     hello_world.c
100755 blob 6611b8e     hello_world.pl
100755 blob f3d7a14     hello_world.py
100755 blob 9f3f770     hello_world.sh
```

From here, there are various ways to resurrect the changes. You can either checkout the commit and create a branch; then, you'll have a pointer so you can easily find it again. You can also checkout specific files from the commit with `git checkout – path/to/file SHA-1`, or you can use the `git show` or `git cat-file` commands to view the files.

How it works...

For every movement of the `HEAD` pointer in the repository, Git stores the commit pointed to and the action for getting there. This can be commit, checkout, reset, revert, merge, rebase, and so on. The information is local to the repository and is not shared on pushes, fetches, and clones. Using the `reflog` command to find the lost commits is fairly easy if you know what you are searching for and the approximate time when you created the commit you are searching for. If you have a lot of reflog history, many commits, switching branches, and so on, it can be hard to search through the `reflog` command due to the amount of noise from the many updates to `HEAD`. The output of the `reflog` command can be a lot of options, and among them, there are options you can also pass on to the normal `git log` command.

Finding lost changes with git fsck

Another tool exists in Git that can help you find and recover lost commits and even blobs (files), which is `git fsck`. The `fsck` command tests the object database and verifies the SHA-1 ID of the objects and the connections they make. The command can also be used to find objects that are not reachable from any named reference, as it tests all the objects found in the database, which are under the `.git/objects` folder.

Getting ready

Again, we'll use the `hello world` repository. If you make a fresh clone, make sure to run the scripts for this chapter (`04_undo_dirty.sh`), so there will be some objects for `git fsck` to consider. The scripts can be found on the book's homepage. If you just reset the `master` branch after performing the other recipes in the chapter, everything is ready.

We can create the fresh clone as follows:

```
$ git clone https://github.com/dvaske/hello_world_cookbook.git
$ cd hello_world_cookbook
```

We can reset an existing clone as follows:

```
$ cd hello_world_cookbook
$ git checkout master
$ git reset --hard origin master
HEAD is now at 3061dc6 Adds Java version of 'hello world'
```

How to do it...

1. Let's look for the unreachable objects in the database:

   ```
   $ git fsck --unreachable
   Checking object directories: 100% (256/256), done.
   unreachable commit 147240ad0297f85c9ca3ed513906d4b75209e83d
   unreachable blob b16cf63ab66605f9505c17c5affd88b34c9150ce
   unreachable commit 4c3b1e10d8876cd507bcf2072c85cc474f7fb93b
   ```

    The object's ID, the SHA-1 hash, will not be the same if you perform the example on your computer, as the committer, author, and timestamp will be different.

2. We found two commits and one blob. Let's take a closer look at each of them; the blob first:

   ```
   git show b16cf63ab66605f9505c17c5affd88b34c9150ce
   #include <stdio.h>
   ```

```
void say_hello(void) {
        printf("hello, world\n");
}


int main(void){
        say_hello();
        return 0;
}
```

So the blob is the `hello_world.c` file from the example which stashing away your changes before resetting a commit. Here we stashed away the file, performed a reset, and resurrected the file from the stash, but we never actually performed a commit. The `stash` command, however, did add the file to the database, so it could find it again, and the file will continue to be there until the garbage collection kicks in or forever if it is referenced by a commit in the general history.

3. Let's look closer at the two commits:

```
$ git show 147240ad0297f85c9ca3ed513906d4b75209e83d
commit 147240ad0297f85c9ca3ed513906d4b75209e83d
Merge: 3061dc6 4c3b1e1
Author: Aske Olsson <aske@schantz.com>
Date:   Thu Mar 13 23:19:37 2014 +0100

        WIP on master: 3061dc6 Adds Java version of 'hello world'

diff --cc hello_world.c
index 881ef55,881ef55..b16cf63
--- a/hello_world.c
+++ b/hello_world.c
@@@ -1,7 -1,7 +1,10 @@@
  #include <stdio.h>

--int main(void){
++void say_hello(void) {
        printf("hello, world\n");
++}
```

```
++int main(void){
++   say_hello();
       return 0;
--}
++}
```

```
$ git show 4c3b1e10d8876cd507bcf2072c85cc474f7fb93b
commit 4c3b1e10d8876cd507bcf2072c85cc474f7fb93b
Author: Aske Olsson <aske@schantz.com>
Date:    Thu Mar 13 23:19:37 2014 +0100

        index on master: 3061dc6 Adds Java version of 'hello world'
```

Both the commits are actually commits we made when we stashed away our changes in the previous example. The `stash` command creates a commit object with the contents of the staging area, and a merge commit merging HEAD and the commit with the index with the content of the working directory (tracked files only). As we resurrected our stashed changes in the previous example, we no longer have any reference pointing at the preceding commits; therefore, they are found by `git fsck`.

How it works...

The `git fsck` command will test all the objects found under the `.git/objects` folder. When the `--unreachable` option is given, it will report the objects found that can't be reached from another reference; the reference can be a branch, a tag, a commit, a tree, the reflog, or stashed away changes.

See also

▶ Refer to *Chapter 12*, *Tips and Tricks*, for more information on the `git stash` command

9
Repository Maintenance

In this chapter, we will cover the following topics:

- ▶ Pruning remote branches
- ▶ Running garbage collection manually
- ▶ Turning off automatic garbage collection
- ▶ Splitting a repository
- ▶ Rewriting history – changing a single file
- ▶ Creating a backup of your repositories as mirror repositories
- ▶ A quick submodule how-to
- ▶ Subtree merging
- ▶ Submodule versus subtree merging

Introduction

In this chapter, we'll take a look at the various tools for repository maintenance. We will look at how we can easily delete branches in the local repository that have been deleted from the remote repository. We'll also see how we can trigger garbage collection and how to turn it off. We will take a look at how a repository can be split with the `filter-branch` command and how the `filter-branch` command can be used to rewrite the history of a repository. Finally, we'll take a quick look on how to integrate other git projects as subprojects in a git repository with either the submodule functionallity or the subtree strategy.

Pruning remote branches

Often, development in a software project tracked with Git happens on feature branches, and as time goes by, an increasing number of feature branches are merged to the mainline. Usually, these feature branches are deleted in the `main` repository (origin). However, the branches are not automatically deleted from all the clones while fetching and pulling. Git must explicitly be told to delete the branches from the local repository that have been deleted on origin.

Getting ready

First, we'll set up two repositories and use one of them as a remote for the other. We will use the `hello_world_flow_model` repository, but first we'll clone a repository to a local `bare` repository:

```
$ git clone --bare
https://github.com/dvaske/hello_world_flow_model.git
hello_world_flow_model_remote
```

Next, we'll clone the newly cloned repository to a local one with a working directory:

```
$ git clone hello_world_flow_model_remote hello_world_flow_model
```

Now, let's delete a couple of merged feature branches in the `bare` repository:

```
$ cd hello_world_flow_model_remote
$ git branch -D feature/continents
$ git branch -D feature/printing
$ git branch -D release/1.0
$ cd ..
```

Finally, change the directory to your working copy and make sure `develop` is checked out:

```
$ cd hello_world_flow_model
$ git checkout develop
$ git reset --hard origin/develop
```

How to do it...

1. Start by listing all branches using the following command:

   ```
   $ git branch -a
   * develop
   ```

```
remotes/origin/HEAD -> origin/develop
remotes/origin/develop
remotes/origin/feature/cities
remotes/origin/feature/continents
remotes/origin/feature/printing
remotes/origin/master
remotes/origin/release/1.0
```

2. Let's try to fetch or pull and see whether anything happens using the following command:

```
$ git fetch
$ git pull
Current branch develop is up to date.
$ git branch -a
* develop
  remotes/origin/HEAD -> origin/develop
  remotes/origin/develop
  remotes/origin/feature/cities
  remotes/origin/feature/continents
  remotes/origin/feature/printing
  remotes/origin/master
  remotes/origin/release/1.0
```

3. The branches are still there even if they are deleted in the remote repository. We need to tell Git explicitly to delete the branches that are also deleted from the remote repository using the following command:

```
$ git fetch --prune
 x [deleted]          (none)       -> origin/feature/continents
 x [deleted]          (none)       -> origin/feature/printing
 x [deleted]          (none)       -> origin/release/1.0
$ git branch -a
* develop
  remotes/origin/HEAD -> origin/develop
  remotes/origin/develop
  remotes/origin/feature/cities
  remotes/origin/master
```

The branches are now also deleted from our local repository.

How it works...

Git simply checks the remote-tracking branches under the `remotes` or `origin` namespace and removes branches that are not found on the remote any more.

There's more...

There are several ways to remove the branches in Git that have been deleted on the master. It can be done while updating the local repository, as we saw with `git fetch --prune`, and also with `git pull --prune`. It can even be performed with the `git remote prune origin` command. This will also remove the branches from Git that are no longer available on the remote, but it will not update remote-tracking branches in the repository.

Running garbage collection manually

When using Git on a regular basis, you might notice that some commands sometimes trigger Git to perform garbage collection and pack loose objects into a pack file (Git's objects storage). The garbage collection and packing of loose objects can also be triggered manually by executing the `git gc` command. Triggering `git gc` is useful if you have a lot of loose objects. A loose object can, for example, be a blob or a tree or a commit. As we saw in *Chapter 1, Navigating Git*, `blob-`, `tree-`, and `commit` objects are added to Git's database when we add files and create commits. These objects will first be stored as loose objects in Git's object storage as single files inside the `.git/objects` folder. Eventually, or by manual request, Git packs the loose objects into pack files that can reduce disk usage. A lot of loose objects can happen after adding a lot of files to Git, for example, when starting a new project or after frequent adds and commits. Running the garbage collection will make sure loose objects are being packed, and objects not referred to by any reference or object will be deleted. The latter is useful when you have deleted some branches/commits and want to make sure the objects referenced by these are also deleted.

Let's see how we can trigger garbage collection and remove some objects from the database.

Getting ready

First, we need a repository to perform the garbage collection on. We'll use the same repository as the previous example:

```
$ git clone https://github.com/dvaske/hello_world_flow_model.git
$ cd hello_world_flow_model
$ git checkout develop
$ git reset --hard origin/develop
```

How to do it...

1. First, we'll check the repository for loose objects; we can do this with the
   `count-objects` command:

   ```
   $ git count-objects
   51 objects, 204 kilobytes
   ```

2. We'll also check for unreachable objects, which are objects that can't be reached
   from any reference (tag, branch, or other object). The unreachable objects will
   be deleted when the garbage collect runs. We also check the size of the
   `.git` directory using the following command:

   ```
   $ git fsck --unreachable
   Checking object directories: 100% (256/256), done.
   $ du -sh .git
   292K   .git
   ```

3. There are no unreachable objects. This is because we just cloned and haven't
   actually worked in the repository. If we delete the `origin` remote, the remote
   branches (`remotes/origin/*`) will be deleted, and we'll lose the reference to
   some of the objects in the repository; they'll be displayed as unreachable while
   running `fsck` and can be garbage collected:

   ```
   $ git remote rm origin
   $ git fsck --unreachable
   Checking object directories: 100% (256/256), done.
   unreachable commit 127c621039928c5d99e4221564091a5bf317dc27
   unreachable commit 472a3dd2fda0c15c9f7998a98f6140c4a3ce4816
   unreachable blob e26174ff5c0a3436454d0833f921943f0fc78070
   unreachable commit f336166c7812337b83f4e62c269deca8ccfa3675
   ```

4. We can see that we have some unreachable objects due to the deletion of the
   remote. Let's try to trigger garbage collection manually:

   ```
   $ git gc
   Counting objects: 46, done.
   Delta compression using up to 8 threads.
   Compressing objects: 100% (44/44), done.
   Writing objects: 100% (46/46), done.
   Total 46 (delta 18), reused 0 (delta 0)
   ```

5. If we investigate the repository now, we can see the following:

```
$ git count-objects
5 objects, 20 kilobytes
$ git fsck --unreachable
Checking object directories: 100% (256/256), done.
Checking objects: 100% (46/46), done.
unreachable commit 127c621039928c5d99e4221564091a5bf317dc27
unreachable commit 472a3dd2fda0c15c9f7998a98f6140c4a3ce4816
unreachable blob e26174ff5c0a3436454d0833f921943f0fc78070
unreachable commit f336166c7812337b83f4e62c269deca8ccfa3675
$ du -sh .git
120K   .git
```

6. The object count is smaller; Git packed the objects to the pack-file stored in the `.git/objects/pack` folder. The size of the repository is also smaller as Git compresses and optimizes the objects in the pack-file. However, there are still some unreachable objects left. This is because the objects will only be deleted if they are older than what is specified in the `gc.pruneexpire` configuration option that defaults to two weeks (`config value: 2.weeks.ago`). We can override the default or configured option by running the `--prune=now` option:

```
$ git gc --prune=now
Counting objects: 46, done.
Delta compression using up to 8 threads.
Compressing objects: 100% (26/26), done.
Writing objects: 100% (46/46), done.
Total 46 (delta 18), reused 46 (delta 18)
```

7. Investigating the repository gives the following output:

```
$ git count-objects
0 objects, 0 kilobytes
$ git fsck --unreachable
Checking object directories: 100% (256/256), done.
Checking objects: 100% (46/46), done.
$ du -sh .git
100K   .git
```

The unreachable objects have been deleted, there are no loose objects, and the repository size is smaller now that the objects have been deleted.

How it works...

The `git gc` command optimizes the repository by compressing file revisions and deleting objects that are no longer referred to. The objects can be commits and so on. On an abandoned (deleted) branch, blobs from invocations of `git add`, commits discarded/redone with `git commit -amend`, or other commands that can leave objects behind. Objects are, by default, already compressed with zlib when they are created, and when moved into the pack-file, Git makes sure only to store the necessary change. If, for example, you change only a single line in a large file, it would waste a bit of space while storing the entire file in the pack-file again. Instead, Git stores the newest file as a whole in the pack-file and only the delta for the older version. This is pretty smart as you are more likely to require the newest version of the file, and Git doesn't have to do delta calculations for this. This might seem like a contradiction to the information from *Chapter 1, Navigating Git*, where we learned that Git stores snapshots and not deltas. However, remember how the snapshot is made. Git hashes all the files content in blobs, makes tree and commit objects, and the commit object describes the full tree state with the root-tree `sha-1` hash. The storing of the objects inside the pack-files have no effect on the computation of the tree state. When you checkout an earlier version or commit, Git makes sure the `sha-1` hashes match the branch or commit or tag you requested.

Turning off automatic garbage collection

The automatic triggering of garbage collection can be turned off so it will not run unless manually triggered. This can be useful if you are searching the repository for a lost commit/file and want to make sure that it is not being garbage collected while searching (running Git commands).

Getting ready

We'll use the `hello_world_flow_model` repository again for this example:

```
$ git clone https://github.com/dvaske/hello_world_flow_model.git
Cloning into 'hello_world_flow_model'...
remote: Reusing existing pack: 51, done.
remote: Total 51 (delta 0), reused 0 (delta 0)
Unpacking objects: 100% (51/51), done.
Checking connectivity... done.
$ cd hello_world_flow_model
$ git checkout develop
Already on 'develop'
Your branch is up-to-date with 'origin/develop'.
$ git reset --hard origin/develop
HEAD is now at 2269dcf Merge branch 'release/1.0' into develop
```

How to do it...

1. To switch off the automatic garbage collection triggering, we need to set the `gc.auto` configuration to 0. First, we'll check the existing setting, and then we can set it and verify the configuration using the following commands:

```
$ git config gc.auto
$ git config gc.auto 0
$ git config gc.auto
0
```

2. Now we can try to run `git gc` with the `--auto` option, as it will be called when normally triggered from other command:

```
$ git gc --auto
```

3. As expected, nothing happens as the configuration disables automatic garbage collection. We can still trigger it manually though (without the `--auto` flag):

```
$ git gc
Counting objects: 51, done.
Delta compression using up to 8 threads.
Compressing objects: 100% (49/49), done.
Writing objects: 100% (51/51), done.
Total 51 (delta 23), reused 0 (delta 0)
```

Splitting a repository

Sometimes a project tracked with Git is not one logical project but several projects. This may be fully intentional and there is nothing wrong with it, but there can also be cases where the projects tracked in the same Git repository really should belong to two different repositories. You can imagine a project where the code base grows and at some point in time, one of the subprojects could have value as an independent project. This can be achieved by splitting the subfolders and/or files that contain the project that should have its own repository with the full history of commits touching the files and/or folders.

Getting ready

In this example, we'll use the JGit repository so we'll have some history to filter through. The subfolders we split out to are not really projects, but serve well as an example for this exercise.

1. First, clone the Jgit repository and create local branches of the remote ones using the following command:

```
git clone https://git.eclipse.org/r/jgit/jgit
Cloning into 'jgit'...
```

```
remote: Counting objects: 1757, done

remote: Finding sources: 100% (148/148)

remote: Total 46381 (delta 4), reused 46317 (delta 4)

Receiving objects: 100% (46381/46381), 10.86 MiB | 411.00 KiB/s,
done.

Resolving deltas: 100% (24829/24829), done.

Checking connectivity... done.

$ cd jgit

$ git checkout master

Already on 'master'

Your branch is up-to-date with 'origin/master'.
```

2. Save the name of the current branch in the `current` variable:

```
$ current=$(git rev-parse --symbolic-full-name --abbrev-ref HEAD)
```

3. In the following step, we create local branches from all the remote branches in the repository:

```
$ for br in $(git branch -a | grep -v $current | grep remotes |
grep -v HEAD);

    do

        git branch ${br##*/} $br;

    done

Branch stable-0.10 set up to track remote branch stable-0.10 from
origin.

Branch stable-0.11 set up to track remote branch stable-0.11 from
origin.

Branch stable-0.12 set up to track remote branch stable-0.12 from
origin.

...
```

First, we filtered the branches. From all the `git branch -a` branches, we exclude branches that match the `$current` variable somewhere in the name, `grep -v $current`. Then, we include only the branches that match `remote` with `grep remotes`. Finally, we exclude all branches with HEAD in `grep -v HEAD`. For each of the branches, `$br` we create a local branch with the name given after the last "/" in the full name of the branch: `git branch ${br##*/} $br`. For example, `remotes/origin/stable-0.10` becomes the local branch `stable-0.10`.

4. Now we'll prepare a small script that will delete everything but the input to the shell script from the Git index. Save the following to the file `clean-tree` in the folder that contains the Jgit repository (not the repository itself):

```bash
#!/bin/bash

# Clean the tree for unwanted dirs and files
# $1 Files and dirs to keep
clean-tree () {
    # Remove everything but $1 from the git index/staging area
    for f in $(git ls-files | grep -E -v "$1" | grep -o -E
"^[^/\"]+" | sort -u); do
        git rm -rq --cached --ignore-unmatch $f
    done
}

clean-tree $1
```

The small script filters all the files currently in the staging area, `git ls-files`, excluding the ones that match the input `$1`, `grep -E -v "$1"`. It lists only the first part of their name/path up to the first "/", `grep -o -E "^[^/\"]+"`, and finally sorts them by unique entries using `sort -u`. The entries in the remaining list, $f, removed from the staging are of Git, `git rm -rq --cached --ignore-unmatch $f`. The `--cached` option tells Git to remove from the staging area and `--ignore-unmatched` tells Git not to fail if the file does not exist in the staging area. The `-rq` option is recursive and quiet respectively.

 The staging area contains all the files tracked by Git in the last snapshot (commit) and files (modified or new) you have added with `git add`. However, you only see changes between the latest commit and the staging area when you run `git status`, and changes between the working tree and the staging area.

5. Make the file executable using the following command:

```
$ chmod +x clean-tree
```

6. Now we are ready to split out a subpart of the repository.

How to do it...

1. First, we'll decide which folders and files to keep in the new repository; we'll delete everything from the repository except those files. We'll store the files and folders to be kept in a string separated by | so that we can feed it to grep as a regular expression, as shown in the following command:

    ```
    keep="org.eclipse.jgit.http|LICENSE|.gitignore|README.md|.
    gitattributes"
    ```

2. Now we are ready to start the conversion of the repository. We'll use the git filter-branch command that can rewrite the entire history of the repository; just what we need for this task.

     Always remember to make sure you have a backup of the repository you are about to run git filter-branch on in case something goes wrong.

3. We'll use the --index-filter option to filter the branch. The option allows us to rewrite the index or staging area just before each commit is recorded, and we'll do this with the clean-tree script we created previously. We'll also preserve tags using cat as tag-name-filter. We will perform the rewrite on all branches. And remember to use the absolute path to the clean-tree script:

    ```
    $ git filter-branch --prune-empty  --index-filter "\"path/to/
    clean-tree\" \"$keep\"" --tag-name-filter cat -- --all
    Rewrite 720734983bae056955bec3b36cc7e3847a0bb46a (13/3051)
    Rewrite 6e1571d5b9269ec79eadad0dbd5916508a4fee82 (23/3051)
    Rewrite 2bfe561f269afdd7f4772f8ebf34e5e25884942b (37/3051)
    Rewrite 2086fdaedd5e71621470865c34ad075d2668af99 (60/3051)
    ...
    ```

4. The rewrite takes a bit of time as all commits need to be processed, and once the rewrite is done we can see that everything, except the files and folders we wanted to keep, is deleted.

    ```
    git ls-tree --abbrev HEAD
    100644 blob f57840b   .gitattributes
    100644 blob ea8c4bf   .gitignore
    100644 blob 1b85c64   LICENSE
    100644 blob 6e6c0c7   README.md
    040000 tree 8bb062e   org.eclipse.jgit.http.apache
    040000 tree 2dff82d   org.eclipse.jgit.http.server
    040000 tree 91a9a3e   org.eclipse.jgit.http.test
    ```

5. The cleanup isn't done just yet; Git filter-branch saves all the original references, branches and tags, under the `refs/original` namespace in the repository. After verifying, the new history looks good, and we can get rid of the original refs as these point to objects that are not in our current history, and take up a lot of disk space. We'll delete all the original refs and run the garbage collector to clean the repository for old objects:

```
$ du -sh .git
  17M  .git
```

6. Delete original references, `refs/original`, and remove old objects with `git gc`, as shown in the following command:

```
$ git for-each-ref --format="%(refname)" refs/original/ |\
xargs -n 1 git update-ref -d
$ git reflog expire --expire=now --all
$ git gc --prune=now
Counting objects: 3092, done.
Delta compression using up to 8 threads.
Compressing objects: 100% (1579/1579), done.
Writing objects: 100% (3092/3092), done.
Total 3092 (delta 1238), reused 1721 (delta 796)
```

7. Check the size of the repository after garbage collection:

```
$ du -sh .git
796K  .git
```

8. The repository is now clean of all old objects, the size is greatly reduced, and the history is preserved for the files and directories we listed to keep.

How it works...

The `git filter-branch` command has different filter options depending on what needs to be done when rewriting the repository. In this example, where we are only removing files and folders from the repository; the index-filter is highly useable as it allows us to rewrite the index just before recording a commit in the database without actually checking out the tree on disk, saving a lot of disk I/O. The clean-tree script we prepared previously is then used to remove the unwanted files and folders from the index. First, we list the contents of the index and filter the files and folders we want to keep. Then, we remove the remaining files and folders (`$f`) from the index with the following command:

```
git rm -rq --cached --ignore-unmatch $f
```

The `--cached` option tells Git to remove from files the index, and the `-rq` option tells to remove recursive (r) and be quiet (q). Finally, the `--ignore-unmatch` option is used so `git rm` will not exit with an error if it tries to remove a file that is not in the index.

There's more...

There are many more filters for `git filter-branch`; the most common ones and their use cases are:

- `env-filter`: This filter is used to modify the environment where commits are recorded. This is particularly useful when rewriting author and committer information.
- `tree-filter`: The tree-filter is used to rewrite the tree. This is useful if you need to add or modify files in the tree, for example, to remove sensitive data from a repository.
- `msg-filter`: This filter is used to update the commit message.
- `subdirectory-filter`: This filter can be used if you want to extract a single subdirectory to a new repository and keep the history of that subdirectory. The subdirectory will be the root of the new repository.

Rewriting history – changing a single file

In this example, we'll see how we can use Git filter-branch to remove sensitive data from a file throughout the repository history.

Getting ready

For simplicity, we'll use a very simple example repository. It contains a few files. One among them is `.credentials`, which contains a username and password. Start by cloning the repository and changing the directory, as shown in the following command:

```
$ git clone https://github.com/dvaske/remove-credentials.git
$ cd remove-credentials
```

How to do it...

1. As we need to modify a file when rewriting the history of this repository, we'll use the `tree-filter` option to filter branch. The `.credentials` file looks as follows:

   ```
   username = foobar
   password = verysecret
   ```

2. All we need to do is to remove everything after the equals sign on each line of the file. We can use the following `sed` command to do this:

   ```
   sed -i '' 's/^\(.*=\).*$/\1/'
   ```

3. We can now run the filter branch with the following command:

```
$ git filter-branch --prune-empty  --tree-filter "test -f
.credentials && sed -i '' 's/^\(.*=\).*$/\1/' .credentials ||
true" -- --all
```

4. If we look at the file now, we can see the username and password are gone:

```
$ cat .credentials
username =
password =
```

5. As we saw in the last example, we still need to clean up after the filter-branch, by deleting original references, expiring the `reflog`, and triggering garbage collection.

How it works...

For each commit in the repository, Git will check the contents of that commit and run `tree-filter`. If the filter fails, non zero the exit code, `filter-branch` will fail. Therefore, it is important to remember to handle the cases where `tree-filter` might fail. This is why the previous `tree-filter` checks whether the `.credentials` file exists, runs the `sed` command if it does, and otherwise returns `true` to continue the `filter-branch`.

Back up your repositories as mirror repositories

Though Git is distributed and every clone essentially is a backup, there are some tricks that can be useful when backing up Git repositories. A normal Git repository has a working copy of the files it tracks and the full history of the repository in the `.git` folder of that repository. The repositories on the server, the one you push to and pull from, will usually be `bare` repositories. A `bare` repository is a repository without a working copy. Roughly, it is just the `.git` folder of a normal repository. A `mirror` repository is almost the same as a `bare` repository, except it fetches all the references under `refs/*`, where a bare only fetches the references that fall under `refs/heads/*`. We'll now take a closer look at a normal, a `bare`, and a `mirror` clone of the Jgit repository.

Getting ready

We'll start by creating three clones of the Jgit repository, a normal, a bare, and a mirror clone. When we create the first clone, we can use that as a reference repository for the other clones. In this way, we can share the objects in the database, and we don't have to transfer the same data three times:

```
$ git clone https://git.eclipse.org/r/jgit/jgit
```

```
$ git clone --reference jgit --bare https://git.eclipse.org/r/jgit/jgit
$ git clone --mirror --reference jgit https://git.eclipse.org/r/jgit/jgit
jgit.mirror
```

How to do it...

1. One of the differences between a normal repository and a bare/mirror one is that there are no remote branches in a bare repository; all the branches are created locally. We can see this in the three repositories by listing the branches with the `git` branch as follows:

    ```
    $ cd jgit
    $ git branch
    * master

    $ cd ../jgit.git # or cd ../jgit.mirror
    $ git branch
    * master
      stable-0.10
      stable-0.11
      stable-0.12
    ...
    ```

2. To see the difference between the `bare` and `mirror` repositories, we need to list the different `refspecs` fetch and the different `refs` namespaces. List the fetch `refspec` for `origin` in the mirror repository (`jgit.mirror`):

    ```
    $ git config remote.origin.fetch
    +refs/*:refs/*
    ```

3. List the different `refs` namespaces in the mirror repository:

    ```
    $ git show-ref | cut -f2 -d " " | cut -f1,2 -d / | sort -u
    refs/cache-automerge
    refs/changes
    refs/heads
    refs/meta
    refs/notes
    refs/tags
    ```

4. There is no explicit `refspec` fetch in the configuration for `origin` in the `bare` repository (`jgit.git`). When no configuration entry is found, Git uses the default `refspec` fetch, as it does in a normal repository. We can check the remote URL of `origin` using the following command:

```
$ git config remote.origin.url
https://git.eclipse.org/r/jgit/jgit
```

5. List the different `refs` namespaces in the `bare` repository using the following command:

```
$ git show-ref | cut -f2 -d " " | cut -f1,2 -d / | sort -u
refs/heads
refs/tags
```

6. Finally, we can list the `refspec` fetch and `refs` namespaces for the normal repository (`jgit`):

```
$ git config remote.origin.fetch
+refs/heads/*:refs/remotes/origin/*
$ git show-ref | cut -f2 -d " " | cut -f1,2 -d / | sort -u
refs/heads
refs/remotes
refs/tags
```

7. The mirror repository has four ref namespaces not found in the normal or the bare repositories, `refs- cache-automerge`, `changes`, `meta`, and `notes`. The normal repository is the only one that has the `refs/remote` namespace.

How it works...

The normal and bare repositories are pretty similar, only the mirror sticks out. This is due to the `refspec` fetch on the mirror repository, `+refs/*:refs/*`, which will fetch all refs from the remote and not just `refs/heads/*` and `refs/tags/*` as a normal repository (and bare) does. The many different ref namespaces on the Jgit repository is because the Jgit repository is managed by Gerrit Code Review that uses different namespaces for some repository specific content, such as `changes` branches for all commits submitted for code review, metadata on code review score, and so on.

The `mirror` repositories are good to know when you would like a quick way to back up a Git repository, and make sure you have everything included without needing more access than the Git access to the machine that hosts the Git repository.

There's more...

The repositories on GitHub store extra information in some `refs` namespaces. If a repository has had a pull request made, the pull request will be recorded in the `refs/pull/*` namespace. Let's look at it in the following code:

```
$ git clone --mirror git@github.com:jenkinsci/extreme-feedback-plugin.git
$ cd extreme-feedback-plugin.git
$ git show-ref | cut -f2 -d " " | cut -f1,2 -d / | sort -u
refs/heads
refs/meta
refs/pull
refs/tags
```

A quick submodule how-to

When developing a software project, you sometimes find yourself in a situation where you need to use another project as a subpart of your project. This other project can be anything from the another project you are developing to a third-party library. You want to keep the projects separate even though you need to use one project from the other. Git has a mechanism for this kind of project dependency called submodules. The basic idea is that you can clone another Git repository into your project as a subdirectory, but keep the commits from the two repositories separate, as shown in the following diagram:

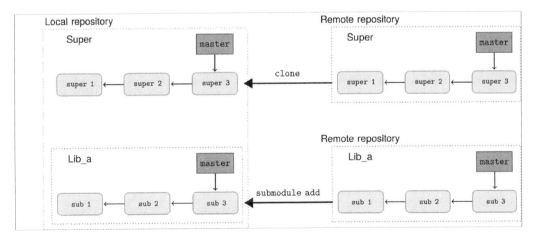

Getting ready

We'll start by cloning an example repository to be used as the super project:

```
$ git clone https://github.com/dvaske/super.git
$ cd super
```

How to do it...

1. We'll add a subproject, `lib_a`, to the super project as a Git submodule:

   ```
   $ git submodule add git://github.com/dvaske/lib_a.git lib_a
   Cloning into 'lib_a'...
   remote: Counting objects: 18, done.
   remote: Compressing objects: 100% (14/14), done.
   remote: Total 18 (delta 4), reused 17 (delta 3)
   Receiving objects: 100% (18/18), done.
   Resolving deltas: 100% (4/4), done.
   Checking connectivity... done.
   ```

2. Let's check `git status` using the following command:

   ```
   $ git status
   On branch master
   Your branch is up-to-date with 'origin/master'.

   Changes to be committed:
     (use "git reset HEAD <file>..." to unstage)


       new file:    .gitmodules
       new file:    lib_a
   ```

3. We can take a closer look at the two files in the Git index; `.gitmodules` is a regular file, so we can use `cat`:

   ```
   $ cat .gitmodules
   [submodule "lib_a"]
     path = lib_a
     url = git://github.com/dvaske/lib_a.git
   $ git diff --cached lib_a
   diff --git a/lib_a b/lib_a
   new file mode 160000
   ```

```
index 0000000..0d96e7c
--- /dev/null
+++ b/lib_a
@@ -0,0 +1 @@
+Subproject commit 0d96e7cfc4d4db64002e63af0f7325d33bdaf84f
```

The `.gitmodules` files contains information about all the submodules registered in the repository. The `lib_a` file stores which commit the submodule's HEAD is pointing to when added to the super project. Whenever the submodule is updated with new commits (created locally or fetched), the super project will state the submodule as changed while running `git status`. If the changes to the submodule can be accepted, the submodule revision in the super project is updated by adding the submodule file and committing this to the super project.

4. We'll update the submodule, `lib_a`, to the latest change on the develop branch using the following command:

```
$ cd lib_a
$ git checkout develop
Branch develop set up to track remote branch develop from origin
by rebasing.
Switched to a new branch 'develop'
$ cd ..
$ git status
On branch master
Your branch is ahead of 'origin/master' by 1 commit.
   (use "git push" to publish your local commits)


Changes not staged for commit:
   (use "git add <file>..." to update what will be committed)
   (use "git checkout -- <file>..." to discard changes in working
directory)


   modified:   lib_a (new commits)


no changes added to commit (use "git add" and/or "git commit -a")
```

5. Let's just check whether there are any updates to the submodule:

```
$ git submodule update
Submodule path 'lib_a': checked out
'0d96e7cfc4d4db64002e63af0f7325d33bdaf84f'
```

6. Oops! Now we actually reset our submodule to the state as described in the file for that submodule. We need to switch to the submodule again, check develop, and create a commit in the super project this time:

```
$ cd lib_a
$ git status
HEAD detached at 0d96e7c
nothing to commit, working directory clean
$ git checkout develop
Previous HEAD position was 0d96e7c... Fixes book title in README
Switched to branch 'develop'
Your branch is up-to-date with 'origin/develop'.
$ cd ..
$ git status
On branch master
Your branch is ahead of 'origin/master' by 1 commit.
  (use "git push" to publish your local commits)

Changes not staged for commit:
  (use "git add <file>..." to update what will be committed)
  (use "git checkout -- <file>..." to discard changes in working
directory)

  modified:   lib_a (new commits)

no changes added to commit (use "git add" and/or "git commit -a")
$ git add lib_a
$ git commit -m 'Updated lib_a to newest version'
[master 4d371bb] Updated lib_a to newest version
 1 file changed, 1 insertion(+), 1 deletion(-)
```

Notice that the submodule is on default in a detached head state, which means that HEAD is pointing directly to a commit instead of a branch. You can still edit the submodule and record commits. However, if you perform a submodule update in the super repository without first committing a new submodule state, your changes can be hard to find. So, always remember to checkout or create a branch while switching to a submodule to work, then you can just checkout the branch again and get your changes back. Since Git Version 1.8.2, it has been possible to make submodules track a branch rather than a single commit. Git 1.8.2 was released on the March 13, 2013, and you can check your version by running git --version.

7. To make Git track the branch of a submodule rather than a specific commit, we need to write the name of the branch we want to track in the `.gitmodules` file for the submodule; here we'll use the `stable` branch:

```
$ git config -f .gitmodules submodule.lib_a.branch stable
$ cat .gitmodules
[submodule "lib_a"]
  path = lib_a
  url = git://github.com/dvaske/lib_a.git
  branch = stable
```

8. We can now add and commit the submodule, and then try to update it using the following command:

```
$ git add .gitmodules
$ git commit -m 'Make lib_a module track its stable branch'
[master bf9b9ba] Make lib_a module track its stable branch
 1 file changed, 1 insertion(+)
$ git submodule update --remote
Submodule path 'lib_a': checked out
'8176a16db21a48a0969e18a51f2c2fb1869418fb'
$ git status
On branch master
Your branch is ahead of 'origin/master' by 3 commits.
  (use "git push" to publish your local commits)

Changes not staged for commit:
  (use "git add <file>..." to update what will be committed)
  (use "git checkout -- <file>..." to discard changes in working
directory)

    modified:   lib_a (new commits)

no changes added to commit (use "git add" and/or "git commit -a")
```

The submodule is still in the detached HEAD state. However, when updating the submodule with `git submodule update --remote`, changes from the submodule's remote repository will be fetched and the submodule will be updated to the latest commit on the branch it is tracking. We still need to record a commit to the super repository, specifying the state of the submodule.

There's more...

When you are cloning a repository that contains one or more submodules, you need to explicitly fetch them after the clone. We can try this with our newly created submodule repository:

```
$ git clone super super_clone
Cloning into 'super_clone'...
done.
```

Now, initialize and update the submodules:

```
$ cd super_clone
$ git submodule init
Submodule 'lib_a' (git://github.com/dvaske/lib_a.git) registered for path 'lib_a'
$ git submodule update --remote
Cloning into 'lib_a'...
remote: Counting objects: 18, done.
remote: Compressing objects: 100% (14/14), done.
remote: Total 18 (delta 4), reused 17 (delta 3)
Receiving objects: 100% (18/18), done.
Resolving deltas: 100% (4/4), done.
Checking connectivity... done.
Submodule path 'lib_a': checked out
'8176a16db21a48a0969e18a51f2c2fb1869418fb'
```

The repository is ready for development!

 When cloning the repository, the submodules can be initialized and updated directly after the clone if the `--recursive` or `--recurse-submodules` option is given.

Subtree merging

An alternative to submodules is subtree merging. Subtree merging is a strategy that can be used while performing merges with Git. The subtree merge strategy is useful when merging a branch (or as we'll see in this recipe another project) into a subdirectory of a Git repository instead of the root directory. When using the subtree merge strategy, the history of the subproject is joined with the history of the super project, while the subproject's history can be kept clean except for commits indented to go upstream.

Getting ready

We'll use the same repositories as in the last recipe, and we'll reclone the super project to get rid of the submodule setup:

```
$ git clone https://github.com/dvaske/super.git
$ cd super
```

How to do it...

We'll add the subproject as a new remote and fetch the history:

```
$ git remote add lib_a git://github.com/dvaske/lib_a.git
$ git fetch lib_a
warning: no common commits
remote: Reusing existing pack: 18, done.
remote: Total 18 (delta 0), reused 0 (delta 0)
Unpacking objects: 100% (18/18), done.
From git://github.com/dvaske/lib_a
 * [new branch]      develop    -> lib_a/develop
 * [new branch]      master     -> lib_a/master
 * [new branch]      stable     -> lib_a/stable
```

We can now create a local branch, `lib_a_master`, which points to the same commit as the `master` branch in `lib a` (`lib_a/master`):

```
$ git checkout -b lib_a_master lib_a/master
Branch lib_a_master set up to track remote branch master from lib_a by rebasing.
Switched to a new branch 'lib_a_master'
```

We can check the content of our working tree using the following command:

```
$ ls
README.md   a.txt
```

If we switch back to the `master` branch, we should see the content of the super repository in our directory:

```
$ git checkout master
Switched to branch 'master'
Your branch is up-to-date with 'origin/master'.
$ ls
README.md   super.txt
```

Git changes branches and populates the working directory as normal even though the branches are originally from two different repositories. Now, we want to merge the history from `lib_a` into a subdirectory. First, we prepare a merge commit by merging with the `ours` strategy and make sure the commit isn't completed (we need to bring in all the files).

```
$ git merge -s ours --no-commit lib_a_master
Automatic merge went well; stopped before committing as requested
```

In short what the `ours` strategy tells Git to do the following: Merge in this branch, but keep the resulting tree the same as the tree on the tip of this branch. So, the branch is merged, but all the changes it introduced are discarded. In our previous command line, we also passed the `--no-commit` option. This option stops Git from completing the merge, but leaves the repository in a merging state. We can now add the content of the `lib_a` repository to the `lib_a` folder in the repository root. We do this with `git read-tree` to make sure the two trees are exactly the same as follows:

```
$ git read-tree --prefix=lib_a/ -u lib_a_master
```

Our current directory structure looks as follows:

```
$ tree
.
|-- README.md
|-- lib_a
|    |-- README.md
|    '-- a.txt
'-- super.txt
```

It is time to conclude the merge commit we started using the following command:

```
$ git commit -m 'Initial add of lib_a project'
[master 5066b7b] Initial add of lib_a project
```

Now the subproject is added. Next, we'll see how we can update the super project with new commits from the subproject and how to copy commits made in the super project to the subproject.

We need to add and commit some changes to the super project using the following command:

```
$ echo "Lib_a included\!" >> super.txt
$ git add super.txt
$ git commit -m "Update super.txt"
[master 83ef9a4] Update super.txt
 1 file changed, 1 insertion(+)
```

Some changes are made to the subproject committed in the super project:

```
$ echo "The b file in lib_a" >> lib_a/b.txt
$ git add lib_a/b.txt
$ git commit -m "[LIB_A] Enhance lib_a with b.txt"
[master debe836] [LIB_A] Enhance lib_a with b.txt
 1 file changed, 1 insertion(+)
 create mode 100644 lib_a/b.txt
```

The current history looks like the following screenshot:

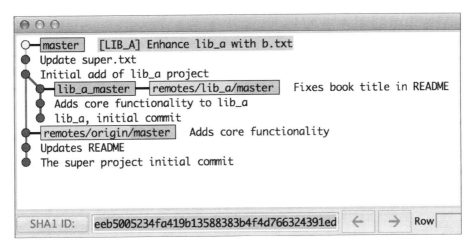

The merge can be seen in the previous screenshot and the two root commits of the repository, the original root commit and the root from `lib_a`.

Now, we will learn to integrate new commits into the super repository made in the subproject, `lib_a`. Normally, we would do this by checking out the `lib_a_master` branch and performing `pull` on this to get the latest commit from the remote repository. However, as we are working with example repositories in this recipe, no new commits are available on the `master` branch. Instead, we'll use the `develop` and `stable` branches from `lib_a`. We'll now integrate commits from the `develop` branch on `lib_a`. We do this directly using the `lib_a/develop` reference in the repository as follows:

```
$ git merge -m '[LIB_A] Update lib_a project to latest state' -s \
subtree lib_a/develop
Merge made by the 'subtree' strategy.
 lib_a/a.txt | 2 ++
 1 file changed, 2 insertions(+)
```

Our `master` branch has now been updated with the commits from `lib_a/develop` as shown in the following screenshot:

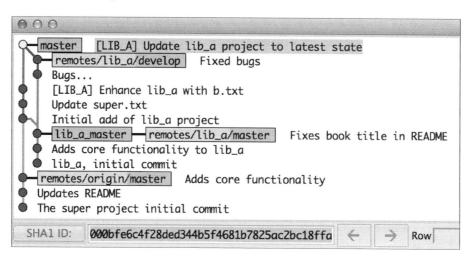

Now, it is time to add the commits we made in the `lib_a` directory back to the `lib_a` project. First, we'll change the `lib_a_master` branch and merge that with `lib_a/develop` to be as up to date as possible:

```
$ git checkout lib_a_master
$ git merge lib_a/develop
Updating 0d96e7c..ab47aca
Fast-forward
 a.txt | 2 ++
 1 file changed, 2 insertions(+)
```

Now we are ready to merge changes from the super project to the subproject. In order not to merge the history of the super project to the subproject, we'll use the `--squash` option. This option stops Git from completing the merge, and unlike the previous case where we also stopped a merge from recording a commit, it does not leave the repository in a merging state. The state of the working directory and staging area are, however, set as though a real merge has happened.

```
$ git merge --squash -s subtree --no-commit master
Squash commit -- not updating HEAD
Automatic merge went well; stopped before committing as requested
```

Now, we can record a commit with all the changes done in `lib_a` from the super project:

```
$ git commit -m 'Enhance lib_a with b.txt'
[lib_a_master 01e45f7] Enhance lib_a with b.txt
 1 file changed, 1 insertion(+)
 create mode 100644 b.txt
```

The history for the `lib_a` repository is seen in the following screenshot:

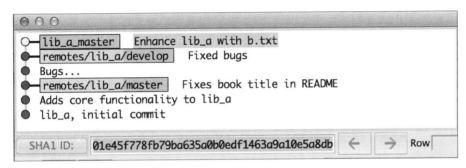

We can integrate more changes from `lib_a/stable` into the super project, but first we'll update the `lib_a_master` branch so we can integrate them from here:

```
$ git merge lib_a/stable
Merge made by the 'recursive' strategy.
 a.txt | 2 ++
 1 file changed, 2 insertions(+)
```

A new commit was added to the subproject, as shown in the following screenshot:

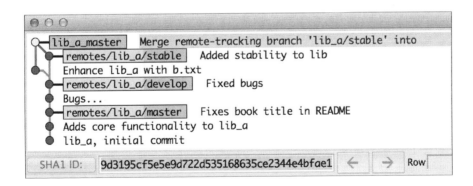

The last task is to integrate the new commit on `lib_a_master` to the master branch in the super repository. This is done as in the previous case with the `subtree` strategy option to `git` merge:

```
$ git checkout master
$ git merge -s subtree -m '[LIB_A] Update to latest state of lib_a'
lib_a_master
Merge made by the 'subtree' strategy.
 lib_a/a.txt | 2 ++
 1 file changed, 2 insertions(+)
```

The resulting history is shown in the following screenshot:

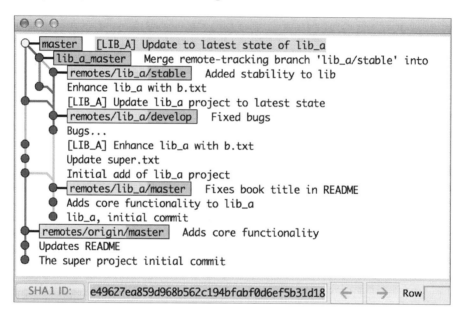

How it works...

When using the subtree strategy, Git finds out which subtree in your repository, the branch you are trying to merge fits in. This is why we added the content of the `lib_a` repository with the `read-tree` command to make sure we got the exact same SHA-1 ID for the `lib_a` directory in the super project as the root tree in the `lib_a` project.

We can verify this by finding the SHA-1 of the `lib_a` tree in the super project in the commit where we merged in the subproject:

```
$ git ls-tree a3662eb94abf0105a25309653b5d2ce67a4028d2
100644 blob 456a5df638694a699fff7a7ff31a496630b12d01  README.md
```

```
040000 tree 7d66ad11cb22c6d101c7ac9c309f7dce25231394   lib_a
100644 blob c552dead26fdba634c91d35708f1cfc2c4b2a100   super.txt
```

The ID of the root tree at `lib_a/master` can be found out by using the following command:

```
$ git cat-file -p lib_a/master
tree 7d66ad11cb22c6d101c7ac9c309f7dce25231394
parent a7d76d9114941b9d35dd58e42f33ed7e32a9c134
author Aske Olsson <aske.olsson@switch-gears.dk> 1396553189 +0200
committer Aske Olsson <aske.olsson@switch-gears.dk> 1396553189 +0200

Fixes book title in README
```

See also

Another way of using subtree merging is with the `git subtree` command. This is not enabled by default in Git installations, but is distributed with Git since 1.7.11. You can see how to install and use it at the following links:

- ▶ For installation, go to `https://github.com/git/git/blob/master/contrib/subtree/INSTALL`
- ▶ To understand how to use a subtree, go to `https://github.com/git/git/blob/master/contrib/subtree/git-subtree.txt`

Submodule versus subtree merging

There is no easy answer to the question of whether or not to use submodules or subtree merging for a project. When choosing submodule, a lot of extra pressure is put on the developers working on the project as they need to make sure they keep the submodule and the super project in sync. When choosing to add a project by subtree merging, no or little extra complexity is added for developers. The repository maintainer, however, needs to make sure the subproject is up to date and that commits are added back to the subproject. Both methods work and are in use, and it is probably just a matter of getting used to either method before finding it natural to use. A completely different solution is to use the build system of the super project to fetch the necessary dependencies, as for example, **Maven** or **Gradle** does.

10
Patching and Offline Sharing

In this chapter, we will cover the following topics:

- ▶ Creating patches
- ▶ Creating patches from branches
- ▶ Applying patches
- ▶ Sending patches
- ▶ Creating Git bundles
- ▶ Using a Git bundle
- ▶ Creating archives from a tree

Introduction

With the distributed nature of Git and the many existing hosting options available for Git, it is very easy to share the history between machines when they are connected through a network. In cases where the machines that need to share history are not connected or can't use the transport mechanisms supported, Git provides other methods to share the history. Git provides an easy way to format patches from the existing history, sending those with an e-mail and applying them to another repository. Git also has a bundle concept, where a bundle that contains only part of the history of a repository can be used as a remote for another repository. Finally, Git provides a simple and easy way to create an archive for a snapshot of the folder/subfolder structure for a given reference.

With these different methods provided by Git, it becomes easy to share the history between repositories, especially where the normal push/pull methods are not available.

Creating patches

In this recipe, we'll learn how to make patches out of commits. Patches can be sent via e-mails for quick sharing or copied to sneakernet devices (USB sticks, memory cards, external hard disk drives, and so on) if they need to be applied on an offline computer or the like. Patches can be useful methods to review code as the reviewer can apply the patch on his repository, investigate the diff, and check the program. If the reviewer decides the patch is good, he can publish (push) it to a public repository, given the reviewer is the maintainer of the repository. If the reviewer rejects the patch, he can simply reset his branch to the original state and inform the author of the patch that more work is needed before the patch can be accepted.

Getting ready

In this example, we'll clone and use a new repository. The repository is just an example repository for the Git commands and only contains some example commits:

```
$ git clone https://github.com/dvaske/offline-sharing.git
$ cd offline-sharing
$ git checkout master
```

How to do it...

Let's see the history of the repository as shown by Gitk:

```
$ gitk --all
```

The history of the repository can be seen in the following screenshot:

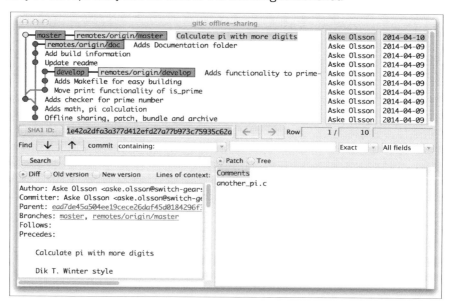

There are three branches in the repository: `master`, `develop`, and `doc`. All of them differ by one or more commits to the others. On the `master` branch, we can now create a patch file for the latest commit on the `master` branch and store it in the `latest-commit` folder, as shown in the following command:

```
$ git format-patch -1 -o latest-commit
latest-commit/0001-Calculate-pi-with-more-digits.patch
```

If we look at the file created by the patch command, we will see the following command:

```
$ cat latest-commit/0001-Calculate-pi-with-more-digits.patch

From 1e42a2dfa3a377d412efd27a77b973c75935c62a Mon Sep 17 00:00:00 2001
From: Aske Olsson <aske.olsson@switch-gears.dk>
Date: Thu, 10 Apr 2014 09:19:29 +0200
Subject: [PATCH] Calculate pi with more digits


Dik T. Winter style


Build: gcc -Wall another_pi.c -o pi
Run: ./pi
---
 another_pi.c | 21 +++++++++++++++++++++
 1 file changed, 21 insertions(+)
 create mode 100644 another_pi.c

diff --git a/another_pi.c b/another_pi.c
new file mode 100644
index 0000000..86df41b
--- /dev/null
+++ b/another_pi.c
@@ -0,0 +1,21 @@
+/* Pi with 800 digits
+ * Dik T. Winter style, but modified sligthly
+ * https://crypto.stanford.edu/pbc/notes/pi/code.html
+ */
+ #include <stdio.h>
+
```

```
+void another_pi (void) {

+      printf("800 digits of pi:\n");

+      int a=10000, b=0, c=2800, d=0, e=0, f[2801], g=0;

+      for ( ;b-c; )f[b++]=a/5;

+          for (;d=0,g=c*2;c-=14,printf("%.4d",e+d/a),e=d%a)

+              for (b=c; d+=f[b]*a, f[b]=d%--g,d/=g--,--b; d*=b);

+

+      printf("\n");

+}

+

+int main (void){

+      another_pi();

+

+      return 0;

+}

--

1.9.1
```

The previous snippet is the content of the patch file produced. It contains a header much like an e-mail with the `From`, `Date`, and `Subject` fields, a body with the commit message and after the 3 dashes (`---`), the actual patch, and finally ending with 2 dashes (`--`), and the Git version used to generate the patch. The patch generated by `git format-patch` is in the **UNIX** mailbox format but with a magic fixed timestamp to identify that it comes from `git format-patch` rather than a real mailbox. You can see the time stamp in the first line after the `sha-1` ID **Mon Sep 17 00:00:00 2001**.

How it works...

When generating the patch, Git will diff the commit at HEAD with its parent commit and use this diff as the patch. The `-1` option tells Git only to generate patches for the last commit and `-o latest-commit` tells Git to store the patch in the folder `latest-commit`. The folder will be created if it does not exist.

There's more...

If you want to create patches for several commits, say the last 3 commits, you just pass on `-3` to `git format-patch` instead of the `-1`.

Format the latest three commits as patches in the `latest-commits` folder:

```
$ git format-patch -3 -o latest-commits
latest-commits/0001-Adds-math-pi-calculation.patch
latest-commits/0002-Adds-checker-for-prime-number.patch
latest-commits/0003-Calculate-pi-with-more-digits.patch
$ ls -la latest-commits
total 24
drwxr-xr-x   5 aske    staff     170 Apr 11 21:55 .
drwxr-xr-x   8 aske    staff     272 Apr 11 21:55 ..
-rw-r--r--   1 aske    staff     676 Apr 11 21:55 0001-Adds-math-pi-
calculation.patch
-rw-r--r--   1 aske    staff    1062 Apr 11 21:55 0002-Adds-checker-for-prime-
number.patch
-rw-r--r--   1 aske    staff    1041 Apr 11 21:55 0003-Calculate-pi-with-more-
digits.patch
```

Creating patches from branches

Instead of counting the number of commits you need to make patches for, you can create the patches by specifying the target branch when running the format-patch command.

Getting ready

We'll use the same repository as in the previous example:

```
$ git clone https://github.com/dvaske/offline-sharing.git
$ cd offline-sharing
```

Create the master branch locally without checking out:

```
$ git branch master origin/master
```

Make sure we have develop checked out:

```
$ git checkout develop
```

How to do it...

We'll pretend that we have been working on the `develop` branch and have made some commits. Now, we need to format patches for all these commits so we can send them to the repository maintainer or carry them to another machine.

Let's see the commits on `develop` not on `master`:

```
$ git log --oneline master..develop
c131c8b Adds functionality to prime-test a range of numbers
274a7a8 Adds Makefile for easy building
88798da Move print functionality of is_prime
```

Now, instead of running `git format-patch -3` to get patches made for these 3 commits, we'll tell Git to create patches for all the commits that are not on the `master` branch:

```
$ git format-patch -o not-on-master master
not-on-master/0001-Move-print-functionality-of-is_prime.patch
not-on-master/0002-Adds-Makefile-for-easy-building.patch
not-on-master/0003-Adds-functionality-to-prime-test-a-range-of-numbers.
patch
```

How it works...

Git makes a list of commits from `develop` that are not on the `master` branch, much like we did before creating the patches, and makes patches for these. We can check the content of the folder `not-on-master`, which we specified as the output folder (`-o`) and verify that it contains the patches as expected:

```
$ ls -1 not-on-master
0001-Move-print-functionality-of-is_prime.patch
0002-Adds-Makefile-for-easy-building.patch
0003-Adds-functionality-to-prime-test-a-range-of-numbers.patch
```

There's more...

The `git format-patch` command has many options and besides the `-<n>` option to specify the number of commits in order to create patches for and the `-o <dir>` for the target directory, some useful options are as follows:

- ▶ `-s, --signoff`: Adds a `Signed-off-by` line to the commit message in the patch file with the name of the committer. This is often required when mailing patches to the repository maintainers. This line is required for patches to be accepted when they are sent to the Linux kernel mailing list and the Git mailing list.

- ▶ `-n, --numbered`: Numbers the patch in the subject line as `[PATCH n/m]`.

- ▶ `--suffix=.<sfx>`: Sets the suffix of the patch; it can be empty and does not have to start with a dot.

- ▶ `-q, --quiet`: Suppresses the printing of patch filenames when generating patches.

- ▶ `--stdout`: Prints all commits to the standard output instead of creating files.

Applying patches

Now we know how to create patches from commits. It is time to learn to apply them.

Getting ready

We'll use the repository from the previous examples along with the generated patches as follows:

```
$ cd offline-sharing
$ git checkout master
$ ls -1a
.
..
.git
Makefile
README.md
another_pi.c
latest-commit
math.c
not-on-master
```

How to do it...

First, we'll checkout the `develop` branch and apply the patch generated from the `master` branch (`0001-Calculate-pi-with-more-digits.patch`) in the first example. We use the Git command `am` to apply the patches; `am` is short for `apply from mailbox`:

```
$ git checkout develop
Your branch is up-to-date with 'origin/develop'.
$ git am latest-commit/0001-Calculate-pi-with-more-digits.patch
Applying: Calculate pi with more digits
```

We can also apply the `master` branch to the series of patches that was generated from the `develop` branch as follows:

```
$ git checkout master
Switched to branch 'master'
Your branch is up-to-date with 'origin/master'.
```

```
$ git am not-on-master/*
Applying: Move print functionality of is_prime
Applying: Adds Makefile for easy building
Applying: Adds functionality to prime-test a range of numbers
```

How it works...

The `git am` command takes the mailbox file specified in the input and applies the patch in the file to the files needed. Then, a commit is recorded using the commit message and author information from the patch. The committer identity of the commit will be the identity of the person performing the `git am` command. We can see the author and committer information with `git log`, but we need to pass the `--pretty=fuller` option to also view the committer information:

```
$ git log -1 --pretty=fuller
commit 5af5ee2746b67893b0550d8a63110c48fd1b667c
Author:     Aske Olsson <aske.olsson@switch-gears.dk>
AuthorDate: Wed Apr 9 21:50:18 2014 +0200
Commit:     Aske Olsson <aske.olsson@switch-gears.dk>
CommitDate: Fri Jun 13 22:50:45 2014 +0200

    Adds functionality to prime-test a range of numbers
```

There's more...

The `git am` command applies the patches in the files specified and records the commits in the repository. However, if you only want to apply the patch to the working tree or the staging area and not record a commit, you can use the `git apply` command.

We can try to apply the patch from the `master` branch to the `develop` branch once again; we just need to reset the `develop` branch first:

```
$ git checkout develop
Switched to branch 'develop'
Your branch is ahead of 'origin/develop' by 1 commit.
  (use "git push" to publish your local commits)
$ git reset --hard origin/develop
```

```
HEAD is now at c131c8b Adds functionality to prime-test a range of
numbers
$ git apply latest-commit/0001-Calculate-pi-with-more-digits.patch
```

Now, we can check the state of the repository with the `status` command:

```
$ git status
On branch develop
Your branch is up-to-date with 'origin/develop'.

Untracked files:
  (use "git add <file>..." to include in what will be committed)

  another_pi.c
  latest-commit/
  not-on-master/

nothing added to commit but untracked files present (use "git add" to
track)
```

We successfully applied the patch to the working tree. We can also apply it to the staging area and the working tree using the `--index` option, or only to the staging area using the `--cached` option.

Sending patches

In the previous example, you saw how to create and apply patches. You can, of course, attach these patch files directly to an e-mail, but Git provides a way to send the patches directly as e-mails with the `git send-email` command. The command requires some setting up, but how you do that is heavily dependent on your general mail and SMTP configuration. A general guide can be found in the Git help pages or visit `http://git-scm.com/docs/git-send-email`.

Getting ready

We'll set up the same repository as in the previous example:

```
$ git clone https://github.com/dvaske/offline-sharing.git
Cloning into 'offline-sharing'...
```

```
remote: Counting objects: 32, done.
remote: Compressing objects: 100% (25/25), done.
remote: Total 32 (delta 7), reused 30 (delta 6)
Unpacking objects: 100% (32/32), done.
Checking connectivity... done.
$ cd offline-sharing
```

How to do it...

First, we'll send the same patch as the one we created in the first example. We'll send it to ourselves using the e-mail address we specified in our Git configuration. Let's create the patch again with `git format-patch` and send it with `git send-email`:

```
$ git format-patch -1 -o latest-commit
latest-commit/0001-Calculate-pi-with-more-digits.patch
```

Save the e-mail address from the Git configuration to a variable as follows:

```
$ emailaddr=$(git config user.email)
```

Send the patch using the e-mail address in both the to and from fields:

```
$ git send-email --to $emailaddr --from $emailaddr latest-commit/0001-
Calculate-pi-with-more-digits.patch
latest-commit/0001-Calculate-pi-with-more-digits.patch
(mbox) Adding cc: Aske Olsson <aske.olsson@switch-gears.dk> from line
'From: Aske Olsson <aske.olsson@switch-gears.dk>'
OK. Log says:
Server: smtp.gmail.com
MAIL FROM:<aske.olsson@switch-gears.dk>
RCPT TO:<aske.olsson@switch-gears.dk>
From: aske.olsson@switch-gears.dk
To: aske.olsson@switch-gears.dk
Subject: [PATCH] Calculate pi with more digits
Date: Mon, 14 Apr 2014 09:00:11 +0200
Message-Id: <1397458811-13755-1-git-send-email-aske.olsson@switch-gears.
dk>
X-Mailer: git-send-email 1.9.1
```

An e-mail check will reveal an e-mail in the inbox, as shown in the following screenshot:

How it works...

As we saw in the previous examples, `git format-patch` creates the patch files in the Unix mbox format, so only a little extra effort is required to allow Git to send the patch as an e-mail. When sending e-mails with `git send-email`, make sure your **MUA (Mail User Agent)** does not break the lines in the patch files, replace tabs with spaces, and so on. You can test this easily by sending a patch to yourself and checking whether it can be applied cleanly to your repository.

There's more...

The `send-email` command can of course be used to send more than one patch at a time. If a directory is specified instead of a single patch file, all the patches in that directory will be sent. We don't even have to generate the patch files before sending them; we can just specify the same range of revisions we want to send as we would have specified for the `format-patch` command. Then, Git will create the patches on the fly and send them. When we send a series of patches this way, it is good practice to create a cover letter with a bit of explanation about the patch series that follows. The cover letter can be created by passing `--cover-letter` to the `send-email` command. We'll try sending patches for the commits on `develop` since it is branched from `master` (the same patches as in the second example) as follows:

```
$ git checkout develop
Switched to branch 'develop'
Your branch is up-to-date with 'origin/develop'.
$ git send-email --to aske.olsson@switch-gears.dk --from \
aske.olsson@switch-gears.dk --cover-letter --annotate origin/master
/tmp/path/for/patches/0000-cover-letter.patch
/tmp/path/for/patches/0001-Move-print-functionality-of-is_prime.patch
/tmp/path/for/patches/0002-Adds-Makefile-for-easy-building.patch
/tmp/path/for/patches/0003-Adds-functionality-to-prime-test-a-range-of-
numbers.patch
(mbox) Adding cc: Aske Olsson <aske.olsson@switch-gears.dk> from line
'From: Aske Olsson <aske.olsson@switch-gears.dk>'
OK. Log says:
Server: smtp.gmail.com
MAIL FROM:<aske.olsson@switch-gears.dk>
RCPT TO:<aske.olsson@switch-gears.dk>
From: aske.olsson@switch-gears.dk
To: aske.olsson@switch-gears.dk
```

```
Subject: [PATCH 0/3] Cover Letter describing the patch series

Date: Sat, 14 Jun 2014 23:35:14 +0200

Message-Id: <1397459884-13953-1-git-send-email-aske.olsson@switch-gears.
dk>

X-Mailer: git-send-email 1.9.1

...
```

We can check our e-mail inbox and see the four mails we sent: the cover letter and the 3 patches, as shown in the following screenshot:

[PATCH 3/3] Adds functionality to prime-test a range of numbers - From: Aske Olsson <aske.olsson@switch-gears.dk> --- math	11:35 pm
[PATCH 2/3] Adds Makefile for easy building - From: Aske Olsson <aske.olsson@switch-gears.dk> --- Makefile | 10 ++++++++++	11:35 pm
[PATCH 1/3] Move print functionality of is_prime - From: Aske Olsson <aske.olsson@switch-gears.dk> Moves print functionality	11:35 pm
[PATCH 0/3] Cover Letter describing the patch series - From: Aske Olsson <aske.olsson@switch-gears.dk> Best math I ever did	11:35 pm
[PATCH] Adds functionality to prime-test a range of numbers - From: Aske Olsson <aske.olsson@switch-gears.dk> --- math.c |	11:32 pm

Before sending the patches, the cover letter is filled out and by default has [PATCH 0/3] (if sending 3 patches) in the subject line. A cover letter with only the default template subject and body won't be sent as default. In the scripts that come with this chapter, the `git send-email` command invokes the `--force` and `--confirm=never` options. This was done for script automation to force Git to send the mails even though the cover letter has not been changed from the default. You can try to remove these options, put in the `--annotate` option, and run the scripts again. You should then be able to edit the cover letter and e-mails that contain the patches before sending.

Creating Git bundles

Another method to share the repository history between repositories is to use the `git bundle` command. A Git bundle is a series of commits that can work as a remote repository, but without having the full history of a repository included in the bundle.

Getting ready

We'll use a fresh clone of the `offline-sharing` repository as follows:

```
$ git clone https://github.com/dvaske/offline-sharing.git
$ cd offline-sharing
$ git checkout master
```

How to do it...

First, we'll create a root bundle, as shown in the following command, so that the history in the bundle forms a complete history and the initial commit is also included:

```
$ git bundle create myrepo.bundle master
Counting objects: 12, done.
Delta compression using up to 8 threads.
Compressing objects: 100% (11/11), done.
Writing objects: 100% (12/12), 1.88 KiB | 0 bytes/s, done.
Total 12 (delta 1), reused 0 (delta 0)
```

We can verify the bundle content with `git bundle verify`:

```
$ git bundle verify myrepo.bundle
The bundle contains this ref:
1e42a2dfa3a377d412efd27a77b973c75935c62a refs/heads/master
The bundle records a complete history.
myrepo.bundle is okay
```

To make it easy to remember which commit we included as the latest commit in the bundle, we create a tag that points to this commit; the commit is also pointed to by the `master` branch:

```
$ git tag bundleForOtherRepo master
```

We have created the root bundle that contains the initial commits of the repository history. We can now create a second bundle that contains the history from the tag we just created to the tip of the `develop` branch. Note that in the following command, we use the same name for the bundle file, `myrepo.bundle`, and this will overwrite the old bundle file:

```
$ git bundle create myrepo.bundle bundleForOtherRepo..develop
Counting objects: 12, done.
Delta compression using up to 8 threads.
Compressing objects: 100% (9/9), done.
Writing objects: 100% (9/9), 1.47 KiB | 0 bytes/s, done.
Total 9 (delta 2), reused 0 (delta 0)
```

It might seem strange to overwrite the bundle file just after creating it, but there is some sense in naming the bundle files by the same name. As you will also see in the next recipe, when using a bundle file, you add it to your repository as a remote, the URL being the file path of the bundle. The first time you do this is with the root bundle file and the URL. The file path of the bundle file will be stored as the URL of the remote repository. So, the next time you need to update the repository, you just overwrite the bundle file and perform `fetch` from the repository.

If we verify the bundle, we can see which commit needs to exist in the target repository before the bundle can be used:

```
$ git bundle verify myrepo.bundle
The bundle contains this ref:
c131c8bb2bf8254e46c013bfb33f4a61f9d4b40e refs/heads/develop
The bundle requires this ref:
ead7de45a504ee19cece26daf45d0184296f3fec
myrepo.bundle is okay
```

We can check the history and see that the `ead7de4` commit is where `develop` is branched off so it makes sense that this commit is the basis for the bundle we have just created:

```
$ gitk master develop
```

The previous command gives the following output:

How it works...

The `bundle` command creates a binary file with the history of the specified commit range included. When creating the bundle as a range of commits that does not include the initial commit in the repository (for example, `bundleForOtherRepo..develop`), it is important to make sure the range matches the history in the repository where the bundle is going to be used.

Using a Git bundle

In the last example, we saw how we could create bundles from the existing history that contains a specified range of history. Now, we'll learn to use these bundles either to create a new repository or to add the history to an existing one.

Getting ready

We'll use the same repository and methods as in the last example to create bundles, but we'll recreate them in this example to be able to use them one at a time. First, we'll prepare the repository and the first bundle, as shown in the following commands:

```
$ rm -rf offline-sharing
$ git clone https://github.com/dvaske/offline-sharing.git
Cloning into 'offline-sharing'...
remote: Counting objects: 32, done.
remote: Compressing objects: 100% (25/25), done.
remote: Total 32 (delta 7), reused 30 (delta 6)
Unpacking objects: 100% (32/32), done.
Checking connectivity... done.
$ cd offline-sharing
$ git checkout master
Branch master set up to track remote branch master from origin by
rebasing.
Switched to a new branch 'master'
$ git bundle create myrepo.bundle master
Counting objects: 12, done.
Delta compression using up to 8 threads.
Compressing objects: 100% (11/11), done.
Writing objects: 100% (12/12), 1.88 KiB | 0 bytes/s, done.
Total 12 (delta 1), reused 0 (delta 0)
$ git tag bundleForOtherRepo master
```

How to do it...

Now, let's create a new repository from the bundle file we just created. We can do that with the `git clone` command and by specifying the URL to the remote repository as the path to the bundle. We'll see how to do that in the following code snippet:

```
$ cd ..
$ git clone -b master offline-sharing/myrepo.bundle offline-other
Cloning into 'offline-other'...
Receiving objects: 100% (12/12), done.
Resolving deltas: 100% (1/1), done.
Checking connectivity... done.
```

The new repository is created in the `offline-other` folder. Let's check the history of that repository by using the following command:

```
$ cd offline-other
$ git log --oneline --decorate --all
1e42a2d (HEAD, origin/master, master) Calculate pi with more digits
ead7de4 Adds checker for prime number
337bfd0 Adds math, pi calculation
7229805 Offline sharing, patch, bundle and archive
```

The repository contains, as expected, all the history of the `master` branch in the original repository. We can now create a second bundle, the same as in the previous example, that contains history from the tag we created (`bundleForOtherRepo`) to the tip of the `develop` branch:

```
$ cd ..
$ cd offline-sharing
$ git bundle create myrepo.bundle bundleForOtherRepo..develop
Counting objects: 12, done.
Delta compression using up to 8 threads.
Compressing objects: 100% (9/9), done.
Writing objects: 100% (9/9), 1.47 KiB | 0 bytes/s, done.
Total 9 (delta 2), reused 0 (delta 0)
$ git bundle verify myrepo.bundle
The bundle contains this ref:
c131c8bb2bf8254e46c013bfb33f4a61f9d4b40e refs/heads/develop
The bundle requires this ref:
ead7de45a504ee19cece26daf45d0184296f3fec
myrepo.bundle is okay
```

As we also saw in the previous example, the bundle requires that the
`ead7de45a504ee19cece26daf45d0184296f3fec` commit exists in the repository we'll
use with the bundle. Let's check the repository we created from the first bundle for this
commit by using the following command:

```
$ cd ..
$ cd offline-other
$ git show -s ead7de45a504ee19cece26daf45d0184296f3fec
commit ead7de45a504ee19cece26daf45d0184296f3fec
Author: Aske Olsson <aske.olsson@switch-gears.dk>
Date:   Wed Apr 9 21:28:51 2014 +0200

    Adds checker for prime number
```

The commit exists. Now we can use the new bundle file as it has the same filename and
path as the first bundle we created. We can just use `git fetch` in the `offline-other`
repository as follows:

```
$ git fetch
Receiving objects: 100% (9/9), done.
Resolving deltas: 100% (2/2), done.
From /path/to/repo/offline-sharing/myrepo.bundle
 * [new branch]      develop      -> origin/develop
```

We can now checkout, `develop`, and verify that the history for the `develop` and `master`
branch matches the one in the original repository:

```
$ git checkout develop
Branch develop set up to track remote branch develop from origin by
rebasing.
Switched to a new branch 'develop'
$ gitk --all
```

The previous command gives the following output:

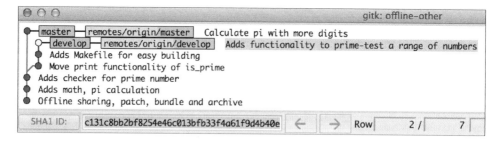

There's more...

The bundle is useful to update the history for repositories on machines where the normal transport mechanisms can't be used due to missing network connections between the machines, firewall rules, and so on. There are, of course, other methods than the Git bundle to transport the history to remote machines. A bare repository on a USB stick could also be used, or even plain patches can be applied to the repository. The advantage of the Git bundle is that you don't have to write the entire history to a bare repository each time you need to update a remote, but only the part of history that is missing.

Creating archives from a tree

Sometimes, it is useful to have a snapshot of the directory structure as specified by a particular commit, but without the corresponding history. This can, of course, be done by checking the particular commit followed by deleting/omitting the .git folder when creating an archive. But with Git, there is a better way to do this, which is built in so it is possible to create an archive from a particular commit or reference. When using Git to create the archive, you also make sure that the archive only contains the files tracked by Git and not any untracked files or folders you might have in your working directory.

Getting ready

We'll use the same offline-sharing repository as used in the previous examples in this chapter:

```
$ git clone https://github.com/dvaske/offline-sharing.git
Cloning into 'offline-sharing'...
remote: Counting objects: 32, done.
remote: Compressing objects: 100% (25/25), done.
remote: Total 32 (delta 7), reused 30 (delta 6)
Unpacking objects: 100% (32/32), done.
Checking connectivity... done.
$ cd offline-sharing
```

How to do it...

We'll start by creating an archive of the directory structure on the latest commit on the master branch. The offline-sharing repository is checked out on the develop branch by default, so we'll use the reference origin/master to specify the ref for the archive:

```
$ git archive --prefix=offline/ -o offline.zip origin/master
```

The `--prefix` option prepends the specified prefix to each file in the archive, effectively adding an `offline` directory as a root directory for the files in the repository, and the `-o` option tells Git to create the archive in the `offline.zip` file which of course, is compressed in the zip format. We can investigate the zip archive to check whether the files contain the following:

```
$ unzip -l offline.zip
Archive:  offline.zip
1e42a2dfa3a377d412efd27a77b973c75935c62a
   Length      Date    Time    Name
 --------      ----    ----    ----
        0   04-10-14 09:19   offline/
      162   04-10-14 09:19   offline/README.md
      485   04-10-14 09:19   offline/another_pi.c
      672   04-10-14 09:19   offline/math.c
 --------                    -------
     1319                    4 files
```

If we look in the Git repository in the `origin/master` commit, we can see that the files are the same; the `-l` option tells Git to specify each file's size as follows:

```
$ git ls-tree -l origin/master
100644 blob c79cad47938a25888a699142ab3cdf764dc99193 162      README.md
100644 blob 86df41b3a8bbfb588e57c7b27742cf312ab3a12a 485      another_pi.c
100644 blob d393b41eb14561e583f1b049db716e35cef326c3 672      math.c
```

There's more...

The archive command can also be used to create an archive for a subdirectory of the repository. We can use this on the `doc` branch of the repository to zip the content of the `Documentation` folder:

```
$ git archive --prefix=docs/ -o docs.zip origin/doc:Documentation
```

Again, we can list the contents of the zip file and the `Documentation` tree at `origin/doc` as follows:

```
$ unzip -l docs.zip
Archive:  docs.zip
   Length      Date    Time    Name
 --------      ----    ----    ----
```

```
    0   04-13-14 21:14   docs/
   99   04-13-14 21:14   docs/README.md
  152   04-13-14 21:14   docs/build.md
--------                 -------
  251                    3 files
$ git ls-tree -l origin/doc:Documentation
100644 blob b65b4fc78c0e39b3ff8ea549b7430654d413159f 99   README.md
100644 blob f91777f3e600db73c3ee7b05ea1b7d42efde8881 152  build.md
```

There are other format options besides the zip format for the archive, for example, tar, tar.gz, and so on. The format can be specified with the `--format=<format>` option or as a suffix to the output file name with the `-o` option. The following two commands will produce the same output file:

```
$ git archive --format=tar.gz HEAD > offline.tar.gz
$ git archive -o offline.tar.gz HEAD
```

The Git archive command behaves a bit differently if a commit/tag ID or a tree ID is passed as an identifier. If a commit or tag ID is given, the ID will be stored in a global extended pax header for the tar format and as a file comment for the zip format. If only the tree ID is given, no extra information will be stored. You can actually see this in the previous examples where the first ID was given a branch as a reference. As the branch points to a commit, the ID of this commit was written as a comment to the file and we can actually see it in the output of the archive listing:

```
$ unzip -l offline.zip
Archive:  offline.zip
1e42a2dfa3a377d412efd27a77b973c75935c62a
  Length      Date    Time    Name
--------      ----    ----    ----
        0   04-10-14 09:19   offline/
      162   04-10-14 09:19   offline/README.md
      485   04-10-14 09:19   offline/another_pi.c
      672   04-10-14 09:19   offline/math.c
--------                    -------
     1319                    4 files
```

In the second example, we also passed a branch as a reference, but furthermore we specified the `Documentation` folder as the subfolder we wanted to create an archive from. This corresponds to passing the ID of the tree to the archive command; hence, no extra information will be stored in the archive.

11

Git Plumbing and Attributes

In this chapter, we will cover the following topics:

- ▶ Displaying the repository information
- ▶ Displaying the tree information
- ▶ Displaying the file information
- ▶ Writing a blob object to the database
- ▶ Writing a tree object to the database
- ▶ Writing a commit object to the database
- ▶ Keyword expansion with attribute filters
- ▶ Metadata diff of binary files
- ▶ Storing binaries elsewhere
- ▶ Checking the attributes of a file
- ▶ Attributes for exporting an archive

Introduction

Git distinguishes between porcelain commands and plumbing commands. Porcelain commands are the ones you will normally use as add, commit, checkout, rebase, merge, and so on. Plumbing commands are all the helper functions that execute the low-level work. If you run `git help` in a terminal, you'll get a list of approximately 20 commands—the normal porcelain commands. You can also list all the Git commands with the `-a`, `--all` option; this results in about 150 commands.

In the previous chapters of the book, we already used some Git plumbing commands, but without much explanation. In this chapter, we'll take a closer look at some of the more useful commands to display information about files and trees in the repository. We'll also learn how we can create history without the use of the add and commit Git porcelain commands. Finally, we'll look into another area of Git: attributes. We'll see how we can replace keywords or strings in files on add or checkout, how we can diff binary files using textual metadata, and how we can transparently store binary files outside the repository, though added with git add. We'll see how to check the attributes of files in the repository and how we can use attributes while exporting our repository with git archive.

Displaying the repository information

It is fairly common to have some scripts that use repository information, for example, builds or release note generation. This small example will show some examples of the rev-parse command that can be very useful for scripting.

Getting ready

Clone the data-model repository from *Chapter 1, Navigating Git*:

```
$ git clone https://github.com/dvaske/data-model.git
$ cd data-model
```

How to do it...

First, let's figure out the ID of the commit at HEAD:

```
$ git rev-parse HEAD
34acc370b4d6ae53f051255680feaefaf7f7850d
```

This can, of course, also be obtained by git log -1 --format=%H, but with the rev-parse command, you don't need all the options. We can also get the current branch from the rev-parse command:

```
$ git rev-parse --symbolic-full-name HEAD
refs/heads/master
```

We can also just get the abbreviated name:

```
$ git rev-parse --symbolic-full-name --abbrev-ref HEAD
master
```

We can also get the ID of other refs:

```
$ git rev-parse origin/feature/2
82cd5662900a50063ff4bb790539fe4a6d470d56
```

There's more...

The `rev-parse` command can also be used to give some information about the repository, especially the directory structure relative to the current working directory.

We can find the top-level directory from a subdirectory using the following snippet:

```
$ cd a_sub_directory
$ pwd
/path/to/repo/data-model/a_sub_directory
$ git rev-parse --show-toplevel
/path/to/repo/data-model
```

We can also get the number of `cd ..` we need to get to the root directory using the following command:

```
$ git rev-parse --show-cdup
../
```

And we can get the relative path from the root directory to the current working directory using the following command:

```
$ git rev-parse --show-prefix
a_sub_directory/
```

Finally, we can get Git to show the path to the `.git` directory:

```
$ git rev-parse --git-dir
/path/to/repo/data-model/.git
```

We can check whether the current repository is a bare repository using the following command:

```
$ git rev-parse --is-bare-repository
false
```

Displaying the tree information

It can sometimes be useful to show or find information on certain trees and files in Git. Here, the `ls-tree` and `diff-tree` commands come in handy. Essentially, these are plumbing commands, and they can sometimes be very useful when scripting or browsing.

Getting ready

We'll use the same repository as the previous example:

```
$ git clone https://github.com/dvaske/data-model.git
```

We also need a `bare` repository for some examples; it will by default, with the `--bare` option, be cloned to `data-model.git`, so remember which repository you are currently working on:

```
$ git clone --bare https://github.com/dvaske/data-model.git
$ cd data-model
```

How to do it...

To show the content of the current tree in the Git context, we can use the `ls-tree` command. We'll pass `--abbrev` to the command to limit the SHA-1 ID to its abbreviated form. This is usually seven characters:

```
$ git ls-tree --abbrev HEAD
100644 blob f21dc28   README.md
040000 tree abc267d   a_sub_directory
100644 blob b50f80a   another-file.txt
100644 blob 92f046f   cat-me.txt
100644 blob bb2fe94   hello_world.c
```

The columns in the output are as follows:

▶ **Mode**: In mode, `tree` is `040000`, a regular file is `100644`, and an executable file is `100755`

▶ **Type**: This is the object type tree or blob

▶ **SHA-1 ID**: This is the object identifier, that is, the SHA-1 of the object

▶ **Path**: This is the file or the directory name

It's also possible to print the sizes of blobs in a column between the ID and the filename using the `-l, --long` option as follows:

```
$ git ls-tree --abbrev -l HEAD
100644 blob f21dc28     312   README.md
040000 tree abc267d       -   a_sub_directory
100644 blob b50f80a      26   another-file.txt
100644 blob 92f046f      78   cat-me.txt
100644 blob bb2fe94     101   hello_world.c
```

It is also possible to recursively list all the files with the `ls-tree` command:

```
$ git ls-tree --abbrev -r HEAD
100644 blob f21dc28   README.md
100644 blob 6dc3bfb   a_sub_directory/readme
100644 blob b50f80a   another-file.txt
100644 blob 92f046f   cat-me.txt
100644 blob bb2fe94   hello_world.c
```

By default, the recursive option for `ls-tree` doesn't print tree objects, only blobs. To get this information as well while recursively listing the contents, pass the `-t` option as shown in the following command:

```
$ git ls-tree --abbrev -r -t HEAD
100644 blob f21dc28   README.md
040000 tree abc267d   a_sub_directory
100644 blob 6dc3bfb   a_sub_directory/readme
100644 blob b50f80a   another-file.txt
100644 blob 92f046f   cat-me.txt
100644 blob bb2fe94   hello_world.c
```

The `ls-tree` command makes it easy to find a file in a repository, `normal` or `bare`. If for example, you need a single file in a bare repository and don't want to clone it, you can run `ls-tree` on the project and `grep` for the filename you need, or supply the path for the file if you know it. With the `SHA-1` ID of the file, you can display the contents of the file, with either `cat-file` or `show`, and redirect the output to a file. Let's see an example of this; we're looking for the `readme` file in the `a_sub_directory` directory. We'll use the `bare` repository, `data-model.git`, we created in the *Getting started* section of this recipe:

```
$ cd data-model.git
$ git ls-tree -r HEAD a_sub_directory/readme
```

```
100644 blob 6dc3bfbc6db8253b7789af1dee44caf8ec6ffb6e  a_sub_directory/
readme
$ git cat-file -p 6dc3bfbc6db8253b7789af1dee44caf8ec6ffb6e
A file in a sub directory
```

We can also perform diffs of trees and see the result in the same type of view as the `ls-tree` command. Switch back to the normal repository, and we'll investigate the `diff-tree` command:

```
$ cd ..
$ cd data-model
```

Start by performing a diff of the HEAD commit with the `feature/2` branch in the data-model repo:

```
$ git diff-tree --abbrev HEAD origin/feature/2
:000000 100644 0000000... 07ec769... A  HelloWorld.java
:100644 100644 f21dc28... c4e7c18... M  README.md
:040000 000000 abc267d... 0000000... D  a_sub_directory
:100644 000000 b50f80a... 0000000... D  another-file.txt
:100644 000000 92f046f... 0000000... D  cat-me.txt
:100644 000000 bb2fe94... 0000000... D  hello_world.c
:000000 100755 0000000... cf5edaa... A  hello_world.pl
:000000 100755 0000000... 2bec0da... A  hello_world.py
```

The output here differs from the output of `ls-tree`. There are two columns for mode and ID, one for each side of the diff. In this case, the branches are `master` and `origin/feature/2`. The second last column describes the state of the file in diff, A = added, D = deleted, M = modified, and R = renamed. If we just want to see the diff in files, without the mode and ID, we can specify the `--name-status` or the `--name-only` option:

```
$ git diff-tree --name-status HEAD origin/feature/2
A  HelloWorld.java
M  README.md
D  a_sub_directory
D  another-file.txt
D  cat-me.txt
D  hello_world.c
A  hello_world.pl
A  hello_world.py
```

```
$ git diff-tree --name-only HEAD origin/feature/2
HelloWorld.java
README.md
a_sub_directory
another-file.txt
cat-me.txt
hello_world.c
hello_world.pl
hello_world.py
```

The specific output format of the `ls-tree` and `diff-tree` commands makes them very useful for scripting in the cases where the file or tree information is needed.

Displaying the file information

While `git ls-tree` can give information about tree objects in the repository, it can't be used to display information about the index and working area. The `git ls-files` command can do this, and we will explore this next.

Getting ready

Again, we'll use the `data-model` repository from the previous example.

How to do it...

For specific file information, we can use the `ls-files` command to get information about files in the working tree and the staging area. By default, `git ls-files` will show the files in the staging area, as shown in the following command:

```
$ git ls-files
README.md
a_sub_directory/readme
another-file.txt
cat-me.txt
hello_world.c
```

Note this includes all files in the staging area (the tree state at the latest commit, HEAD) and files added since. The status command shows the changes between HEAD and staging area and the staging area and working tree. We can try to create a new file and see what happens using the following command:

```
$ echo 'Just testing...' > test.txt
$ git ls-files
README.md
a_sub_directory/readme
another-file.txt
cat-me.txt
hello_world.c
```

If we add the test.txt file to the staging area, we get the following output:

```
$ git add test.txt
$ git ls-files
README.md
a_sub_directory/readme
another-file.txt
cat-me.txt
hello_world.c
test.txt
```

By default, ls-files shows only the current content of the staging area, but let's see some other options. We can filter the output to only show modified files with the -m, --modified option, as shown in the following command:

```
$ echo "Another fine line" >> another-file.txt # Update tracked file
$ git ls-files -m
another-file.txt
```

The ls-files command can also show files not tracked by Git but that exist in the work area. If we can remove the test.txt file from the staging area, the file is untracked and we can see that it shows up in the ls-files output with the -o, --others option:

```
$ git reset HEAD test.txt
$ git ls-files --others
test.txt
```

The `ls-files` command can also be used to show which files are ignored by Git with the `-i`, `--ignored` option. So, we'll add an exclude pattern on `.txt` files to `.gitignore` and check the output of `ls-files` with the standard exclude patterns (`.gitignore` in each directory, `.git/info/exclude`, and `~/.gitignore`):

```
$ echo '*.txt' >> .gitignore
$ git ls-files -i --exclude-standard
another-file.txt
cat-me.txt
```

This showed two files already tracked by Git that match the exclude pattern, probably not really what we wanted. Let's try it again but this time on untracked files with the `-o`, `--others` option:

```
$ git ls-files -o -i --exclude-standard
test.txt
```

This matches, as expected, the untracked files in the working directory, which are ignored in the `.gitignore` file.

Let's clean up for the next example:

```
$ git reset --hard origin/master
$ git clean -xfd
```

There's more...

The `ls-files` command can also come in handy when performing merges that result in conflicts. With the `--unmerged` option, the output will only show files that have merge conflicts that haven't been fixed (added). To explore this, we can merge the `feature/2` branch into `master`:

```
$ git merge origin/feature/2
Auto-merging README.md
CONFLICT (content): Merge conflict in README.md
Recorded preimage for 'README.md'
Automatic merge failed; fix conflicts and then commit the result.
```

We can check `git status` to see which files have conflicts:

```
$ git status
On branch master
Your branch is up-to-date with 'origin/master'.
```

```
You have unmerged paths.
  (fix conflicts and run "git commit")


Changes to be committed:

  new file:    HelloWorld.java
  new file:    hello_world.pl
  new file:    hello_world.py


Unmerged paths:
  (use "git add <file>..." to mark resolution)


  both modified:        README.md
```

Let's see what the `--unmerged` option gives in the output:

```
$ git ls-files --unmerged
100644 23493f6b1edfafbee958d6dacaa863b1156850b7 1   README.md
100644 f21dc2804e888fee6014d7e5b1ceee533b222c15 2   README.md
100644 c4e7c18f3b31cd1d6fabeda4d7b009e3b4f12edb 3   README.md
```

As expected, the output only shows the conflicted file, README.md, but in three versions. The output is pretty similar to that of `ls-tree`, which we saw earlier; the first column and second column represent the file mode and the SHA-1 ID, respectively. The third column is different though and is the stage number of the object. Here stage 0 represents the current working tree (not shown previously), but when a conflict arises, the stage number is used to distinguish between the different versions. Stage 1 represents the file where the other differences derive from, that is, the `merge-base` for that file. Stage 2 and 3 represent the same files, but with different revisions, as they were in their respective branches before the merge. If we want, we can check the revisions of the file with the `cat-file` or the `show` command. The `--unmerged` option also makes it easy to get a list of unmerged files when filtered a bit:

```
$ git ls-files --unmerged | cut -f 2 | sort -u
README.md
```

The output is much cleaner than `git status`, which also shows possible content in the staging area and untracked files.

Writing a blob object to the database

In this example, we'll see how we can use plumbing commands to add blob objects to the database. This is, of course, used internally by the `git add` command; however, this can also be useful if you, for example, need to add the public part of your GPG key to the Git repository so that signed tags can be verified. You can then, after you've added the `key`, tag the blob ID so that the other committers can find it.

Getting ready

We'll create and use a new repository for this example and the next couple of examples. Let's create a new repository in the `myplumbing` folder:

```
$ git init myplumbing
Initialized empty Git repository in /path/to/myplumbing/.git/
$ cd myplumbing
$ git status
On branch master

Initial commit

nothing to commit (create/copy files and use "git add" to track)
```

How to do it...

Git uses the `hash-object` plumbing command to write objects to its database. We can use it to update the database with the content of files, or pass the content directly on `stdin`. First, let's just see what is currently stored in the database (`.git/objects`) using the following command:

```
$ find .git/objects
.git/objects
.git/objects/info
.git/objects/pack
$ find .git/objects -type f
```

The database is empty as expected when we have just created the repository. Now, we can write an object to the database:

```
echo 'This is the content of my file' | git hash-object -w --stdin
70bacd9f51c26d602f474bbdc9f60644aa449e97
```

We can also try to use the `hash-object` command on a regular file:

```
$ echo 'This content is good' > mytest.txt
$ git hash-object -w mytest.txt
926e8ffd3258ed6edd1e254438f02fd24e417acc
```

We can update the file and write the new content to the database:

```
$ echo 'This content is better' > mytest.txt
$ git hash-object -w mytest.txt
6b3da706d14c3820597ec7109f163bc144dcbb22
```

How it works...

The `hash-object` function will create a SHA-1 hash of the input given and if the `-w` switch is used, write it to the database. The command defaults to blob objects. We can investigate the contents of the database using the following command:

```
find .git/objects -type f
.git/objects/6b/3da706d14c3820597ec7109f163bc144dcbb22
.git/objects/70/bacd9f51c26d602f474bbdc9f60644aa449e97
.git/objects/92/6e8ffd3258ed6edd1e254438f02fd24e417acc
```

We can see that the database contains the three objects we just created. As you can see, Git stores each object as a file where the two first digits of the SHA-1 are used as a subdirectory and the remaining 38 objects as the filename. To check the object in Git's database, we can use the `cat-file` command, just like we did in *Chapter 1, Navigating Git*. To check the contents of an object, we use the `-p` (pretty print) switch:

```
git cat-file -p 70bacd9f51c26d602f474bbdc9f60644aa449e97
This is the content of my file
```

We can also use the `cat-file` command to check the type of an object:

```
git cat-file -t 926e8ffd3258ed6edd1e254438f02fd24e417acc
blob
```

There's more...

We can use the `cat-file` command to update files in our working directory, so to revert `mytest.txt` to the first version, use the following command:

```
$ git cat-file -p 926e8ffd3258ed6edd1e254438f02fd24e417acc > mytest.txt
$ cat mytest.txt
This content is good
```

Writing a tree object to the database

Now, we have manually created objects in the Git database, but as nothing point to these objects, we have to remember them by their SHA-1 identifier. Furthermore, only the content of the files is stored in the database, so we learn to create a tree object that will refer to the blobs created.

Getting ready

We'll use the same repository of the last examples with the objects we created in the database.

How to do it...

We'll start by adding the first version of `mytest.txt` as follows:

```
$ git update-index --add --cacheinfo 100644 \
926e8ffd3258ed6edd1e254438f02fd24e417acc mytest.txt
```

Now we can write the content of the staging area to the database:

```
$ git write-tree
4c4493f8029d491d280695e263e24772ab6962ce
```

We can update and write a tree for the second version of `mytest.txt` as follows:

```
$ git update-index --cacheinfo 100644 \
6b3da706d14c3820597ec7109f163bc144dcbb22 mytest.txt
$ git write-tree
2b9697438318f3a62a5e85d14a3b52d69b962907
```

Finally, we can use the object we created from `stdin` and we'll put it in a subdirectory, `sub`, with the name `other.txt`:

```
$ git update-index --add --cacheinfo 100644 \
70bacd9f51c26d602f474bbdc9f60644aa449e97 sub/other.txt
$ git write-tree
9387b1a7619c6d899d83fe8d1437864bcd88736c
```

How it works...

The `update-index` command updates the staging area with the files or content specified. The `--add` command tells Git to add a new file to the index, and the `--cacheinfo` switch is used to tell the command to use an existing object from the database. The `100644` command is used to create a normal file. Other types are `100755` (the executable file) and `040000` (a subdirectory), and so on. We could also have used a file directly for the `update-index` command, and then just provided the filename and omitted `--cacheinfo`, `filetype`, and `identifier`.

We can check the objects created with the `cat-file` command and verify their types, as shown in the following snippet:

```
$ git cat-file -p 4c4493f8029d491d280695e263e24772ab6962ce
100644 blob 926e8ffd3258ed6edd1e254438f02fd24e417acc  mytest.txt
$ git cat-file -t 4c4493f8029d491d280695e263e24772ab6962ce
tree
$ git cat-file -p 2b9697438318f3a62a5e85d14a3b52d69b962907
100644 blob 6b3da706d14c3820597ec7109f163bc144dcbb22  mytest.txt
$ git cat-file -t 2b9697438318f3a62a5e85d14a3b52d69b962907
tree
$ git cat-file -p 9387b1a7619c6d899d83fe8d1437864bcd88736c
100644 blob 6b3da706d14c3820597ec7109f163bc144dcbb22  mytest.txt
040000 tree 4cbaf806ece93e483f2515a7cc7326e194844797  sub
$ git cat-file -t 9387b1a7619c6d899d83fe8d1437864bcd88736c
tree
```

Writing a commit object to the database

Now that we have created both blob and tree objects, the next step in the data model is to create the actual commit object.

Getting ready

Again, we'll use the repository created in the previous examples with the different objects written to the database.

How to do it...

As we saw in *Chapter 1, Navigating Git*, a commit object consists of the author and committer information, a root tree object, a parent commit (except for the first commit), and a commit message. We have the root tree object generated in the last example, and Git will pick up the author and committer information from the configuration. So, all we need to do is create a commit message and write the commit object. We can do this for each of the tree objects we created previously:

```
$ echo 'Initial commit - Good contents' | git commit-tree 4c4493f8
40f4783c37e7cb9d07a4a71100acf4c474a376b0
$ echo 'Second commit - Better contents' | git commit-tree -p \
40f4783 2b969743
991ad244c6fdc84a983543cd8f2e89deca0eff29
$ echo 'Adds a subdirectory' | git commit-tree -p 991ad244 9387b1a7
e89518224a971df09a00242355b62278964d6811
```

How it works...

Three commit objects are created. The `-p` switch in the latter two commands tells Git to use the commit specified as a parent commit for the one to be created. Git will use the author and committer information it can find through the configuration options. We can verify that the commits were created with the `cat-file` command, just like we did with the blobs and trees:

```
$ git cat-file -p 40f4783c37e7cb9d07a4a71100acf4c474a376b0
tree 4c4493f8029d491d280695e263e24772ab6962ce
author Aske Olsson <aske.olsson@switch-gears.dk> 1398270736 +0200
committer Aske Olsson <aske.olsson@switch-gears.dk> 1398270736 +0200

Initial commit - Good contents
$ git cat-file -t 40f4783c37e7cb9d07a4a71100acf4c474a376b0
commit
$ git cat-file -p 991ad244c6fdc84a983543cd8f2e89deca0eff29
tree 2b9697438318f3a62a5e85d14a3b52d69b962907
parent 40f4783c37e7cb9d07a4a71100acf4c474a376b0
author Aske Olsson <aske.olsson@switch-gears.dk> 1398270736 +0200
```

```
committer Aske Olsson <aske.olsson@switch-gears.dk> 1398270736 +0200

Second commit - Better contents
$ git cat-file -t 991ad244c6fdc84a983543cd8f2e89deca0eff29
commit
$ git cat-file -p e89518224a971df09a00242355b62278964d6811
tree 5c23c103aeaa360342f36fe13a673fa473f665b8
parent 991ad244c6fdc84a983543cd8f2e89deca0eff29
author Aske Olsson <aske.olsson@switch-gears.dk> 1398270736 +0200
committer Aske Olsson <aske.olsson@switch-gears.dk> 1398270736 +0200

Adds a subdirectory
$ git cat-file -t e89518224a971df09a00242355b62278964d6811
commit
```

As we specified, parent commits for the last two commit objects we made we actually created Git's history in the repository, which we can view with the `log` command. We'll need to tell the log command to show the history from the latest commit, as we haven't updated any branches to point to it:

```
$ git log e89518224a971df09a00242355b62278964d6811
commit e89518224a971df09a00242355b62278964d6811
Author: Aske Olsson <aske.olsson@switch-gears.dk>
Date:   Wed Apr 23 18:32:16 2014 +0200

    Adds a subdirectory

commit 991ad244c6fdc84a983543cd8f2e89deca0eff29
Author: Aske Olsson <aske.olsson@switch-gears.dk>
Date:   Wed Apr 23 18:32:16 2014 +0200

    Second commit - Better contents

commit 40f4783c37e7cb9d07a4a71100acf4c474a376b0
Author: Aske Olsson <aske.olsson@switch-gears.dk>
Date:   Wed Apr 23 18:32:16 2014 +0200

    Initial commit - Good contents
```

Keyword expansion with attribute filters

With version control systems such as Subversion, RCS, and so on, it is possible to insert a number of keywords in a file, and these will then be expanded/collapsed on checkout/add. The same functionality can be achieved with Git, though a bit of setting up is required, as it is not built into Git's core. The attributes functionality of Git can be used to create filters for the keyword substitution. In the following example, we'll see how we can easily exchange the $Date$ keyword with a string such as $Date: Sun Apr 27 14:17:24 2014 +0200$ on checkout.

Getting ready

In this example, we'll use the repository located at `https://github.com/dvaske/attributes_example.git`. Take a look at the `keyword` branch using the following command:

```
$ git clone https://github.com/dvaske/attributes_example.git
$ cd attributes_example
$ git checkout keyword
```

How to do it...

First, let's create the filters needed to substitute the keyword on add and checkout. The filters are in Git called **clean** and **smudge**. The clean filter runs on add (check-in) to make sure whatever is added to Git is cleaned. The smudge filter runs on checkout and can expand all the keywords in the file, smudging the file. Configure the clean filter for Git (local to this repository):

```
git config filter.date-keyword.clean 'perl -pe \
"s/\\\$Date[^\\\$]*\\\$/\\\$Date\\\$/"'
```

Configure the clean filter for Git (local to this repository):

```
git config filter.date-keyword.smudge 'perl -pe \
"s/\\\$Date[^\\\$]*\\\$/\\\$Date: 'git log -1 --all --format=%ad \
-- $1'\\\$/"'
```

With the filters configured, we now need to tell Git which files to run those filters on. We will write this information in the `.gitattributes` file in the root of the repository. We'll add any `c` or `java` file affected by these filters:

```
echo "*.c filter=date-keyword" > .gitattributes
echo "*.java filter=date-keyword" >> .gitattributes
```

Now the content of any `c` or `java` file will be passed through the filters on add and checkout.

How it works...

We can check how it works by investigating the files in the workspace. Let's take a closer look at `HelloWorld.java`:

```
$ cat HelloWorld.java
/* $Date$ */


public class HelloWorld {
    public static void main(String[] args) {
        System.out.println("Hello, world!");
    }
}
```

Nothing has happened to the file, though the filters are in place, as the filters only run on `add`/`checkout`. We can delete the file and check it out again to see the filters in action:

```
$ rm HelloWorld.java
$ git checkout HelloWorld.java
$ cat HelloWorld.java
/* $Date: Sun Apr 27 14:32:49 2014 +0200$ */


public class HelloWorld {
    public static void main(String[] args) {
        System.out.println("Hello, world!");
    }
}
```

If we change `Helloworld` in the two files and add them to the staging area, we can verify that the java file has been cleaned when added using the following command:

```
$ git add HelloWorld.java
$ git diff -U5 --cached
index 233cc49..3905c75 100644
--- a/HelloWorld.java
+++ b/HelloWorld.java
@@ -1,7 +1,7 @@
 /* $Date$ */
```

```
public class HelloWorld {
    public static void main(String[] args) {
-       System.out.println("Hello, world!");
+       System.out.println("Hello again, world!");
    }
}
```

As expected, we can see that when added, the file has been cleaned of the date information.

There's more...

We can continue to change `hello world` in the c file, also to: `hello again world` and add the c file and the `.gitattributes` file to the staging area. Then, we can create a commit as follows:

```
$ git add hello_world.c
$ git add .gitattributes
$ git commit -m 'Add date-keyword filter for *.c and *.java files'
[keyword 28a0009] Add date-keyword filter for *.c and *.java files
 3 files changed, 4 insertions(+), 2 deletions(-)
 create mode 100644 .gitattributes
```

How does the `hello_world.c` file look in the working tree now? As we only changed a line in the file and added it afterwards, the file was never put through a checkout cycle, so we shouldn't expect the `$Date$` string to be expanded.

```
$ cat hello_world.c
/* $Date$ */

#include <stdio.h>

int main(void)
{
    printf("hello, world\n");
    return 0;
}
```

If we switch branch to `master` and then back to `keyword`, the files will have been through the checkout filter:

```
$ git checkout master
Switched to branch 'master'
Your branch is up-to-date with 'origin/master'.
$ git checkout keyword
Switched to branch 'keyword'
Your branch is ahead of 'origin/keyword' by 1 commit.
  (use "git push" to publish your local commits)
$ head -1 hello_world.c
/* $Date: Thu May 1 22:59:21 2014 +0200$ */
$ head -1 HelloWorld.java
/* $Date: Thu May 1 22:59:21 2014 +0200$ */
```

From the previous output, you can now see the `Date` keyword expanded to a timestamp.

Metadata diff of binary files

Binary files can be hard to diff, depending on the type of the file. Often, the only option is to load two instances of the program to show the files and check the differences visually. In this recipe we'll see how we can use EXIF metadata to diff images in the repository.

Getting ready

We'll use the same repository as we did in the last example and either re-clone it or checkout the `exif` branch:

```
$ git clone https://github.com/dvaske/attributes_example.git
$ cd attributes_example
$ git checkout exif
```

How to do it...

In order to use the EXIF data while diffing binary files, we need to set up a filter to tell Git what to do when a file of `*.jpg` is to be diffed. EXIF data is metadata embedded in images and is often used by digital cameras to record timestamps, the size of an image, and so on.

We'll write the following line to `.gitattributes`:

```
*.jpg diff=exif-diff
```

This only tells Git that JPG files should use the `exif-diff` filter; we still need to set it up. To extract the EXIF metadata, there are different programs such as `exiftool`, `jhead`, and so on. In this example, we're using `exiftool`, so make sure you have it installed and available on your PATH. To set up the `exiftool` diff filter, we create the following Git `config`:

```
git config diff.exif-diff.textconv exiftool
```

From now on, every time `jpg` is to be diffed, you'll just see a comparison of `exifdata`. To see the actual change in the image, you still have to show the two images and visually compare them.

How it works...

Now that the filter is set up, we can try to check the output of it. The last two commits in the repository on the `exif` branch contain pictures that have had their size changed; let's see how they looks with the `exif-diff` filter. First, check `log` for the last two commits:

```
$ git log --name-status -2
commit 0beb82c65d8cd667e1ffe61860a42a106be3c1a6
Author: Aske Olsson <aske.olsson@switch-gears.dk>
Date:   Sat May 3 14:55:50 2014 +0200

    Changes sizes of images

M       europe_needles.jpg
M       hello_world.jpg
M       pic_credits.txt

commit a25d0defc70b9a1842463c1e9894a88dfb897cd8
Author: Aske Olsson <aske.olsson@switch-gears.dk>
Date:   Sun Apr 27 16:02:51 2014 +0200

    Adds pictures to repository

    Picture credits found in pic_credits.txt

M       README.md
A       europe_needles.jpg
A       hello_world.jpg
A       pic_credits.txt
```

Let's look at the diff between the two commits (the output you get might not match the following output 1:1 and depends on the `exiftool` version, OS, and so on. The following output is generated with `exiftool 9.61` on OS X 10.9.3):

```
$ git diff HEAD^..HEAD
diff --git a/europe_needles.jpg b/europe_needles.jpg
index 7291028..44e98e3 100644
--- a/europe_needles.jpg
+++ b/europe_needles.jpg
@@ -1,11 +1,11 @@
 ExifTool Version Number         : 9.54
-File Name                       : Gnepvw_europe_needles.jpg
-Directory                       : /var/folders/3r/6f35b4t11rv2nmbrx5x32t
4w0000gn/T
-File Size                       : 813 kB
+File Name                       : europe_needles.jpg
+Directory                       : .
+File Size                       : 328 kB
 File Modification Date/Time     : 2014:05:03 22:08:05+02:00
-File Access Date/Time           : 2014:05:03 22:08:05+02:00
+File Access Date/Time           : 2014:05:03 22:08:06+02:00
 File Inode Change Date/Time     : 2014:05:03 22:08:05+02:00
-File Permissions                : rw-------
+File Permissions                : rw-r--r--
 File Type                       : JPEG
 MIME Type                       : image/jpeg
 JFIF Version                    : 1.01
@@ -79,8 +79,8 @@ Sub Sec Time Original           : 00
 Sub Sec Time Digitized          : 00
 Flashpix Version                : 0100
 Color Space                     : sRGB
-Exif Image Width                : 1620
-Exif Image Height               : 1080
+Exif Image Width                : 1024
+Exif Image Height               : 683
 ...
```

There's more...

It is also possible to set up diffing of binary files for other types than images. As long as some useful data from the file type can be extracted, it's possible to create a custom diff filter for that file type. With the `catdoc` program, Microsoft Word files can, for example, be translated from the `.doc` format to plain text, which makes it easy to diff the text content in two files, but not their formatting.

Storing binaries elsewhere

Though binaries can't easily be diffed, there is nothing to prevent them from being stored in a Git repository, and there are no issues in doing so. However, if one or more binaries in a repository are updated frequently, it can cause the repository to grow quickly in size, making clones and updates slow as a lot of data needs to be transferred. By using the clean and smudge filters for the binaries, it is possible to move them to another location while adding them to Git and fetch them from that location while checking out the specific version of the file.

Getting ready

We'll use the same repositories as in the previous example, but the `no_binaries` branch:

```
$ git clone https://github.com/dvaske/attributes_example.git
$ cd attributes_example
$ git checkout no_binaries
```

How to do it...

First, we need to set up the clean and smudge filters for the files. Then, we are only going to run the filter on `jpg` files in this example, so let's set it up and create the configuration:

```
$ echo '*.jpg filter=binstore' > .gitattributes
```

Create configuration

```
$ git config filter.binstore.clean "./put-bin"
$ git config filter.binstore.smudge "./get-bin"
```

We also need to create the actual filter logic, the `put-bin` and `get-bin` files, to handle the binary files on `add` and `checkout`. For this example, the implementation is very simple (no error handling, retries, and so on, is implemented).

The clean filter (to store the binaries somewhere else) is a simple bash script that stores the binary it receives on `stdin` to a directory called `binstore` at the same level as the Git repository. Git's own `hash-object` function is used to create a SHA-1 ID for the binary. The ID is used as filename for the binary in the `binstore` folder and is written as the output of the filer, as the content of the binary file when stored in Git.

The filter logic for the `put-bin` file can be created as follows:

```
#!/bin/bash
dest=$(git rev-parse --show-toplevel)/../binstore
mkdir -p $dest
tmpfile=$(git rev-parse --show-toplevel)/tmp
cat > $tmpfile
sha=$(git hash-object --no-filters $tmpfile)
mv $tmpfile $dest/$sha
echo $sha
```

The smudge filter fetches the binaries from the `binstore` storage on the same level as the Git repository. The content of the file stored in Git, the SHA-1 ID, is received on `stdin` and is used to output the content of the file by that name in the `binstore` folder:

The filter logic for the `get-bin` file can be created as follows:

```
#!/bin/bash
source=$(git rev-parse --show-toplevel)/../binstore
tmpfile=$(git rev-parse --show-toplevel)/tmp
cat > $tmpfile
sha=$(cat $tmpfile)
cat $source/$sha
rm $tmpfile
```

Create these two files and put them in the root of the Git repository.

Now, we are ready to add a JPG image to our repository and see that it is stored somewhere else. We can use the `hello_world.jpg` image from the `exif` branch. We can create the file here by querying Git. Find the SHA-1 ID of `hello_world.jpg` at the tip of the `exif` branch:

```
$ git ls-tree --abbrev exif | grep hello_world
100644 blob 5aac2df  hello_world.jpg
```

Create the file by reading the content from Git to a new file:

```
$ git cat-file -p 5aac2df > hello_world.jpg
```

Now, we can add the file, commit the file, and check the external storage, which is placed relative to the current repository at `../binstore`, and see the commit content:

Add `hello_world.jpg` using the following command:

```
$ git add hello_world.jpg
```

Commit the contents of the staging area, the `hello_world.jpg` file:

```
$ git commit -m 'Added binary'
[no_binaries 19e359d] Added binary
 1 file changed, 1 insertion(+)
 create mode 100644 hello_world.jpg
```

Check the content of the `binstore` directory:

```
$ ls -l ../binstore
total 536
-rw-r--r--  1 aske   staff   272509 May  3 23:24
5aac2dff477eebb3da3cb68843b5cc39745d6447
```

Finally, we can check the content of the commit with the `-p` option to display the patch of the commit:

```
$ git log -1 -p
commit 19e359d774c880fa4f37a3f41a874ba632a31c65
Author: Aske Olsson <aske@schantz.com>
Date:   Sat May 3 22:56:46 2014 +0200

    Added binary

diff --git a/hello_world.jpg b/hello_world.jpg
new file mode 100644
index 0000000..19680e5
--- /dev/null
+++ b/hello_world.jpg
@@ -0,0 +1 @@
+5aac2dff477eebb3da3cb68843b5cc39745d6447
```

`hello_world.jpg` is a new file with `5aac2dff477eebb3da3cb68843b5cc39745d6447` content that is similar, as expected, to the name of the file in the `binstore` directory.

How it works...

Each time a `.jpg` file is added, the `put-bin` filter runs. The filter receives the content of the added file on `stdin`, and it has to output the result of the filter (what needs to go into Git) on `stdout`. The following is the filter explained in detail:

```
dest=$(git rev-parse --show-toplevel)/../binstore
mkdir -p "$dest"
```

The previous two lines create the `binstore` directory if it doesn't exist. The directory is created at the same level as the Git repository:

```
tmpfile=$(git rev-parse --show-toplevel)/tmp
cat > $tmpfile
```

The `tmpfile` variable is just a path to a temporary file, `tmp`, located in the root of the repository. The input received on `stdin` is written to this file.

```
sha=$(git hash-object --no-filters $tmpfile)
mv $tmpfile $dest/$sha
```

The previous lines use Git's hashing function to generate a hash for the content of the binary file. We'll use the hash of the file as an identifier when we move it to the `binstore` folder where the SHA-1 will function as the filename of the binary.

```
echo $sha
```

Finally, we output the hash of the file to `stdout`, and this will be what Git stores as the content of the file in the Git database.

The smudge filter to populate our working tree with the correct file contents also receives the content (from Git) on `stdin`. The filter needs to find the file in the `binstore` directory and write the content to `stdout` for Git to pick it up as the smudged file.

```
src=$(git rev-parse --show-toplevel)/../binstore
tmpfile=$(git rev-parse --show-toplevel)/tmp
cat > $tmpfile
```

The first three lines define the path to the `binstore` folder and a temporary file to which the content received from Git is written.

```
sha=$(cat $tmpfile)
```

The hash of the file we need to get is extracted in the previous line.

```
cat $src/$sha
rm $tmpfile
```

Finally, we can output the real contents of the file to `stdout` and remove the temporary file.

There's more...

The previous filters work transparently with Git on `add` and `checkout`, but there are some caveats when using Git attributes, and especially filters like the previous ones, which are:

- Even though the `.gitattributes` file can be added and distributed inside the repository, the configuration of the filters can't. The configuration of the filters was the first step of the example, which tells Git which command to run for clean and smudge when the filter is used:

  ```
  $ git config filter.binstore.clean "./put-bin"
  $ git config filter.binstore.smudge "./get-bin"
  ```

- The configuration can be either local to the repository, global for the user, or global for the system, as we saw in *Chapter 2, Configuration*. However, none of these configurations can be distributed along with the repository, so it is very important that the configuration is set up just after clone. Otherwise, the risk of adding a file without running through the filters is too high.

- In this example, the storage location of the binaries is just a local directory next to the repository. A better way of doing this could be to copy the binaries to a central storage location either with, for example, `scp` or through a web service. This, however, limits the user from adding and committing when offline as the binaries cannot be stored in the central repository. A solution to this could be a `pre-push` hook that could transfer all the binaries to a binary database before a push happens.

- Finally, there is no error handling in the previous two filters. If one of them fails, it might make sense to abort the `add` or `checkout` and warn the user.

See also

There are also other ways of handling binaries in a repository that might be worth considering. These usually introduce extra commands to add and retrieve the binaries. The following are the examples of binary handlers:

- git-annex handler at `https://git-annex.branchable.com/`
- git-media handler at `https://github.com/schacon/git-media`
- git-bin handler at `https://github.com/Mighty-M/git-bin`

Checking the attributes of a file

Checking the `.gitattributes` file (or other places where attributes can be defined) to see whether a specific file is affected by an attribute can be quite cumbersome, especially if there are many entries in these files. Git has a built-in method that can be used to tell whether a file has any attribute associated.

Getting ready

We'll use the `attributes_example` repository:

```
$ git clone https://github.com/dvaske/attributes_example.git
$ cd attributes_example
```

How to do it...

We'll start by setting up all the attributes we had in the last example:

```
$ echo '*.jpg filter=binstore' > .gitattributes
$ echo '*.jpg diff=exif-diff' >> .gitattributes
$ echo "*.c filter=date-keyword" >> .gitattributes
$ echo "*.java filter=date-keyword" >> .gitattributes
```

Now we are ready to check different files. We'll start on the `keyword` branch and check the two code files using the following command:

```
$ git checkout keyword
Branch keyword set up to track remote branch keyword from origin by
rebasing.
Switched to a new branch 'keyword'
$ git check-attr -a hello_world.c HelloWorld.java
hello_world.c: filter: date-keyword
HelloWorld.java: filter: date-keyword
```

Let's also see the jpg files on the `exif` branch:

```
$ git checkout exif
Branch exif set up to track remote branch exif from origin by rebasing.
Switched to a new branch 'exif'
$ git check-attr -a hello_world.jpg europe_needles.jpg
hello_world.jpg: diff: exif-diff
```

```
hello_world.jpg: filter: binstore
europe_needles.jpg: diff: exif-diff
europe_needles.jpg: filter: binstore
```

It is also possible to check a file against a specific attribute with the following command:

```
$ git check-attr diff hello_world.jpg
hello_world.jpg: diff: exif-diff
$ git check-attr filter hello_world.jpg
hello_world.jpg: filter: binstore
```

If we check a file without attributes or against an attribute not associated with the file, the output is empty:

```
$ git check-attr -a README.md
$
```

Attributes to export an archive

While exporting a snapshot of a Git repository with the archive command (refer to *Chapter 10, Patching and Offline Sharing*), it is possible to change the way the archive is made.

Getting ready

We'll use the `attributes_example` repository:

```
$ git clone https://github.com/dvaske/attributes_example.git
$ cd attributes_example
```

How to do it...

First, we'll set up the attributes needed in `.gitattributes` and commit the file on the `exif` branch:

```
$ git checkout exif
Branch exif set up to track remote branch exif from origin by rebasing.
Switched to a new branch 'exif'
$ echo 'europe_needles.jpg export-ignore' >> .gitattributes
$ git add .gitattributes
$ git commit -m 'Add .gitattributes'
[exif 783b7f7] Add .gitattributes
 1 file changed, 1 insertion(+)
 create mode 100644 .gitattributes
```

Now, we can create an archive from the tip of the `exif` branch, and the `europe_needles.jpg` file shouldn't be included, as shown in the following snippet:

```
$ git archive -o attr.zip exif
$ unzip -l attr.zip
Archive:  attr.zip
783b7f73110e23f56675f0014ab3f1d0aba21d7f
  Length      Date    Time     Name
 --------     ----    ----     ----
       33  05-06-14 21:33   .gitattributes
      325  05-06-14 21:33   README.md
   272509  05-06-14 21:33   hello_world.jpg
      543  05-06-14 21:33   pic_credits.txt
 --------                  -------
   273410                  4 files
```

The `europe_needles.jpg` file isn't there! This is very useful when creating archives of the source code without including test, the proprietary code, IPR, and so on.

There's more...

We can also do keyword substitution while exporting an archive. We need to use the `export-subst` attribute. We can set it up on the `README.md` file in the following way:

```
$ echo "README.md export-subst" >> .gitattributes
$ echo "Last commit: \$Format:%H$" >> README.md
$ echo "Last commit date: \$Format:%cd$" >> README.md
$ git add .gitattributes README.md
$ git commit -m "Commit info for git archive"
[exif 8c01a48] Commit info for git archive
 2 files changed, 3 insertions(+)
```

Create the archive. Check the content of the `README.md` file in the archive and the last commit on the `exif` branch using the following command:

```
$ git archive -o attr.zip exif
$ unzip -p attr.zip README.md
```

```
Git Attributes
==============


A few examples on using git attributes.


Pictures used found on flickr.com,
check pic_credits.txt for details.


Pictures only changes in size, not altered
only exif data is used as examples of diff'ing
pictures based on exif data.


Example repository for the book: Git Version Control Cookbook
Last commit: d3dda23601a3cc16295bdd7f4f9812544ea69d53
Last commit date: Tue May 6 21:52:25 2014 +0200 $
$
$ git log -1 --format=Commit: %H%nDate: %cd
Commit: d3dda23601a3cc16295bdd7f4f9812544ea69d53
Date: Tue May 6 21:52:25 2014 +0200
```

Recording the commit ID in the archive is very useful. This is especially the case if you are using the archive for testing so you know which revision or ID of the repository you are using, and you can report issues against this revision or ID.

12
Tips and Tricks

In this chapter, we will cover the following topics:

- ▶ Using git stash
- ▶ Saving and applying stashes
- ▶ Debugging with git bisect
- ▶ Using the blame command
- ▶ Color UI in the prompt
- ▶ Autocompletion
- ▶ Bash prompt with status information
- ▶ More aliases
- ▶ Interactive add
- ▶ Interactive add with Git GUI
- ▶ Ignoring files
- ▶ Showing and cleaning ignored files

Introduction

In this chapter, you will find some tips and tricks that can be useful in everyday Git work. From stashing away your changes when you get interrupted with an important task over efficient bug hunting with `bisect` and `blame`, to color and status information in your prompt. We'll also look at aliases, how you can create clean commits by selecting which lines should be included in the commit, and finally how you can ignore files.

Using git stash

In this example, we explore the `git stash` command and learn how we can use it to quickly put away uncommitted changes and retrieve these again. This can be useful when being interrupted with an urgent task and you are not yet ready to commit the work you currently have in your working directory. With the `git stash` command, you save the state of your current working directory with/without a staging area and restore a clean state of the working tree.

Getting ready

In this example, we'll use the `cookbook-tips-tricks` repository. We'll use the `master` branch, but before we are ready to try the `stash` command, we need to create some changes in the working directory and the staging area:

```
$ git clone https://github.com/dvaske/cookbook-tips-tricks.git
$ cd cookbook-tips-tricks
$ git checkout master
```

Make some changes to `foo` and add them to the staging area:

```
$ echo "Just another unfinished line" >> foo
$ git add foo
```

Make some changes to `bar` and create a new file:

```
$ echo "Another line" >> bar
$ echo "Some content" > new_file
$ git status
On branch master
Your branch is up-to-date with 'origin/master'.

Changes to be committed:
  (use "git reset HEAD <file>..." to unstage)

    modified:   foo


Changes not staged for commit:
  (use "git add <file>..." to update what will be committed)
```

```
(use "git checkout -- <file>..." to discard changes in working
directory)
```

 modified: bar

Untracked files:
 (use "git add <file>..." to include in what will be committed)

 new_file

We can see that we have one file added to the staging area, foo, one modified file, bar, and an untracked file in the work area as well, new_file.

How to do it...

With the preceding state of our repository, we can stash away the changes so that we can work on something else. The basic command will put away changes from the staging area and changes made to the tracked files; it leaves untracked files in the working directory:

```
$ git stash
Saved working directory and index state WIP on master: d611f06 Update foo
and bar
HEAD is now at d611f06 Update foo and bar
$ git status
On branch master
Your branch is up-to-date with 'origin/master'.

Untracked files:
  (use "git add <file>..." to include in what will be committed)

    new_file

nothing added to commit but untracked files present (use "git add" to
track)
```

Now we can work on something else and create and commit this. We'll change the first line of the foo file and create a commit with this change:

```
$ sed -i '' 's/First line/This is the very first line of the foo file/'
foo
```

```
$ git add foo
$ git commit -m "Update foo"
[master fa4b595] Update foo
 1 file changed, 1 insertion(+), 1 deletion(-)
```

We can see the current work we have stashed away with the `git stash list` command:

```
$ git stash list
stash@{0}: WIP on master: 09156a4 Update foo and bar
```

To get back the changes we stashed away, we can pop them from the `stash` stack:

```
$ git status
On branch master
Your branch is ahead of 'origin/master' by 1 commit.
  (use "git push" to publish your local commits)


Untracked files:
  (use "git add <file>..." to include in what will be committed)


    new_file
nothing added to commit but untracked files present (use "git add" to
track)
$ git stash pop
Auto-merging foo
On branch master
Your branch is ahead of 'origin/master' by 1 commit.
  (use "git push" to publish your local commits)


Changes not staged for commit:
  (use "git add <file>..." to update what will be committed)
  (use "git checkout -- <file>..." to discard changes in working
directory)


    modified:   bar
    modified:   foo
```

```
Untracked files:
  (use "git add <file>..." to include in what will be committed)


    new_file
no changes added to commit (use "git add" and/or "git commit -a")
Dropped refs/stash@{0} (91b68271c8968fed01032ad02322292f35be8830)
```

Now, the stashed changes are available again in the working repository and the stash entry is deleted. Note that the changes are applied only to the working directory, though one of the files was staged when we created the stash.

How it works...

We have created two commits: one for the index and one for the work area. In Gitk, we can see the commits that stash creates to put the changes away:

We can also see the state of the branches after we created the commit, as shown in the following screenshot:

Git actually creates two commits under the `refs/stash` namespace. One commit contains the content of the staging area. This commit is called `index on master`. The other commit is the work in progress in the working directory, `WIP on master`. When Git puts away the changes by creating commits, it can use its normal resolution methods to apply the stashed changes back to the working directory. This means that if a conflict arises when applying the stash, it needs to be solved in the usual way.

There's more...

In the preceding example, we saw only the very basic usage of the `stash` command, putting away changes to untracked files and changes added to the staging area. It is also possible to include untracked files in the `stash` command. This can be done with the `--include-untracked` option. We can add `foo` to the staging area; firstly, to have the same state as when we created the stash earlier and then to create a stash that includes untracked files:

```
$ git add foo
$ git stash --include-untracked
Saved working directory and index state WIP on master: 691808e Update foo
HEAD is now at 691808e Update foo
$ git status
On branch master
Your branch is ahead of 'origin/master' by 1 commit.
  (use "git push" to publish your local commits)

nothing to commit, working directory clean
```

Now, we can see that `new_file` has disappeared from the working directory. It is included in the stash and we can check this with Gitk. It will show up as another commit of untracked files:

```
$ gitk master stash
```

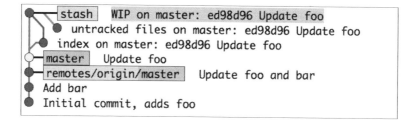

We can also make sure that the changes we added to the staging area are added back to the staging area after we apply the stash, so we end up with the exact same state as before we stashed away our changes:

```
$ git stash pop --index
On branch master
```

```
Your branch is ahead of 'origin/master' by 1 commit.
  (use "git push" to publish your local commits)


Changes to be committed:
  (use "git reset HEAD <file>..." to unstage)


    modified:    foo


Changes not staged for commit:
  (use "git add <file>..." to update what will be committed)
  (use "git checkout -- <file>..." to discard changes in working
directory)


    modified:    bar


Untracked files:
  (use "git add <file>..." to include in what will be committed)


    new_file


Dropped refs/stash@{0} (ff331af57406948619b0671dab8b4f39da1e8fa2)
```

It is also possible to only put away the changes in the working directory, keeping the changes in the staging area. We can do this either for only the tracked files or by stashing away untracked files (`--include-untracked`) as follows:

```
$ git stash --keep-index --include-untracked
Saved working directory and index state WIP on master: 00dd8f8 Update foo
HEAD is now at 00dd8f8 Update foo
$ git status
On branch master
Your branch is ahead of 'origin/master' by 1 commit.
  (use "git push" to publish your local commits)


Changes to be committed:
  (use "git reset HEAD <file>..." to unstage)


    modified:    foo
```

Saving and applying stashes

When stashing away work, we can easily have more than one state of work stashed away at a time. However, the default names for the stashed away changes aren't always helpful. In this example, we'll see how we can save stashes and name them so that it is easy to identify them again when listing the content of the stash. We'll also learn how to apply a stash without deleting it from the stash list.

Getting ready

We'll use the same repository as in the previous example, continuing from the state we left it in:

```
$ cd cookbook-tips-tricks
$ git status
On branch master
Your branch is ahead of 'origin/master' by 1 commit.
  (use "git push" to publish your local commits)

Changes to be committed:
  (use "git reset HEAD <file>..." to unstage)

    modified:   foo


$ git stash list
stash@{0}: WIP on master: 4447f69 Update foo
```

How to do it...

To save the current state to a stash with a description we can remember a later point in time, use the following command:

```
$ git stash save 'Updates to foo'
Saved working directory and index state On master: Updates to foo
HEAD is now at 4447f69 Update foo
```

Our stash list now looks like the following:

```
$ git stash list
stash@{0}: On master: Updates to foo
stash@{1}: WIP on master: 2302181 Update foo
```

We can change `bar` and create a new stash:

```
echo "Another change" >> bar
$ git stash save 'Made another change to bar'
Saved working directory and index state On master: Made another change to
bar
HEAD is now at 2302181 Update foo
$ git stash list
stash@{0}: On master: Made another change to bar
stash@{1}: On master: Updates to foo
stash@{2}: WIP on master: 2302181 Update foo
```

We can apply the stashes back to the working tree (and staging area with the `--index` option) without deleting them from the stash list:

```
$ git stash apply 'stash@{1}'
On branch master
Your branch is ahead of 'origin/master' by 1 commit.
  (use "git push" to publish your local commits)


Changes not staged for commit:
  (use "git add <file>..." to update what will be committed)
  (use "git checkout -- <file>..." to discard changes in working
directory)


    modified:   foo


no changes added to commit (use "git add" and/or "git commit -a")
$ git stash apply --quiet 'stash@{0}'
$ git stash list
stash@{0}: On master: Made another change to bar
stash@{1}: On master: Updates to foo
stash@{2}: WIP on master: 2302181 Update foo
```

The stashes are still in the stash list, and they can be applied in any order and referred to with the `stash@{stash-no}` syntax. The `--quiet` option suppresses the status output after the stashes have been applied.

There's more...

For the stashes applied with `git stash apply`, the stash needs to be deleted with `git stash drop`:

```
$ git stash drop 'stash@{1}'
Dropped stash@{1} (e634b347d04c13fc0a0d155a3c5893a1d3841fcd)
$ git stash list
stash@{0}: On master: Made another change to bar
stash@{1}: WIP on master: 1676cdb Update foo
```

Keeping the stashes in the stash list by using `stash apply` and explicitly deleting them with `git stash drop` has some advantage over just using `stash pop`. When using the `pop` option, the stashes in the list are automatically deleted if they can be successfully applied, but if it fails and triggers the conflict resolution mode, the stash applied is not dropped from the list and continues to exist on the stash stack. This might later lead to accidentally using the wrong stash because it was thought to be gone. By consistently using `git stash apply` and `git stash drop`, you can avoid this scenario when done.

> The `git stash` command can also be used to apply debug information to an application. Let's pretend you have been bug hunting and have added a lot of debug statements to your code in order to track down the bug. Instead of deleting all those debug statements, you can save them as a Git stash:
>
> `git stash save "Debug info stash"`
>
> Then, if you later need debug statements, you can just apply the stash and you are ready to debug.

Debugging with git bisect

The `git bisect` command is an excellent tool to find which commit caused a bug in the repository. The tool is particularly useful if you are looking at a long list of commits that may contain the bug. The `bisect` command performs a binary search through the commit history to find the commit that introduced the bug as fast as possible. The binary search method, or bisection method as it is also called, is a search method where an algorithm finds the position of a key in a sorted array. In each step of the algorithm, the key is compared to the middle value of the array and if they match, the position is returned. Otherwise, the algorithm repeats its search in the subarray to the right or left of the middle value, depending on whether the middle value was greater or lower than the key. In the Git context, the list of commits in the history makes up for the array of values to be tested, and the key can be a test if the code can be complied successfully at the given commit. The binary search algorithm has a performance of $O(\log n)$.

Getting ready

We'll use the same repository as seen in the last example, but from a clean state:

```
$ git clone https://github.com/dvaske/cookbook-tips-tricks.git
$ cd cookbook-tips-tricks
$ git checkout bug_hunting
```

The `bug_hunting` branch contains 23 commits since it branched off from the `master` branch. We know that the tip of the `bug_hunting` branch contains the bug and it was introduced in some commit since it branched off from `master`. The bug was introduced in the following commit:

```
commit 83c22a39955ec10ac1a2a5e7e69fe7ca354129af
Author: HAL 9000 <aske.olsson@switch-gears.dk>
Date:    Tue May 13 09:53:45 2014 +0200

    Bugs...
```

The bug is easily seen in the `map.txt` file in the middle of Australia. The following snippet of the file shows the bug:

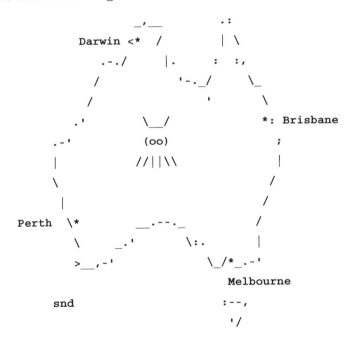

Now, all we need is some way to reproduce/detect the bug so we can test the different commits. This could, for example, simply be to compile the code, run tests, and so on. For this example, we'll create a test script to check for bugs in the code (a simple `grep` for `oo` should do it in this example; see for yourself if you can find the bug in the `map.txt` file):

```
echo "! grep -q oo map.txt" > ../test.sh
chmod +x ../test.sh
```

It is best to create this test script outside the repository to prevent interactions between checkouts, compilation, and so on in the repository.

How to do it...

To begin bisecting, we simply type:

```
$ git bisect start
```

To mark the current commit (`HEAD -> bug_hunting`) as bad, we type:

```
$ git bisect bad
```

We also want to mark the last known good commit (`master`) as good:

```
$ git bisect good master
Bisecting: 11 revisions left to test after this (roughly 4 steps)
[9d2cd13d4574429dd0dcfeeb90c47a2d43a9b6ef] Build map part 11
```

This time, something happened. Git did a checkout of `9d2cd13`, which it wants us to test and mark as good or bad. It also tells us there are 11 revisions to test after this and it can be done in approximately four steps. This is how the bisecting algorithm works; every time a commit is marked as good or bad, Git will checkout the middle one between the just marked one and the current one of opposite value. In this way, Git quickly narrows down the number of commits to check. It also knows that there are approximately four steps, and this makes sense since with 11 revisions left, the maximum number of tries is $log_2(11) = 3.46$ before the faulty commit is found.

We can test with the `test.sh` script we created previously, and based on the return value, mark the commit as good or bad:

```
$ ../test.sh; test $? -eq 0 && git bisect good || git bisect bad
# git bisect good
Bisecting: 5 revisions left to test after this (roughly 3 steps)
[c45cb51752a4fe41f52d40e0b2873350b95a9d7c] Build map part 16
```

The test marks the commit as good and Git checks out the next commit to be marked, until we hit the commit that introduces the bug:

```
$ ../test.sh; test $? -eq 0 && git bisect good || git bisect bad
# git bisect bad
Bisecting: 2 revisions left to test after this (roughly 2 steps)
[83c22a39955ec10ac1a2a5e7e69fe7ca354129af] Bugs...
$ ../test.sh; test $? -eq 0 && git bisect good || git bisect bad
# git bisect bad
Bisecting: 0 revisions left to test after this (roughly 1 step)
[670ab8c42a6cb1c730c7c4aa0cc26e5cc31c9254] Build map part 13
$ ../test.sh; test $? -eq 0 && git bisect good || git bisect bad
# git bisect good
83c22a39955ec10ac1a2a5e7e69fe7ca354129afis the first bad commit
commit 83c22a39955ec10ac1a2a5e7e69fe7ca354129af
Author: HAL 9000 <aske.olsson@switch-gears.dk>
Date:   Tue May 13 09:53:45 2014 +0200

    Bugs...


:100644 100644 8a13f6bd858aefb70ea0a7d8f601701339c28bb0
1afeaaa370a2e4656551a6d44053ee0ce5c3a237 M  map.txt
```

After four steps, Git has identified the `1981eac1` commit as the first bad commit. We can end the bisect session and take a closer look at the commit:

```
$ git bisect reset
Previous HEAD position was 670ab8c... Build map part 13
Switched to branch 'bug_hunting'
Your branch is up-to-date with 'origin/bug_hunting'.
$ git show 83c22a39955ec10ac1a2a5e7e69fe7ca354129af
commit 83c22a39955ec10ac1a2a5e7e69fe7ca354129af
Author: HAL 9000 <aske.olsson@switch-gears.dk>
Date:   Tue May 13 09:53:45 2014 +0200

    Bugs...


diff --git a/map.txt b/map.txt
```

```
index 8a13f6b..1afeaaa 100644

--- a/map.txt

+++ b/map.txt

@@ -34,6 +34,6 @@ Australia:
                 .-./        |.        :   :,
             /                 '-._/        \_
           /                      '            \
    -                   .'                         *: Brisbane
    -              .-'                              ;
    -              |                                |
    +                   .'         \__/             *: Brisbane
    +              .-'           (oo)                ;
    +              |            //||\\              |
```

Clearly, there is a bug introduced with this commit.

The following annotated screenshot shows the steps taken by the bisect session:

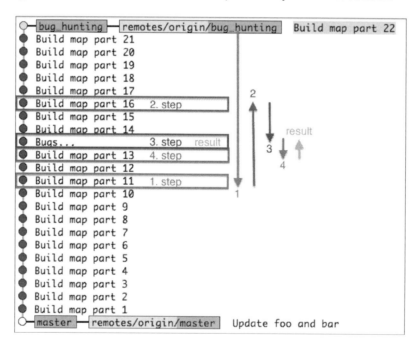

Note that the bisection algorithm actually hits the faulty commit in the third step, but it needs to look further to make sure that the commit isn't just a child commit of the faulty commit, and in fact is the commit that introduced the bug.

There's more...

Instead of running all the bisecting steps manually, it is possible to do it automatically by passing Git a script, makefile, or test to run on each commit. The script needs to exit with a **zero-status** to mark a commit as good and a **non-zero** status to mark it as bad. We can use the `test.sh` script we created at the beginning of this chapter for this. First, we set up the good and bad commits:

```
$ git bisect start HEAD master
Bisecting: 11 revisions left to test after this (roughly 4 steps)
[9d2cd13d4574429dd0dcfeeb90c47a2d43a9b6ef] Build map part 11
```

Then we tell Git to run the test.sh script and automatically mark the commits:

```
$ git bisect run ../test.sh
running ../test.sh
Bisecting: 5 revisions left to test after this (roughly 3 steps)
[c45cb51752a4fe41f52d40e0b2873350b95a9d7c] Build map part 16
running ../test.sh
Bisecting: 2 revisions left to test after this (roughly 2 steps)
[83c22a39955ec10ac1a2a5e7e69fe7ca354129af] Bugs...
running ../test.sh
Bisecting: 0 revisions left to test after this (roughly 1 step)
[670ab8c42a6cb1c730c7c4aa0cc26e5cc31c9254] Build map part 13
running ../test.sh
83c22a39955ec10ac1a2a5e7e69fe7ca354129afis the first bad commit
commit 83c22a39955ec10ac1a2a5e7e69fe7ca354129af
Author: HAL 9000 <aske.olsson@switch-gears.dk>
Date:    Tue May 13 09:53:45 2014 +0200

    Bugs...

:100644 100644 8a13f6bd858aefb70ea0a7d8f601701339c28bb0
1afeaaa370a2e4656551a6d44053ee0ce5c3a237 M  map.txt
bisect run success
```

Git found the same commit and we can now exit the bisecting session:

```
$ git bisect reset
Previous HEAD position was 670ab8c... Build map part 13
Switched to branch 'bug_hunting'
```

Using the blame command

The `bisect` command is good when you don't know where in your code there is a bug, but you can test for it and thereby find the commit that introduced it. If you already know where in the code the bug is but want to find the commit that introduced it, you can use `git blame`. The `blame` command will annotate every line in the file with the latest commit that touched that line, making it easy to find the commit ID and then the full context of the commit.

Getting ready

We'll use the same repository and branch as in the bisect example:

```
$ git clone https://github.com/dvaske/cookbook-tips-tricks.git
$ cd cookbook-tips-tricks
$ git checkout bug_hunting
```

How to do it...

We know that the bug is in `map.txt` on lines 37-39. To annotate each line in the file with the commit ID and author, we'll run `git blame` on the file. We can further limit the search to specific lines with the `-L <from>,<to>` option:

```
$ git blame --date short -L 30,47 map.txt
828f25e7 (Dave Bowman       2014-05-13 30) Australia:
9d2cd13d (Frank Poole       2014-05-13 31)
9d2cd13d (Frank Poole       2014-05-13 32)
9d2cd13d (Frank Poole       2014-05-13 33)                           _'__         .:
fec0bd22 (Frank Poole       2014-05-13 34)            Darwin <* /        | \
fec0bd22 (Frank Poole       2014-05-13 35)                .-./     |.      : :,
fec0bd22 (Frank Poole       2014-05-13 36)               /          '-._/    \_
83c22a39 (HAL 9000          2014-05-13 37)             /     .'       \_/          \
83c22a39 (HAL 9000          2014-05-13 38)            .-'       (oo)         *: Brisbane
83c22a39 (HAL 9000          2014-05-13 39)            |        //||\\         ;
4c543b9c (Dave Bowman       2014-05-13 40)            \                      /
4c543b9c (Dave Bowman       2014-05-13 41)            |                     /
4c543b9c (Dave Bowman       2014-05-13 42)     Perth  \*      __.--._      /
7ad3da42 (Heywood R. Floyd  2014-05-13 43)            \   _.'      \:.   /
7ad3da42 (Heywood R. Floyd  2014-05-13 44)             >__,-'         \_/*_.-'
7ad3da42 (Heywood R. Floyd  2014-05-13 45)                              Melbourne
c45cb517 (Heywood R. Floyd  2014-05-13 46)       snd                  :--,
c45cb517 (Heywood R. Floyd  2014-05-13 47)                            '/
```

From the output, it can be clearly seen that the commit with the ID `83c22a39` by `HAL 9000` introduced the bug.

There's more...

The `blame` command can be used even if the file has been refactored and the code has been moved around. With the `-M` option, the `blame` command can detect lines that have been moved around in the file and with the `-C` option, Git can detect lines that were moved or copied from other files in the same commit. If the `-C` option is used three times `-CCC`, the `blame` command will find lines that were copied from other files in any commit.

Color UI in the prompt

By default, Git has no colors when displaying information in the terminal. However, displaying colors is a feature of Git that is only a configuration away.

Getting ready

We'll use the `cookbook-tips-tricks` repository:

```
$ git clone https://github.com/dvaske/cookbook-tips-tricks.git
$ cd cookbook-tips-tricks
```

How to do it...

First, we'll edit and add `foo`:

```
$ echo "And another line" >> foo
$ git add foo
```

Change `foo` some more, but don't add it to the staging area:

```
$ echo "Last line ...so far" >> foo
```

Create a new file called `test`:

```
$ touch test
```

The `git status` command will show us the status:

```
$ git status
On branch master
Your branch is up-to-date with 'origin/master'.

Changes to be committed:
```

```
        (use "git reset HEAD <file>..." to unstage)


        modified:    foo


Changes not staged for commit:
    (use "git add <file>..." to update what will be committed)
    (use "git checkout -- <file>..." to discard changes in working
directory)


        modified:    foo


Untracked files:
    (use "git add <file>..." to include in what will be committed)


        test
```

We can set the `color.ui` configuration to `auto` or `true` to get color in the UI when required:

```
$ git config --global color.ui true
$ git status
On branch master
Your branch is up-to-date with 'origin/master'.

Changes to be committed:
    (use "git reset HEAD <file>..." to unstage)


        modified:    foo


Changes not staged for commit:
    (use "git add <file>..." to update what will be committed)
    (use "git checkout -- <file>..." to discard changes in working
directory)


        modified:    foo


Untracked files:
    (use "git add <file>..." to include in what will be committed)


        test
```

There's more...

The `color.ui` configuration works with a long range of Git commands `diff`, `log`, and `branch` included. The following is an example of `git log` when setting `color.ui` to `true`:

```
$ git log --oneline --decorate --graph
* c111003 (HEAD, origin/master, origin/HEAD, master) Update foo and bar
* 270e97b Add bar
* 43fd490 Initial commit, adds foo
```

Autocompletion

Git comes with built-in support for auto-completion of Git commands for the `bash` and `zsh` shells. So if you use either of these shells, you can enable the auto-completion feature and let the `<tab>` option help you complete commands.

Getting ready

Generally, the auto-completion feature is distributed with the Git installation, but it is not enabled by default on all platforms or distributions. To enable it, we need to find the `git-completion.bash` file distributed/installed with the Git installation.

Linux

For Linux users, the location may vary depending on the distribution. Generally, the file can be found at `/etc/bash_completion.d/git-completion.bash`.

Mac

For mac users, it can generally be found at `/Library/Developer/CommandLineTools/usr/share/git-core/git-completion.bash`.

If you installed Git from Homebrew, it can be found at `/usr/local/Cellar/git/1.9.1/etc/bash_completion.d/git-completion.bash`.

Windows

With the **Msysgit** installation on Windows, the completion functions are already enabled in the Git bash shell it bundles.

If you can't find the file on your system, you can grab the latest version from `https://github.com/git/git/blob/master/contrib/completion/git-completion.bash` and install it in your home directory.

How to do it...

To enable the completion feature, you need to run the `source` command on the completion file, which you can do by adding the following lines to your `.bashrc` or `.zshrc` file depending on your shell and the location of the Git completion file:

```
if [ -f /etc/bash_completion.d/git-completion.bash ]; then
    source /etc/bash_completion.d/git-completion.bash
fi
```

How it works...

Now, you are ready to try. Switch to an existing Git repository, for example, `cookbook-tips-tricks` and type the following commands:

```
$ git che<tab><tab>
```

```
checkout        cherry        cherry-pick
```

You can add another `c<tab>` and the command will autocomplete to `checkout`. But the autocompletion feature doesn't only complete commands, it can also help you complete branch names, and so on, so you can continue with the checkout and write `mas<tab>`. You should be able to see the output completed to the `master` branch unless you are in a repository where there are several branches starting with `mas`.

There's more...

The completion feature also works with options; this is quite useful if you can't remember the exact option but you may remember some of it, for example, when using `git branch`:

```
git branch --<tab><tab>
```

```
--abbrev=              --merged              --set-upstream-to=
--color                --no-abbrev           --track
--contains             --no-color            --unset-upstream
--edit-description     --no-merged           --verbose
--list                 --no-track
```

Bash prompt with status information

Another cool feature Git provides is to have the prompt display status information if the current working directory is a Git repository.

Getting ready

For the status information prompt to work, we also need to source another file, `git-prompt.sh`, which is usually distributed with the Git installation and located in the same directory as the completion file.

How to do it...

In your `.bashrc` or `.zshrc` file, add the following code snippet, again depending on your shell and the location of the `git-prompt.sh` file:

```
if [ -f /etc/bash_completion.d/git-prompt.sh ]; then
    source /etc/bash_completion.d/git-prompt.sh
fi
```

How it works...

To make use of the command prompt, we must change the `PS1` variable; usually this is set to something like this:

```
PS1='\u@\h:\w\$ '
```

The preceding command shows the current user, an @ sign, the host name, the current working directory relative to the user's home directory, and finally a $ character:

```
aske@yggdrasil:~/cookbook-tips-tricks$
```

We can change this to add a branch name after the working directory by adding `$(__git_ps1 " (%s)")` to the `PS1` variable:

```
PS1='\u@\h:\w$(__git_ps1 " (%s)") \$ '
```

Our prompt will now look like this:

```
aske@yggdrasil:~/cookbook-tips-tricks (master) $
```

It is also possible to show the state of the working tree, index, and so on. We can enable these features by exporting some environment variables in the `.bashrc` file that `git-prompt.sh` picks up.

The following environment variables can be set:

Variable	Value	Effect
GIT_PS1_SHOWDIRTYSTATE	Nonempty	Shows * for unstaged changes and + for staged changes
GIT_PS1_SHOWSTASHSTATE	Nonempty	Shows a $ character if something is stashed
GIT_PS1_SHOWUNTRACKEDFILES	Nonempty	Shows a % character if there are untracked files in the repository
GIT_PS1_SHOWUPSTREAM	auto verbose name Legacy Git svn	Auto shows whether you are behind (<) or ahead (>) of the upstream branch. A <> value is displayed if the branch is diverged and = if it is up to date. Verbose shows the number of commits behind/ahead. Name shows the upstream name. Legacy is verbose for old versions of Git. Git compares HEAD to @{upstream}. SVN compares HEAD to svn upstream.
GIT_PS1_DESCRIBE_STYLE	contains branch describe default	Displays extra information when on a detached HEAD. Contains is relative to a newer annotated tag (v1.6.3.2~35). Branch is relative to a newer tag or branch (master~4). Describe is relative to an older annotated tag (v1.6.3.1-13-gdd42c2f). Default is the tag that matches exactly.

Let's try to set some of the variables in the ~/.bashrc file:

```
export GIT_PS1_SHOWUPSTREAM=auto
export GIT_PS1_SHOWDIRTYSTATE=enabled
PS1='\u@\h:\w$(__git_ps1 " (%s)") \$ '
```

Let us see the ~/.bashrc file in action:

```
aske@yggdrasil:~ $ cd cookbook-tips-tricks/
aske@yggdrasil:~/cookbook-tips-tricks (master=) $ touch test
aske@yggdrasil:~/cookbook-tips-tricks (master=) $ git add test
aske@yggdrasil:~/cookbook-tips-tricks (master +=) $ echo "Testing" > test
```

```
aske@yggdrasil:~/cookbook-tips-tricks (master *+=) $ git commit -m "test"
[master 5c66d65] test
 1 file changed, 0 insertions(+), 0 deletions(-)
 create mode 100644 test
aske@yggdrasil:~/cookbook-tips-tricks (master *>) $
```

When using the `__git_ps1` option, Git will also display information when merging, rebasing, bisecting, and so on. This is very useful and a lot of `git status` commands suddenly become unnecessary as you have the information right there in the prompt.

There's more...

What is a terminal these days without some colors? The `git-prompt.sh` script also supports this. All we need to do is set the `GIT_PS1_SHOWCOLORHINTS` variable to a nonempty value and instead of using `PS1`, we need to use `PROMPT_COMMAND`. Let's change `~/.bashrc`:

```
export GIT_PS1_SHOWUPSTREAM=auto
export GIT_PS1_SHOWDIRTYSTATE=enabled
export GIT_PS1_SHOWCOLORHINTS=enabled
PROMPT_COMMAND='__git_ps1 "\u@\h:\w" "\\\$ "'
```

If we redo the same scenario as the previous one, we get the following:

```
aske@yggdrasil:~$ cd cookbook-tips-tricks/
aske@yggdrasil:~/cookbook-tips-tricks (master=)$ touch test
aske@yggdrasil:~/cookbook-tips-tricks (master=)$ git add test
aske@yggdrasil:~/cookbook-tips-tricks (master +=)$ echo "Testing" > test
aske@yggdrasil:~/cookbook-tips-tricks (master *+=)$ git commit -m "test"
[master 0cb59ca] test
 1 file changed, 0 insertions(+), 0 deletions(-)
 create mode 100644 test
aske@yggdrasil:~/cookbook-tips-tricks (master *>)$
```

See also

If you are using `zsh` or just want to try something new with many features, such as completion, Git support, and so on, you should take a look at the `oh-my-zsh` framework available for `zsh` at `https://github.com/robbyrussell/oh-my-zsh`.

More aliases

In *Chapter 2, Configuration*, we saw how we can create aliases and a few examples of them. In this example, we will see some more examples of the useful aliases.

Getting ready

Clone the `cookbook-tips-tricks` repository and checkout the `aliases` branch:

```
$ git clone https://github.com/dvaske/cookbook-tips-tricks.git
$ cd cookbook-tips-tricks
$ git checkout aliases
```

How to do it...

Here, we'll see some examples of aliases with a short description of each of them and an example of how to use them. The aliases are just made for the local repository; use `--global` to make them available for all the repositories.

▶ Show the current branch only:

```
$ git config alias.b "rev-parse --abbrev-ref HEAD"
$ git b
aliases
```

▶ Show a compact graph history view with colors:

```
git config alias.graph "log --graph --pretty=format:'%Cred%h%Creset
-%C(yellow)%d%Creset %s %Cgreen(%cr) %C(bold blue)<%an>%Creset'
--abbrev-commit --date=relative"

git graph origin/conflict aliases
```

```
* a43eaa9 - (HEAD, origin/aliases, aliases) Better spaceship design (58 minutes ago) <Aske Olsson>
| * 918fe4e - (origin/conflict) Spaceship upgrade (60 minutes ago) <Aske Olsson>
|/
* 8fc1819 - Adds spaceship (64 minutes ago) <Aske Olsson>
* c73d2ef - Adds directory structure (67 minutes ago) <Aske Olsson>
* c111003 - (origin/master, origin/HEAD, master) Update foo and bar (3 days ago) <Aske Olsson>
* 270e97b - Add bar (3 days ago) <Aske Olsson>
* 43fd490 - Initial commit, adds foo (3 days ago) <Aske Olsson>
```

▶ When resolving a conflicted merge, get a list of the conflicted/unmerged files:

```
$ git config alias.unmerged '!git ls-files --unmerged | cut -f2 |
sort -u'
```

We can see the previous command in action by merging the `origin/conflict` branch:

```
$ git merge origin/conflict
Auto-merging spaceship.txt
CONFLICT (content): Merge conflict in spaceship.txt
Automatic merge failed; fix conflicts and then commit the result.
```

Check the output of `git status` first:

```
$ git status
On branch aliases
Your branch is up-to-date with 'origin/aliases'.

You have unmerged paths.
  (fix conflicts and run "git commit")

Unmerged paths:
  (use "git add <file>..." to mark resolution)

    both modified:      spaceship.txt

no changes added to commit (use "git add" and/or "git commit -a")
```

Let's see what the unmerged alias does:

```
$ git unmerged
spaceship.txt
```

Abort the merge:

```
$ git merge --abort
```

▶ Shorthand status as follows:

```
git config alias.st "status"
git st
On branch aliases
Your branch is up-to-date with 'origin/aliases'.

nothing to commit, working directory clean
```

▶ A shorter status with branch and file information:

```
$ git config alias.s 'status -sb'
```

Modify `foo` and create an untracked file `test`:

```
$ touch test
$ echo testing >> foo
```

Try the `s` alias:

```
$ git s
## aliases...origin/aliases
 M foo
?? test
```

▶ Show the latest commit with some stats:

```
$ git config alias.l1 "log -1 --shortstat"
$ git l1
commit a43eaa9b461e811eeb0f18cce67e4465888da333
Author: Aske Olsson <aske.olsson@switch-gears.dk>
Date:   Wed May 14 22:46:32 2014 +0200


    Better spaceship design


 1 file changed, 9 insertions(+), 9 deletions(-)
```

▶ This gives the same view as the previous but for the five latest commits (the output is not shown):

```
$ git config alias.l5 "log -5 --decorate --shortstat"
```

▶ A commit listing with statistics on the changed files in colors can be displayed using the following command:

```
$ git config alias.ll "log --pretty=format:\"%C(yellow)%h%Cres
et %s %Cgreen(%cr) %C(bold blue)<%an>%Creset %Cred%d%Creset\"
--numstat"
$ git ll -5
```

```
a43eaa9 Better spaceship design (58 minutes ago) <Aske Olsson>  (HEAD, origin/aliases, aliases)
9       9       spaceship.txt

8fc1819 Adds spaceship (64 minutes ago) <Aske Olsson>
43      0       spaceship.txt

c73d2ef Adds directory structure (67 minutes ago) <Aske Olsson>
1       0       sub/directory/example/readme.txt

c111003 Update foo and bar (3 days ago) <Aske Olsson>  (origin/master, origin/HEAD, master)
7       0       bar
7       0       foo

270e97b Add bar (3 days ago) <Aske Olsson>
1       0       bar
```

▸ Show the upstream/tracking branch:

```
$ git config alias.upstream "rev-parse --symbolic-full-name
--abbrev-ref=strict HEAD@{u}"

$ git upstream

origin/aliases
```

▸ Show details of ID/SHA-1 (commit, tag, tree, blob):

```
git config alias.details "cat-file -p"
git details HEAD
tree bdfdaacbb29934b239db814e599342159c4390dd
parent 8fc1819f157f2c3c25eb973c2a2a412ef3d5517a
author Aske Olsson <aske.olsson@switch-gears.dk> 1400100392 +0200
committer Aske Olsson <aske.olsson@switch-gears.dk> 1400100392
+0200

Better spaceship design
```

▸ Show the numbers of "cd-ups", ../, needed to go to the repository root using following command:

```
$ git config alias.root "rev-parse --show-cdup"
$ cd sub/directory/example
$ pwd
/path/to/cookbook-tips-tricks/sub/directory/example
$ git root
../../../
$ cd $(git root)
$ pwd
/path/to/cookbook-tips-tricks
```

▶ The path of the repository on the filesystem:

```
$ git config alias.path "rev-parse --show-toplevel"
$ git path
/path/to/cookbook-tips-tricks
```

▶ Abandon whatever changes we have in the index, working tree, and possibly also the commits and reset the working tree to a known state (commit ID). Do not touch the untracked files. We need a ref as an argument for the state of the repository to be restored, for example, HEAD:

```
$ git config alias.abandon "reset --hard"
$ echo "new stuff" >> foo
$ git add foo
$ echo "other stuff" >> bar
$ git s
## aliases...origin/aliases
 M bar
M  foo
?? test
$ git abandon HEAD
$ git s
## aliases...origin/aliases
?? test
```

Interactive add

The exposed staging area Git offers sometimes lead to confusion, especially when adding a file, changing it a bit, and then adding the file again to be able to commit the changes made after the first add. While this can seem a bit cumbersome to add the file after every little change, it is also a big advantage that you can stage and unstage changes. With the `git add` command, it is even possible to only add some changes to a file in the staging area. This comes in handy especially if you make a lot of changes to a file and for example, want to split the changes into bug fixes, refactoring, and features. This example will show how you can easily do this.

Getting ready

Again, we'll use the `cookbook-tips-tricks` repository. Clone it and check out the interactive branch:

```
$ git clone https://github.com/dvaske/cookbook-tips-tricks.git
$ cd cookbook-tips-tricks
$ git checkout interactive
```

How to do it...

First, we need some changes to be added; we do this by a resetting the latest commit:

```
$ git reset 'HEAD^'
Unstaged changes after reset:
M       liberty.txt
```

Now, we have a modified file. To start the interactive add, we can either run the `git add -i` or `git add -p` filename. The `-i` option brings up an interface where all the different files in the modified state can be added interactively one at a time. The `add -p/--patch` option is simpler and just gives you the option to add parts of the file specified:

```
$ git add -p liberty.txt
diff --git a/liberty.txt b/liberty.txt
index 8350a2c..9638930 100644
--- a/liberty.txt
+++ b/liberty.txt
@@ -8,6 +8,13 @@
            WW)  ,WWW)
            7W) ,WWWW'
            'WWWWWW'
+           9---W)
+       ,,--WPL=YXW===
+     (P),CY:,I/X'F9P
+     WUT===---/===9)
+     -HP+----Y(C=9W)
```

```
+          '9Y3'-'-OWPT-
+          'WWLUIECW
           (:7L7C7'
           ,P--=YWFL
           Y-=:9)UW:L
Stage this hunk [y,n,q,a,d,/,j,J,g,e,?]?
```

Git asks you whether you want to stage the previous change (the hunk), but also shows quite a lot of options, which can expand a little bit if you type `?`:

```
Stage this hunk [y,n,q,a,d,/,j,J,g,e,?]?
y - stage this hunk
n - do not stage this hunk
q - quit; do not stage this hunk nor any of the remaining ones
a - stage this hunk and all later hunks in the file
d - do not stage this hunk nor any of the later hunks in the file
g - select a hunk to go to
/ - search for a hunk matching the given regex
j - leave this hunk undecided, see next undecided hunk
J - leave this hunk undecided, see next hunk
k - leave this hunk undecided, see previous undecided hunk
K - leave this hunk undecided, see previous hunk
s - split the current hunk into smaller hunks
e - manually edit the current hunk
? - print help
```

There are a lot of options, but with the help text, they are quite self-explanatory. Let's add the current hunk, `y`, and look at the next one:

```
Stage this hunk [y,n,q,a,d,/,j,J,g,e,?]? y
@@ -17,16 +24,17 @@
          7WYW))PW W
           7WH)),WC)
            7L--/XY)
+DEBUG: Don't include this line...
             9+-,KY7)
            W9-Y3+7)
            W'=9WI7)
```

```
        ,W   '-YY)
-       W    ::W
-       ,T   :X)
-       ()   '9W   'L.                    ,-
-       (C   =:9   '9L                ,T
-       ()   ,,-7)   7WL              ,F'
-       ()   , T9)     '9WL          ,YF
+       W    ::W                ,
+       ,T   :X)              ()
+       ()   '9W   'L.        ()          ,-
+       (C   =:9   '9L        ()        ,T
+       ()   ,,-7)   7WL      WW        ,F'
+       ()   , T9)     '9WL   --        ,YF
        ()   '-/(W       -==+PE9P7===O)          -,
       'W, ,   T+/WX=L-. ,WP+()+3L3,),=WL  --==-T-
        7)    -,YW '-=9WPL+PT-- ':--L/=9WP=-'
Stage this hunk [y,n,q,a,d,/,K,j,J,g,s,e,?]?
```

Whoa! It looks like there is a debug line there that we should not add. Let's split the hunk, `s`:

```
Stage this hunk [y,n,q,a,d,/,K,j,J,g,s,e,?]? s
Split into 2 hunks.
@@ -17,7 +24,8 @@
        7WYW))PW W
        7WH)),WC)
        7L--/XY)
+DEBUG: Don't include this line...
        9+-,KY7)
        W9-Y3+7)
        W'=9WI7)
        ,W   '-YY)
Stage this hunk [y,n,q,a,d,/,K,j,J,g,e,?]?
```

We don't want the output to be staged, use `n`, but we'll stage the next hunk and all the hunks later in the a file:

```
Stage this hunk [y,n,q,a,d,/,K,j,J,g,e,?]? n
 @@ -20,13 +28,13 @@
```

```
        9+-,KY7)

        W9-Y3+7)

        W'=9WI7)

    ,W   '-YY)

-       W     ::W

-     ,T     :X)

-     ()     '9W   'L.                      ,-

-     (C     =:9    '9L                    ,T

-     ()     ,,-7)    7WL                 ,F'

-     ()     , T9)     '9WL             ,YF

+       W     ::W                 ,

+     ,T     :X)              ()

+     ()     '9W   'L.        ()          ,-

+     (C     =:9    '9L       ()         ,T

+     ()     ,,-7)    7WL     WW        ,F'

+     ()     , T9)     '9WL    --      ,YF

      ()     '-/(W          -==+PE9P7===O)           -,

    'W, ,   T+/WX=L-. ,WP+()+3L3,),=WL   --==-T-

      7)     -,YW '-=9WPL+PT-- ':--L/=9WP=-'
```

Stage this hunk [y,n,q,a,d,/,K,j,J,g,e,?]? a

Let's see the current status and difference between the working directory and staging area:

`$ git status`

On branch interactive

Your branch is behind 'origin/interactive' by 1 commit, and can be fast-forwarded.

  (use "git pull" to update your local branch)

Changes to be committed:

  (use "git reset HEAD <file>..." to unstage)

    modified: liberty.txt

Changes not staged for commit:

  (use "git add <file>..." to update what will be committed)

(use "git checkout -- <file>..." to discard changes in working directory)

```
    modified:    liberty.txt
$ git diff
diff --git a/liberty.txt b/liberty.txt
index 035083e..9638930 100644
--- a/liberty.txt
+++ b/liberty.txt
@@ -24,6 +24,7 @@
        7WYW))PW W
        7WH)),WC)
         7L--/XY)
+DEBUG: Don't include this line...
        9+-,KY7)
       W9-Y3+7)
       W'=9WI7)
```

Perfect! We got all the changes staged except the debug line, so the result can be committed:

```
$ git commit -m 'Statue of liberty completed'
[interactive 1ccb885] Statue of liberty completed
 1 file changed, 36 insertions(+), 29 deletions(-)
```

There's more...

As mentioned earlier, it is also possible to use `git add -i` to interactively add files. If we do this after resetting our branch, we would get the following menu:

```
$ git add -i
           staged      unstaged path
  1:      unchanged      +37/-29 liberty.txt

*** Commands ***
  1: status    2: update    3: revert    4: add untracked
  5: patch     6: diff      7: quit      8: help
What now>
```

The eight options pretty much do what they say. We can choose the patch option to get into the patch menu as we saw previously, but first we have to choose which file to add patches for:

```
What now> p
            staged      unstaged path
  1:      unchanged      +37/-29 liberty.txt
Patch update>> 1
            staged      unstaged path
* 1:      unchanged      +37/-29 liberty.txt
Patch update>>
diff --git a/liberty.txt b/liberty.txt
index 8350a2c..9638930 100644
--- a/liberty.txt
+++ b/liberty.txt
...
```

Once we have chosen the files, we want to add patches so they get a * character in the menu. To begin the patching, just click on `<return>`. When you're done, you'll return to the menu and can quit, review, revert, and so on.

Interactive add with Git GUI

The interactive features of `git add` are really powerful in order to create clean commits that only contain a single logical change even though it was coded as a mix of feature adding and bug fixing. The downside of the interactive `git add` feature is that it is hard to get an overview of all the changes that exist in the file when only being showed one hunk at a time. To get a better overview of the changes and still be able to only add selected hunks (and even single lines), we can use `git gui`. Git GUI is normally distributed with the Git installation (MsysGit on Windows) and can be launched from the command line: `git gui`. If your distribution doesn't have Git GUI available, you can probably install it from the package manager named `git-gui`.

Getting ready

We'll use the same repository as in the last example and reset it to the same state so we can perform the same adds with Git GUI:

```
$ git clone https://github.com/dvaske/cookbook-tips-tricks.git
$ cd cookbook-tips-tricks
$ git checkout interactive
$ git reset HEAD^
```

How to do it...

Load up Git GUI in the `cookbook-tips-tricks` repository. Here, you can see the unstaged changes (files) in the top-left side and the staged changes (files) under it. The main window will display the unstaged changes in the current marked file. You can right-click on a hunk and see a context menu with options for staging and so on. The first hunk shown by Git GUI is much larger than what we saw before with `git add -p`. Choose **Show Less Context** to split the hunk, as shown in the following screenshot:

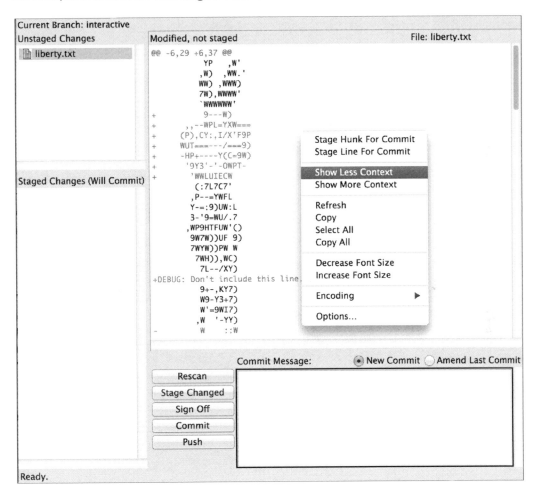

Now, we get a smaller hunk like before, as shown in the following screenshot:

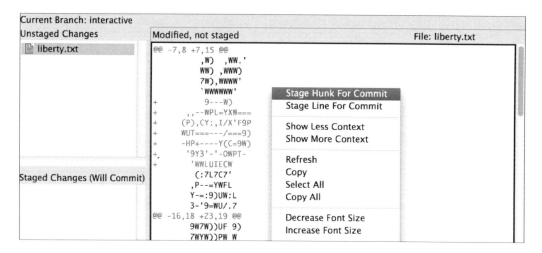

The first hunk we just choose to add, **Stage Hunk For Commit**, and the next hunk moves to the top of the screen:

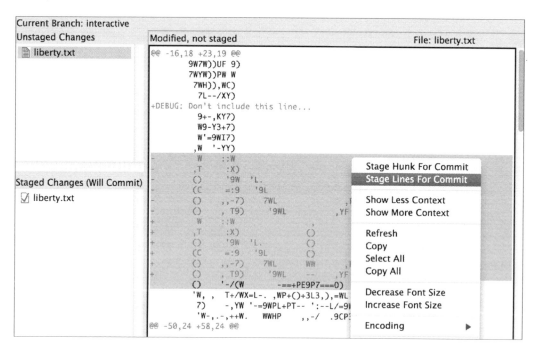

Here, we can select the lines we want to add, instead of performing another split, and stage those lines: **Stage Lines For Commit**. We can add the rest of the hunks except the one with the debug line. Now, we are ready to create a commit and we can do so from the Git GUI. We can just write the commit message in the field at the bottom of the screen and hit **Commit**:

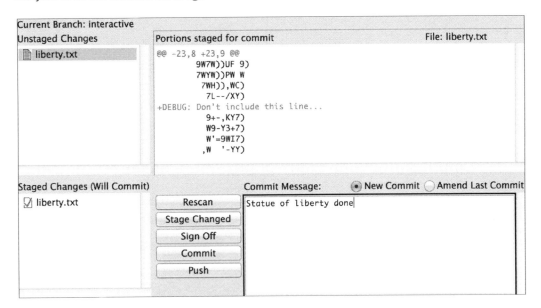

Ignoring files

For every repository, there are usually certain types of files you don't want tracked in the repository. The files can be configuration files, build output, or just backup files created by the editor when editing the file. To avoid these files showing up in the untracked files section of the `git status` output, it is possible to add them to a file called `.gitignore`. Entries in this file that match files in the working directory will not be considered by `git status`.

Getting ready

Clone the `cookbook-tips-tricks` repository and check out the `ignore` branch:

```
$ git clone https://github.com/dvaske/cookbook-tips-tricks.git
$ cd cookbook-tips-tricks
$ git checkout ignore
```

How to do it...

First, we'll create some files and directories:

```
$ echo "Testing" > test.txt
$ echo "Testing" > test.txt.bak
$ mkdir bin
$ touch bin/foobar
$ touch bin/frotz
```

Let's see the output of `git status`:

```
$ git status
On branch ignore
Your branch is up-to-date with 'origin/ignore'.

Untracked files:
  (use "git add <file>..." to include in what will be committed)


    test.txt


nothing added to commit but untracked files present (use "git add" to
track)
```

Only the `test.txt` file showed up in the output. This is because the rest of the files are ignored by Git. We can check the content of `.gitignore` to see how this happened:

```
cat .gitignore
*.config
*.bak

# Java files
*.class

bin/
```

This means that `*.bak`, `*.class`, `*.config`, and everything in the `bin` directory are being ignored by Git.

If we try to add files in a path ignored by Git, for example `bin`, it will complain:

```
$ git add bin/frotz
The following paths are ignored by one of your .gitignore files:
bin/frotz
Use -f if you really want to add them.
```

But, it also tells us an option to use if we really want to add it, `-f`:

```
$ git add -f bin/frotz
$ git status
On branch ignore
Your branch is up-to-date with 'origin/ignore'.

Changes to be committed:
  (use "git reset HEAD <file>..." to unstage)

    new file:   bin/frotz

Untracked files:
  (use "git add <file>..." to include in what will be committed)

    test.txt
```

If we ignore the `foo` file, which is already tracked, and modify it, it still shows up in the status since tracked files are not ignored:

```
$ echo "foo" >> .gitignore
$ echo "more testing" >> foo
$ git status
On branch ignore
Your branch is up-to-date with 'origin/ignore'.

Changes to be committed:
  (use "git reset HEAD <file>..." to unstage)

    new file:   bin/frotz
```

```
Changes not staged for commit:
   (use "git add <file>..." to update what will be committed)
   (use "git checkout -- <file>..." to discard changes in working
directory)

     modified:   .gitignore
     modified:   foo


Untracked files:
   (use "git add <file>..." to include in what will be committed)

     test.txt
```

Let's add and commit foo, .gitignore and the content of the current staging area:

```
$ git add foo .gitignore
$ git commit -m 'Add bin/frotz with force, foo & .gitignore'
[ignore fc60b44] Add bin/frotz with force, foo & .gitignore
 3 files changed, 2 insertions(+)
 create mode 100644 bin/frotz
```

There's more...

It is also possible to ignore files of a repository without the `.gitignore` files. You can put your ignored files in a global ignore file, for example `~/.gitignore_global`, and globally configure Git to also consider entries in this file to be ignored:

```
$ git config --global core.excludesfile ~/.gitignore_global
```

You can also do it per repository in the `.git/info/exclude` file. If you use either of these options, you won't be able to easily share the ignored file; they can't be added to the repository as they are stored outside it. Sharing the `.gitignore` files is much easier; you just add and commit it to Git. But, let's see how the other options work:

```
$ echo "*.test" > .git/info/exclude
$ touch test.test
$ git status
```

```
On branch ignore
Your branch is ahead of 'origin/ignore' by 1 commit.
  (use "git push" to publish your local commits)


Untracked files:
  (use "git add <file>..." to include in what will be committed)


    test.txt


nothing added to commit but untracked files present (use "git add" to
track)
$ ls
bar         bin         foo
test.test   test.txt    test.txt.bak
```

We can see that the `.test` file didn't show up in the `status` output and that the ignored files exists in the working directory.

See also...

There is a wide range of files ignored commonly, for example, to avoid accidentally adding text editor backup files, `*.swp`, `*~.` and `*.bak` are commonly ignored. If you are working on a Java project, you might add `*.class`, `*.jar`, `*.war` to your `.gitignore` and `*.o`, `*.elf`, `*.lib` if you are working on a C project. Github has a repository dedicated to collect Git ignore files for different programming languages and editors/IDEs. You can find it at `https://github.com/github/gitignore`.

Showing and cleaning ignored files

Ignoring files is useful to filter noise from the output of `git status`. But, sometimes it is required to check which files are ignored. This example will show you how to do that.

Getting ready

We'll continue in the repository from the last example.

How to do it...

To show the files we have ignored, we can use the `clean` command. Normally, the `clean` command will remove the untracked files from the working directory but it is possible to run this in a dry-run mode, `-n`, where it just shows what will happen.

```
$ git clean -Xnd
Would remove bin/foobar
Would remove test.test
Would remove test.txt.bak
```

The options used in the preceding command specify the following:

- `-n, --dry-run`: Only lists that will be removed
- `-X`: Removes only the files ignored by Git
- `-d`: Removes the untracked directories in addition to the untracked files

The ignored files can also be listed with the `ls-files` command:

```
$ git ls-files -o -i --exclude-standard
bin/foobar
test.test
test.txt.bak
```

Where the option `-o, --others` shows the untracked files, the option `-i, --ignored` shows only the ignored files, and `--exclude-standard`, use the standard exclusion files `.git/info/exclude` and `.gitignore` in each directory, and the user's global exclusion file.

There's more...

If we need to remove the ignored files, we can of course use `git clean` to do this; instead of the dry-run option, we pass the force option, `-f`:

```
$ git clean -Xfd
Removing bin/foobar
Removing test.test
Removing test.txt.bak
```

To remove all the untracked files and not just the ignored files, use `git clean -xfd`. The lower case x means we don't use the ignore rules, we just remove everything that is not tracked by Git.

Index

Symbols

A

B

binary files
metadata, diffing 264-266
binary handlers
git-annex handler 271
git-bin handler 271
git-media handler 271
bisect command 286
blame command
about 292, 293
using 292
blob object
about 10
writing, to database 255, 256
branch.autosetuprebase configuration 41
branch description
using, in commit message 134-137
branches
differentiating 71, 72
local branches, managing 54-56
merging, git rerere used 65-70
merging, with merge commit 61-65
patches, creating from 227, 228
remote branches 57-60
branch.<name>.rebase configuration 42
branch object 10, 11
bundle command 237

C

cat cat-me.txt command 10
cat-file command
about 8, 15
using 256
changed files
list, obtaining of 23
clean command 318
clean filter 261
clone command 239
commit
author changing, rebase used 86-89
auto squashing 89-94
changes, reverting 179-181
finding, in history 26, 27
push, preventing 148-152
rebasing, to another branch 74, 75
redo 175-177
resetting 167, 168

squashing, interactive rebase used 81-86
tagging, in repository 110-114
undoing 164-167
undoing, while retaining changes in staging
area 169-171
commit message
branch description, using in 134-137
external information, using 144-148
grepping 126-128
template, creating 138-144
commit object
about 8
creating, stages 13-15
writing, to database 258-260
commit template
setting up 159, 160
using 160, 161
configuration, Git
autocorrect 43, 44
object expiry 42
querying 34-36
rebase and merge setup 41
configuration, GLOBAL layer 31-34
configuration, LOCAL layer 31-34
configuration, SYSTEM layer 31-33
current variable 201

D

DAG
about 17
viewing 18-20
dangling commit 167
database
blob object, writing to 255, 256
commit object, writing to 258-260
tree object, writing to 257, 258
data model, Git 5-7
descriptioInCommit branch 134
diff command 65
diff-tree command 250

E

env-filter 205
exif-diff filter 265

Thank you for buying
Git Version Control Cookbook

About Packt Publishing

Packt, pronounced 'packed', published its first book "*Mastering phpMyAdmin for Effective MySQL Management*" in April 2004 and subsequently continued to specialize in publishing highly focused books on specific technologies and solutions.

Our books and publications share the experiences of your fellow IT professionals in adapting and customizing today's systems, applications, and frameworks. Our solution based books give you the knowledge and power to customize the software and technologies you're using to get the job done. Packt books are more specific and less general than the IT books you have seen in the past. Our unique business model allows us to bring you more focused information, giving you more of what you need to know, and less of what you don't.

Packt is a modern, yet unique publishing company, which focuses on producing quality, cutting-edge books for communities of developers, administrators, and newbies alike. For more information, please visit our website: www.packtpub.com.

About Packt Open Source

In 2010, Packt launched two new brands, Packt Open Source and Packt Enterprise, in order to continue its focus on specialization. This book is part of the Packt Open Source brand, home to books published on software built around Open Source licenses, and offering information to anybody from advanced developers to budding web designers. The Open Source brand also runs Packt's Open Source Royalty Scheme, by which Packt gives a royalty to each Open Source project about whose software a book is sold.

Writing for Packt

We welcome all inquiries from people who are interested in authoring. Book proposals should be sent to author@packtpub.com. If your book idea is still at an early stage and you would like to discuss it first before writing a formal book proposal, contact us; one of our commissioning editors will get in touch with you.

We're not just looking for published authors; if you have strong technical skills but no writing experience, our experienced editors can help you develop a writing career, or simply get some additional reward for your expertise.